Returning Home

RETURNING HOME

A Century of African-American Repatriation

Robert Johnson, Jr.

Africa World Press, Inc.

P.O. Box 1892
Trenton, NJ 08607

P.O. Box 48
Asmara, ERITREA

Africa World Press, Inc.

P.O. Box 1892
Trenton, NJ 08607

P.O. Box 48
Asmara, ERITREA

First Printing 2005

Book and Cover design: Saverance Publishing Services

Library of Congress Cataloging-in-Publication Data

Johnson, Robert, Jr., J.D.
Returning home : a century of African-American repatriation / Robert Johnson, Jr.
p. cm.
Includes bibliographical references and index.
ISBN 1-59221-247-6 (cloth) -- ISBN 1-59221-248-4 (pbk.)
1. African Americans--Colonization--Africa. 2. Back to Africa movement. 3. African Americans--Politics and government--19th century. 4. African American political activists--Biography. 5. African American social reformers--Biography. 6. Repatriation--Africa--History--19th century. 7. Return migration--Africa--History--19th century. 8. African Americans--Migrations--History--19th century. 9. Black nationalism--History--19th century. 10. African diaspora. I. Title.

E448.J64 2005
305.896'073009034--dc22

2005024900

Table of Contents

Preface

Over the past twenty-five years, I have sought to distinguish between emigrationism/colonization and repatriation as a philosophical construct within the scholarship on Black Nationalism. As I focused upon John Brown Russwurm, an individual born in Jamaica, educated in Canada and the United States who ultimately moved to Africa where he died and is buried, a philosophical distinction became apparent. While during the nineteenth century when back to Africa sentiments and movements flourished among free Africans, the American Colonization Society provided the financial means for many to realize this dream. In large measure this resulted from slavery and the extremely precarious condition of free Africans in America. Nevertheless, African conceived and/or implemented movements developed in the face of this brutal racial oppression and economic exploitation. These individuals and their movements are the subjects of this book.

Many colleagues helped in helping me develop a more holistic view of these "back to Africa" movements in the nineteenth century. In addition to Professors James Turner and the late J. Congress Mbata at Cornell, my students at University of Massachusetts Boston who struggled through five drafts of the text, helped me sharpen my analysis and broaden my research focus. In particular, I thank Luyen-Nguyen-Huu for his research on resettlement of blacks in Canada, Dasheka Tate for her work on John Brown Russwurm and resettlement in Kansas, Kathryn M. Silva for her excellent research on black women and repatriation in the nineteenth century, Jamal Lee for his work on Edward Jones of Amherst College, and Maryland Camilien and Antonette Kennedy for their extraordinary work on blacks in Boston. Abby Bradbury, a friend and graduate of Middlebury College helped greatly in the research on Alexander Twilight.

In addition, I thank Barbara Krieger at Dartmouth College Library, Special Collections; Barbara Trippel Simmons, Processing Archivist, Amherst College Archives and Special Collections; Susan B. Ravdin, Special Collections, Bowdoin College; Roy Okan, Frederick County Tourism; Frederick County Historical Society for their permission to use the photograph of "Rose," the house slave of Justice Roger Brooke Taney; Maine Historical Society; Laura M. Viscome of Lake Placid-North Elba Historical Society for her kind assistance in providing photographs of John Brown and Lyman Epps, Jr.; and Melissa Vincent for her excellent secretarial assistance with the manuscript.

For the dim regions whence my fathers came
My spirit, bondaged by the body, longs.
Words felt, but never heard, my lips would frame;
My soul would sing forgotten jungle songs.
I would go back to darkness and to peace,
But the great western world holds me in fee,
And I may never hope for full release
While to its alien gods I bend my knee.

Something in me is lost, forever lost,
Some vital thing has gone out of my heart,
And I must walk the way of life a ghost
Among the sons of the earth, a thing apart.

For I was born, far from my native clime,
Under the white man's menace, out of time.

–Claude McKay

INTRODUCTION

Repatriation to Africa, as both a philosophical and pragmatic concept in the nineteenth century, represented the most advanced stage of African-American nationalism. This desire to return to the source of one's origin never died in the nineteenth century, but rather formed the core of national consciousness.

Haitian Revolution

This desire to re-connect with ancestral and traditional ties found expression in the drums of the African in Hispaniola, and in his/her militant resistance to slavery and separation from Africa. As a result, African-American nationalism found its birth in the nineteenth century in the Haitian Revolution. This successful rebellion against the French in 1804 ushered in a new era of African national-sufficiency. Independent Haiti became, not only a symbol of defiance for all African people, but also one of achievement and hope. The message to Africans struggling against European slavery and colonialism was clear: through armed resistance, one could claim one's rightful place among the nations of the world. This was particularly the case when one constituted the majority within a colony like Haiti or on the southern plantations.

African-American Repatriation Ideals

Even when Africans did not constitute the majority population, the Haitian Revolution helped spark national fervor among them. Moreover, among a small percentage of the population in the United States, repatriation movements sprang into existence, especially among Africans who had acquired freedom in the land of the oppressors.

Seven years after Haiti obtained its independence, a prominent, self-made businessman, Paul Cuffe, began planning for a voyage to Africa that would both repatriate free Africans to the continent, and establish commerce between Africans on the continent and those in America. By 1815, Cuffe personally transported thirty-eight Africans to the British Colony of Sierra Leone. First, he believed that returning Africans could aid in the economic development of Africa by implanting Christianity and developing commerce with the West African colonies of Liberia and Sierra Leone. Cuffe, however, did not believe in mass repatriation. Rather, as a Quaker capitalist, he believed that only those with skills should be encouraged to move to Africa and make a contribution to the continent. Irregardless of his motives, Cuffe pioneered the repatriation movements of the nineteenth century, and advanced the cause of African-American nationalism by shifting nationalist fervor from Haiti to Africa.

European-American Separatist Ideals

Even though Cuffe was the first American to repatriate Africans, the resettlement idea had become apart of the American political agenda much earlier than 1815.

In 1777, a committee of the Virginia legislature discussed the idea of emancipation for resettlement of Africans. The committee was chaired by Thomas Jefferson. These early discussions of resettlement by American politicians indicated that European-Americans, including those in high places, questioned whether Africans should ever be integrated into American society. One solution, that gained increasing credibility among these individuals, was resettlement to Africa.

The needs and fears of the American majority found quick relief in the creation of a multi-million dollar organization to accomplish its stated purpose of removing free Africans from the United States. The American Colonization Society represented therefore, the institutional mechanism through which American separatists directed their desire to send Africans back to Africa. To accomplish this goal, an American colony was formed on the west coast of Africa. Therefore, the desire and perceived need to remove Africans from America precipitated a movement for resettlement, which ultimately required the colonization of a portion of the African continent.

Without the Society, resettlement to Africa would have become permanently relegated to a mere trickle of emigrants, since there was a scarcity of African individuals with the financial resources of Paul Cuffe. The Society, on the other hand, through its many auxiliary branches throughout the United States, accumulated financial resources and developed a rationale for African removal that enlisted the support of both African and European individuals in virtually every section of the country. Although many people of varying political persuasions differed in their ultimate stances on resettlement, they overwhelmingly endorsed the scheme.

Some American abolitionists believed that the resettlement of Africans would help end the slave trade. Others, who were alarmed over the sharp increase in African population as a result of slave breeding in the South, believed that resettlement would arrest this rapid increase. The northern industrialists, on the other hand, believed that the colonization of the west coast of Africa would facilitate commercial development of the continent.

However, the underlying basis of all these different views was the assumption that Africans were innately inferior and needed to be separated from the rest of the American population. Despite the humanitarian rhetoric of the American Colonization Society, southern plantation owners were key supporters of the Society, because it addressed their desire to protect their property rights by removing free Africans, whom they considered an economic and political liability to the plantation system. This issue of stability became even more pressing after the Haitian Revolution and the major slave revolts in the first half of the nineteenth century.

African-American Compromise

For the most part, African leaders who ultimately favored colonization as a means for repatriating the sons and daughters of Africa, lacked access to financial resources and therefore had to turn to the American Colonization Society for support. As a result, the militancy of these African repatriates was compromised by the demands of the Society. Even one of the most Afrocentric nationalist leaders of the period, Edward Wilmot Blyden, cooperated with the Society by accepting a position as agent in Liberia. Although these African leaders exercised some degree of political power in the new colony, the ultimate authority rested with the European-American controlled Board of Directors of the American Colonization Society.

Colonization v. Repatriation

Colonization, however, was not synonymous with repatriation. Colonization was a direct result of racism and its resultant African-American removal schemes. The same powerful group of industrialists and politicians, who controlled the slave economy in the United States, controlled the colony in Africa. Although repatriation represented a legitimate outgrowth of African-American nationalism, it was unable to develop freely without any influence from advocates of colonization. White supremacy and its concomitant endorsement of separation among the "races" influenced repatriation efforts as well.

In fact, this desire and rationale for separating Africans by sending them to Africa, predated the nineteenth century. Early leaders such as Abraham Lincoln and Henry Clay favored the separation of Africans or their return to Africa. During the Civil War, when the nation was sharply divided over the question of slavery and the integration of Africans into American society, Lincoln asked the Congress of the United States to allot funds for the settlement of free Africans in Central America.[1] Two other American presidents, George Washington and William Howard Taft, encouraged free Africans to emigrate. President Grant worked diligently after the war to annex Santo Domingo for the settlement of Africans living in America.

These views of prominent American political leaders reflected both the racism of the times and the economic imperatives of the English colony and the new nation. The free African population was growing rapidly and many politicians saw them as a threat to the economic viability of the plantation system. Many feared that any downturn in the economic health of the South would have a catastrophic impact upon the northern economy as well. For example, in the year 1775, Africans comprised forty percent of Virginia's population and one third of those of North Carolina and Georgia. This growth of the African population in America greatly alarmed the European population, who for the most part, felt that it was inconceivable for a race of people who were considered, by even the clergy, to be innately inferior, to live freely among them. Therefore colonization in Africa was a means to rid America of a despised class of people.

Free Africans differed sharply on the questions of resettlement and colonization. As soon as the news spread of the formation of the Society,

Africans organized a response to the colonization program. Some, like Paul Cuffe and Lott Cary, actively supported such schemes in general, while others like Frederick Douglass and Maria Stewart unequivocally fought the efforts of the Society. In 1787 the Free African Society was formed in Newport, Rhode Island to foster unity among free Africans and to adopt a position on the colonization question. These Africans brought to the debate many differing points of view, but central to every position was the recognition that African people's existence in the United States was precarious and that life in Africa would offer more promise, particularly for the majority held in slavery.

Despite the few who steadfastly favored repatriation as early as 1787, the majority rejected any removal schemes. They believed that as free people, they could choose to remain in America, or not, while the majority of their people had no choice but to continue to suffer under brutal racial and economic oppression. Crowded and whipped on the southern plantations, southern Africans experienced brutal degradation that began during the middle passage and continued for more that four hundred years as slavers raped the shores of West Africa of its strongest men and women. Some of the Africans on the slave ships never reached the shores of America, but died from dysentery, smallpox or other communicable diseases. It was not unusual for shiploads of Africans to die from these epidemics or blindness due to eye disease.

Upon reaching the new world, life for the African only changed in degree of oppression. In America, as opposed to the more benign slavery of Brazil and the Caribbean, Africans were not allowed to stay with their families. Ethnic groups were broken up and members disseminated throughout the South to prevent communication, unity and possible retaliation. They were used as property and capital, and their economic worth was measured solely by how much cotton they could pick, or the number of children they could birth. It was not unusual for females to be bred with strong men in order to procreate strong healthy babies for the plantation. Herein the system of slavery reached its most heinous dimension by usurping the maternal instincts of a woman in order to make money.

In the eyes of the law and the society, Africans were not recognized as humans, but as capital. Just as a cow or dog was bred as capital stock, so were human beings. An African could not be a witness against a

European in a court of law. The slave laws prohibited masters from teaching a slave to read and write and punishment for disobeying a European-American man's order was severe. If an African was hit by a European-American man, he was not allowed to hit back. This process of emasculation led inevitably to an identity crisis for African people, in particular, the African man. The more the African became subjected to the brutality of the plantation owner and his overseer, the more he became alienated from his dream of returning to Africa. Some slaves heard tales of freedom in the North, still others longed for a haven among the Native Americans, but Africa increasingly became an unattainable dream.

African-American Nationalist Ideology

Slavery therefore formed the backdrop to the creation of African-American nationalist ideology and its offspring repatriation. The struggle, among free Africans to maintain their humanity in the face of dehumanizing forces, gave impetus to racial identification and national pride. Throughout the nineteenth century free Africans expressed their identification with Africa by referring to themselves as Africans and using the word Africa in the names of their organizations. Although the majority chose to remain in America, they retained their identification with Africa. Many free Africans even chose to refer to themselves as "Africans," i.e. the Free African Society, African Aid Society and African Methodist Episcopal Church.

Despite this identification with Africa, unanimity among free Africans on the issue of repatriation was hard to obtain. For some, the return to Africa would mean that no one would be in America to plead the cause of abolition. Frederick Douglass, more than any other, represented this point of view. He believed that free Africans, through agitation and education could improve both their condition and that of those held in bondage. Although Douglass never desired to personally leave the country, he did investigate the possibility of settlement of some Africans in Haiti. However, his scheme was interrupted by the Civil War, which drew him and other free Africans into the Union cause.

As free Africans became more integrated into American society, they lost their identification with Africa and accepted racial characterizations such as "Negro," a term that was created by Europeans to legally distinguish Africans from themselves. Inevitably, the dream of African identity became emerged into the ambiguous American dream. Once the decision had been made to seek social equality in America, African-American interest in Africa declined and was only rejuvenated during periods of intense crisis and oppression.

For example, during periods of governmental affirmative action to include Africans in the larger society, interest in repatriation declined. An analysis of the period known as "Reconstruction," 1866-1876, when many Africans believed that the government was taking deliberate steps to promote equality, we see evidence of interest in Africa reaching its lowest point as Africans were hoisted into significant political offices, and programs created by the Freedman's Bureau. These governmental programs not only hurt the cause of African repatriation, but also helped America strengthen its social infrastructure after the bloody Civil War. The country was at its weakest point after having lost numerous lives, and almost disintegrating as a political entity. The nation could not afford to have disgruntled free Africans roaming throughout the South without any purpose. Equally, the North had to keep the South under its military and political control. By insuring these Blacks limited political power in the South, the North consolidated its control over the rebellious South between 1866-1876 and stifled any interest in repatriation, thereby insuring the survival of a large, unskilled labor force for the nation.

This ebb and flow of Federal governmental protection and largess during the nineteenth century meant that African conceived and implemented repatriation efforts were sporadic at best. For the most part, except near the end of the century, these repatriation efforts were supported financially by the American Colonization Society. Nevertheless, beginning in 1815 and as a direct result of their own ingenuity, resources and determination, African people began to leave America for Africa. The African repatriation movements of the nineteenth century, and the role of African-American nationalists, such as John Brown Russwurm and Bishop Henry McNeal Turner, provided a rich legacy of self-determination. Despite the role of the American Colonization Society in providing financial support to many of these nationalists, with the exception of Bishop Turner, these African-Americans were willing to merge their futures with that of Africa. For most of them, their new home would be Liberia.

These individuals who took the bold step to seek self-governance in Africa during the nineteenth century are the primary subjects of this book. Repatriation is therefore treated as a step beyond nationalism, an affirmation of the highest phase of the national spirit. It is a step beyond national identification in America, or even in Haiti. It is that ultimate plunge into self-sufficiency, exercised in a place where African people originated and for centuries formed the majority of the world's population. Moreover, it is an attempt to bridge the gulf created by centuries of separation from Africa and its people. In short, repatriation in the nineteenth century was an attempt to re-integrate into African culture and way of life, and by the act of returning to one's source, rejecting "Babylon" and all that it represents. It represented the triumphant act of returning home to the land of one's ancestors, and bidding farewell to chattel slavery, segregation, discrimination, violence and political uncertainty.

Note

1. Eli Ginzberg, Alfred S. Eichner, *The Troublesome Presence* (New York: A Mentor Book, 1964), page 15.

Chapter One

THE HAITIAN REVOLUTION: THE GENESIS OF AFRICAN-AMERICAN NATIONALISM

No event in the nineteenth century contributed more to the development of repatriation movements than the Haitian Revolution. Not only did it lead to the liberation of Africans on the Island of Santo Domingo, but sparked liberation movements throughout the hemisphere, particularly in the United States. In addition, this militant social movement of oppressed Africans precipitated revolutionary national fervor that inspired African freedom fighters throughout the colonized world. The most important result was the establishment of the first African nation-state in the Caribbean in the nineteenth century. Second, the Haitian Revolution proved to the millions of slaves in the Western Hemisphere that freedom could be achieved through militant agitation and armed struggle. Finally, it created a climate of hope for both free and enslaved Africans who dreamed and planned for an eventual exodus from America, leading to the creation of African repatriation movements that were primarily centered in Liberia, West Africa.

Repatriation, therefore, evolved out of this African revolutionary fervor that was spawned by the Haitian Revolution. For Europeans in America, the revolution helped persuade moderate plantation owners to ally with the conservatives who had opposed, on racist grounds, any effort to integrate Africans into American society. For all slaveholders, the Haitian Revolution was a clear indicator that Africans could not be continually oppressed with impunity, but that they would strike out with violent force to achieve their freedom, in the same way that the American colonists had struck out against the British.

For the free African in America, independent Haiti meant that they had an alternative to their precarious existence in the United States. As the first African nation-state in the Western Hemisphere, it meant that

Africans could aspire to govern and provide for themselves. This sentiment led to the creation of repatriation movements in the nineteenth century that led to both a greater exodus of Africans to the continent and a greater sense of African solidarity.

International Echoes of Freedom and Equality

By the end of the eighteenth century, the Western world was satiated with philosophical notions of freedom. In 1776 the British subjects in the American colonies defied the mother country by drafting and issuing the Declaration of Independence. While this document did not pertain to Africans, it did proclaim universal concepts of liberty and equality. Although the question of African freedom was raised at the Constitutional Convention in 1787, two years later, the founding fathers adopted a proslavery constitution for the new republic.[1]

On July 14, 1789, two years before the revolt of the Africans in Santo Domingo, French workers stormed the Bastille in Paris and demanded liberty, equality and fraternity. When the workers rose in revolutionary protest in France, they did not envision that Africans in the French colonies of Santo Domingo, Martinique and Guadaloupe would become allies in their struggle. Nevertheless, pressure among the French began to mount for change in the colonies. In Paris an organization called Friends of the Blacks (Les Amis des Noirs) began a campaign for voting rights for mulattoes in the colonies. These efforts to give mulattoes the right to vote for representatives to the colonial assemblies caused many planters to threaten secession from France.[2]

Many of the colonizers felt that the French National Assembly was moving too quickly in giving the mulattoes the vote. Furthermore, they did not understand why the status quo in the islands should be disturbed. The colony of Santo Domingo had been profitable to France, supplying most of the country's overseas revenue. French nationals had made significant investments in the colony, which resulted in over 3,000 estates being established for sugar, coffee, cotton, tobacco and cocoa.[3] Despite this significant business relationship between the colony and France, the colonists were unhappy with many of the mercantilist policies. For example, France required the colony to ship and purchase goods only from it, and to carry goods only on French ships. In addition, the colonists paid high prices for imports, including slaves, while they received low prices for their goods sold in France.

The French Revolution, however, threatened to alter their comfortable way of life in the colonies. To give the mulattoes the right to vote would mean that their entire social structure would begin to be undermined. Many saw it as critical to their survival that the various social groups and classes continue to be recognized. The French were outnumbered by Africans and it was crucial to the security of their investments that order be maintained at all costs. In addition, sharp class divisions existed among the colonists themselves. For example, one group known as *grand blancs* numbered about 35,000 and consisted of local merchants, noblemen, slaveholders and royal officials. The *petit blancs*, on the other hand, outnumbered the *grand blancs* and consisted of overseers, artisans, shopkeepers, soldiers, small planters and bookkeepers.[4]

The vast majority of the blacks were slaves, numbering 450,000, while mulattoes represented about 45 percent of the entire free population. For the most part, they were offspring of white plantation owners and had received their freedom from their masters, but did not enjoy all of the privileges of the whites. Their existence in the colony, though better off than the blacks, was still precarious. They were still subject to discriminatory laws, excluded from certain occupations and could be reenslaved for certain crimes.[5]

The French Revolution meant different things to the three major groups in Haiti. The colonists hoped for a degree of self-government, mulattoes for free citizenship and Africans for freedom.

Grassroots Revolt

The revolution in Haiti developed among the masses. While leaders such as Toussaint L'Ouverture, Jean Jacques Dessalines and Henri Christophe would play major roles in this struggle, it was the oppressed masses who would strike the initial blow for freedom.

On August 22, 1791, slaves in Le Cap engaged in armed struggle to achieve their freedom. Under the leadership of a voodoo priest and Dutty Boukman, a Jamaican native, they gathered in the forest, swore allegiance to each other and began a crusade that would, by 1804, result in their independence. They swore that they would never submit to the colonists again and that they would fight to death in order to prevent others from suffering the deprivation and punishment that came from slavery. The great West Indian scholar C.L.R. James explained in graphic detail the depravity of the punishment that many slaves had to suffer:

> Whipping was interrupted in order to pass a piece of hot wood on the buttocks of the victim; salt, pepper, citron, cinders, aloes, and hot ashes were poured on the bleeding wounds. Mutilations were common, limbs, ears, and sometimes the private parts, to deprive them of the pleasures which they could indulge in without expense. Their masters poured burning wax on their arms and hands and shoulders, emptied the boiling cane sugar over their heads, burned them alive, roasted them on slow fires, filled them with gunpowder and blew them up with a match; buried them up to the neck and smeared their heads with sugar that the flies might devour them; fastened them near to nests of ants or wasps; made them eat their excrement, drink their urine, and lick the saliva of other slaves. One colonist was known in moments of anger to throw himself on his slaves and stick his teeth into their flesh.[6]

Given the depravity of this cruelty, the slaves thought that they were fighting against demonic forces and therefore called upon divine assistance to overcome such practices. Boukman, encouraged his freedom fighters by stating: "Our god who is good to us orders us to revenge our wrongs. He will direct our arms and aid us. Throw away the symbol of the god of the whites who has so often caused us to weep, and listen to the voices of liberty, which speaks in the hearts of us all."[7]

The French National Assembly became outraged as overnight Africans began burning their masters' houses and cane fields. In an effort to keep the mulattoes from allying with the Africans, on April 4, 1792, the Assembly granted full citizenship rights to the mulattoes in an effort to solidify their support for France. In September 1792, Leger Sonthonax and 6,000 French troops were sent to restore order and seek the assistance of the mulattoes. In June 1793, *petit blancs* revolted in Le Cap, which required Sonthonax to deplore mulattoes and armed slaves against the whites. The fighting was so intense that in August 1793 Sonthonax had to proclaim full African emancipation. His conditional decree was confirmed in 1794 by the French National

Assembly. All slavery was abolished and all men in the colonies became French citizens.

The Rise of Toussaint L'Ouverture

When the revolt began in 1791, Toussaint L'Ouverture, a slave born to West African parents, refused to take part and, in fact, sheltered his master from the rebels. He later transported his master to safety, had a change of heart, and joined the rebels in the mountains. Within a short period, he organized a disciplined band of followers, became skilled in guerrilla warfare and won a number of key victories against the French army.

After emancipation of the slaves on February 4, 1794, Toussaint joined Andre Rigaud in the French campaign against the British. He wanted to insure that the British would not be victorious and therefore reinstitute slavery in Santo Domingo. By 1798 Toussaint had successfully fought back General Thomas Maitland and forced the British to sign a treaty of nonaggression. In the treaty, Toussaint promised that he would not invade Jamaica and that the British would withdraw their troops from Haiti. Throughout his campaign against the British, Toussaint enjoyed the support of the United States, with President John Adams sending ships and supplies to aid Toussaint's army.[8]

The French, however, soon became intolerant of this very egotistical and successful African general. By May 2, 1797, Toussaint held the titles of commander in chief and governor.[9] General Gabriel d'Hedouville was sent, therefore, to rein in Toussaint's power. France wanted Hedouville to prevent Toussaint from forming a strong national identity among the Africans in Haiti. The essential problem was one of control. As long as Toussaint saw himself as a representative of France, he continued to be subject to France and its colonial policies. If he succeeded in forging a national identity for the island's people, France would lose control of important economic resources in the colony. Disagreeing with the French agenda, Toussaint openly challenged Hedouville, who openly encouraged racial conflict between the Africans and the mulattoes. He urged Rigaud, the leader of the mulattoes, to resist Toussaint and promised French support for such an effort.

In April Toussaint took the offensive and invaded Rigaud's stronghold in the south. At the same time, he ignored the authority of Hedouville. The assault upon Rigaud resulted in the death of close to 10,000 mulattoes. By 1801Toussaint had taken over Spanish Santo Domingo as well, which made him the ruler of the entire island.

Upon obtaining control of the island, Toussaint attempted to restore order and government. He openly petitioned France with the idea that the colony could be most profitable if it was independent. He argued that under a revised plantation system, work hours would be regulated. Africans would receive humane treatment and share in the profits.[10] In addition, Toussaint wanted desperately for France to believe that his government could be fair to whites. For example, he did not disturb the estates owned by whites and guaranteed them control over local government and free trade.

Internal Resistance

The African masses resented this favoritism toward French colonists and engaged in a revolt in the north in September 1801 under the leadership of Moise L'Ouverture, who was commandant of the North Province. Toussaint's policy of rapprochement with French colonists was not working. The bitterness was too deep for Africans to forget. Moise summarized the feelings of the Africans in his personal statement of outrage: "Whatever my old uncle may do, I cannot bring myself to be the executioner of my colour. It is always in the interests of the metropolis that he scolds me; but these interests are those of the whites and I shall only love them when they have given me back the eye that they made me lose in battle."[11]

Toussaint had made a fatal mistake in his leadership: He had failed to understand the depths of his people's frustration with any remaining vestiges of colonial rule. The people wanted freedom and they wanted it immediately. The revolt began on September 21, 1801, and quickly spread, but was brought under control by Toussaint, Christophe and Dessalines. Moise was captured and shot. Toussaint would never be able to overcome this unfortunate act in the eyes of the masses. Moise represented the revolution to the people in the north. He believed that Africans should receive compensation for the wrongs they suffered under the French colonists, and that the large estates should be broken up and small parcels given to the people.[12] While he may not have used the term "reparations," this is precisely what Moise stood for as a leader of the revolution. He realized that redistribution of land had to form the foundation of the new nationalism.

The Demise of Toussaint L'Ouverture

The execution of Moise certainly ignited a series of events that ultimately led to the downfall of Toussaint. By killing Moise, Toussaint destroyed his mass revolutionary support. Napoleon Bonaparte knew, therefore, that the old general was weak and could be defeated. In July 1802 the French invaded Le Cap. Toussaint and his troops surrendered without a fight, as the mulattoes and French colonists joined the French. In April 1802 Toussaint officially surrendered to General Charles Victor Leclerc, and was deported to France and placed in a dungeon at Fort de Joux. His last words in Haiti expressed his undying belief in the ultimate outcome of his people's revolution: "In overthrowing me, you have cut down in San Domingo only the trunk of the tree of liberty. It will spring up again by the roots for they are numerous and deep."[13] He died on April 7, 1803.

The Leadership of Jean Jacques Dessalines

The revolution in Santo Domingo was greater than its leaders. The revolutionary fervor, therefore, continued despite the death of Toussaint or Moise. This was particularly the case once the people learned that Bonaparte had either reintroduced slavery or was planning to reinstitute it in the island.

At this time the militant leader Dessalines took charge of the revolution. He quickly earned back the support of the masses. On November 29, 1803, Dessalines issued a preliminary proclamation of independence. On January 1, 1804, he issued a final proclamation in which he claimed the independence of Santo Domingo and renamed the island "Haiti," a Taino name for "land of mountains." Moreover, he wanted to send a stern warning to the French that the revolution could not be compromised. He would not make the same mistakes as Toussaint by accommodating French colonists. Rather, he engaged in a deliberate campaign to kill all French on the island, including women and children.[14]

In his new constitution for Haiti, he recognized universal freedom. It abolished slavery forever, and prevented "white" men from becoming landowners. As a symbol of the new government, Dessalines prohibited the use of the term "Negro" and substituted "black" as an adjective to describe Haitians.

The independence of Haiti sent shock waves throughout the hemisphere. Southerners in the United States scrambled to pass laws forbidding the entrance of Africans from the West Indies. On February 28, 1803, a law was passed that prohibited the importation into the United States of any "negro, mulatto, or other person of color" from the West Indies. For violating the statute, a ship could be forfeited and the captain punished.[15] Finally, on February 20, 1806, a bill passed the Senate and was ultimately signed into law that prohibited trade with Santo Domingo.[16]

While Haitian nationalism for many European-Americans was to be feared, for some of the most prominent free Africans in the United States, it represented promise and freedom. On January 9, 1826, John Brown Russwurm, on the eve of his graduation from Bowdoin College, wrote his European-American uncle, John Sumner Russwurm the following note: "If not particularly invited by the Haytian Government then, I shall study Medicine in Boston previous to an emigration to Hayti."[17] The social movement for African national independence would continue throughout the nineteenth century and become an inspiration for repatriation movements to Africa and a haven for Africans throughout the Western Hemisphere who desired to join an African majority and take control of the political and economic reins of their nation.

Notes

1. Robert Johnson, Jr., *Race, Law and Public Policy* (Baltimore: Black Classic Press, 1998), page 1.
2. Philip Sherlock and Hazel Bennett, *The Story of the Jamaican People* (Kingston, Jamaica: Ian Randle, 1998), page 184.
3. George F. Tyson, Jr., ed., *Toussaint L'Ouverture* (Englewood Cliffs, NJ: Prentice-Hall, 1973), page 3.
4. Tyson, page 4.
5. Tyson, page 6.
6. C.L.R. James, *The Black Jacobins: Toussaint L'Ouverture and the San Domingo Revolution*, 2nd ed., (New York: Vintage Books, 1989), page 12 to 13.

7. Boukman cited in Sherlock and Bennett, page 185.
8. Sherlock and Bennett, page 188.
9. James, page 186.
10. Tyson, pages 17 to 20.
11. Moise cited in James, page 275.
12. James, page 277.
13. James, page 334.
14. Earl Leslie Griggs and Clifford H. Proctor, eds., *Henry Christophe and Thomas Clarkson: A Correspondence* (New York: Greenwood Press, 1968), pages 34 to 37.
15. W.E.B. Du Bois, *The Suppression of the African Slave Trade* (Baton Rouge: Louisiana State University Press, 1969), page 85.
16. Du Bois, pages 92 to 93.
17. Maine Historical Society, John Brown Russwurm Papers.

Chapter Two

PAUL CUFFE AND AFRICAN-AMERICAN REPATRIATION

Repatriation in the nineteenth century, defined as voluntary reintegration of Africans into Africa, began with Paul Cuffe, who initiated the first African-American conceived and financed return-to-Africa scheme. Even though the majority of blacks were being degraded by the nascent forces of capitalism, manifested through slavery, Cuffe was able to merge a keen business sense with genuine nationalist sentiments. Although Cuffe possessed resources sufficient to maintain a standard of living that rivaled the wealthiest in America, he held genuine concern about Africa and its people.

Unlike the vast majority of African-Americans, he had never known slavery. He was born in New Bedford (Westport), Massachusetts, of free parents on January 17, 1759. His father was African and his mother Native American (Indian). His father, Cuffe Slocum, was brought from Africa (probably Ghana) to the Bay State as early as 1728.[1] After purchasing his freedom, Cuffe Slocum married Ruth Moses, a member of the Wampanoags. After marriage, the couple moved to the island of Cuttyhunk (south of New Bedford) and raised ten children. After living in Chilmark on Martha's Vineyard, the family then bought 120 acres in Westport. It was in Westport that young Cuffe spent his formative years. His family provided him with an excellent start in America. As a free man he encountered discrimination and prejudice, but he never allowed racism to dampen his determination to have a positive impact upon the lives of his people.

As one can see from Cuffe's experience, during the nineteenth century not all Africans in the United States were slaves. Like many Europeans, the first Africans voluntarily emigrated to America. For example, in 1619, twenty Africans arrived at Jamestown, Virginia, as indentured servants, which meant that they agreed to work for another person for a contractually determined period of time in exchange for transportation and support. When the contract had been satisfied, many became independent and prosperous farmers. By 1790 approximately 59,000 free Africans resided in the United States, of which 35,000 lived in the South.[2] By 1800 the number had risen to 108,435 and by 1830 to 319,599. Finally by 1860 the number had risen to 488,000, with 46 percent of them in the North. In the states of Maryland and Pennsylvania a large proportion of the free Africans lived in the cities. In 1860, 24,680 of the 83,942 free Africans in the state of Maryland lived in Baltimore, while one third of those in Pennsylvania lived in Philadelphia.[3] Most of the free Africans moved to the cities in an effort to find employment, which made them particularly vulnerable to the fluctuations in the northern economy.

Of those who remained in the South, the majority engaged in agricultural labor. Only a few free Africans owned large farms in the South. In 1830, of the 319,000 free Africans, 3,777 of them owned 1,260 acres in the states of Virginia, North Carolina, Maryland, South Carolina and Louisiana.[4] Consequently, many were unable to compete effectively in the southern economy, but had to engage in subsistence farming.

The largest single group of free Africans was mulatto, born either of mixed African and Indian parentage or African and European. In 1850, 37 percent of the free Africans in the United States were considered mulattoes;[5] 78 percent of those who lived in Louisiana were classified as mulattoes.[6] This figure is consistent with data in Haiti as well.

One means of acquiring freedom was through voluntary manumission. Some plantation owners specified in their wills that certain slaves, who had served them well, should be freed upon their death. Other slaves obtained their freedom by assisting slaveowners in maintaining order and the status quo on the plantation. For example, the Commonwealth of Virginia gave a slave his freedom in 1710 for discovering a plot by other slaves to rebel.[7] This act of manumission, however, was the exception to the rule; the Virginia legislature passed an act in 1723 that no private slaveowner could free his slaves. This law was passed to protect the thriving economic enterprises involving tobacco and cotton. The public policymakers realized that without slave labor, these thriving industries could experience a severe recession if the plantation owners had to pay for the labor of African people. Slavery was essential to the continued economic viability of the South.

Despite these restrictions upon free African labor, Cuffe was determined to obtain an honorable profession in America. More important, despite the vast majority of his people being enslaved, and free Africans being discriminated against, he strove to maintain roots with this African majority and to develop a means to relieve them of their oppression. But first he had to educate himself. In 1775 young Cuffe engaged in employment on a whaling ship where he started to develop an interest in commerce. This interest soon blossomed into a love for marine navigation and he vowed to someday build his own ships. Although many of the European sailors ridiculed him for having big dreams, he ignored them and learned as much as he could about both shipbuilding and navigation.

He encountered many setbacks, but he was not deterred. His love of the sea continued to motivate him to perfect the art of sailing. It was not easy for Africans to learn sailing. The presence of free African sailors in the harbors of Massachusetts and New York caused authorities a great deal of concern. Eventually, Cuffe ran into institutional roadblocks to his dream of becoming a navigator. In 1776 he was placed under arrest for three months by the British for navigating outside the New York Harbor. Even while in jail he continued to learn from his fellow prisoners about shipping and left New York with renewed determination.

His relentless spirit provided additional impetus in his struggle for more just treatment of Africans in his home of Massachusetts. On February 10, 1780, at the age of nineteen, Paul, his brother and other people of color challenged the policy of the Commonwealth of Massachusetts that denied Africans and Indians the right to vote, even though they paid taxes like everyone else in the state. The petition was addressed to the "Honourable Council and House of Representatives in General Court Assembled for the State of Massachusetts Bay in New England." It was brought by "several poor Negroes + molattoes... inhabitants of the Town of Dartmouth." The petitioners acknowledged that they were "chiefly of the African Extract" and that they were being deprived of the "profits" of their labor and the "advantage of inhabiting Estates from their parents"[8] Consequently, they refused to pay any more taxes until they were allowed to vote. On December 15, 1780, a warrant for the arrest of the brothers was issued. On December 19 they were arrested. They had pushed the system as far as they could without jeopardizing their liberties. Realizing that jail would completely stymie their navigational hopes, they paid their taxes and the lawsuit was ultimately dismissed.[9]

The fact that Cuffe had attempted to obtain relief through the legal process was evidence that discrimination existed even in northern states. In his petition to the General Court for the Commonwealth of Massachusetts Bay, he wrote:

> Your petitioners further showeth that we apprehend ourselves to be aggrieved in that while we are not allowed the privilege of freemen of the state, having no vote or influence in the election with those that tax us, yet many of our color, as is well known, have cheerfully entered the field of the battle in the defence (sic) of the common cause, and that (as we conceive) against a similar exertion of power in regard to taxation too well known to need a recital in this place. That these, the most honorable Court, we humbly beseech thee to take this into consideration and set us aside from paying tax or tax fees. Or cause us to be cleared for we ever have been a people that was free from all these things ever since the days of our forefathers.[10]

These setbacks were only temporary because Cuffe pressed forward with his dream of becoming a seaman and a shipbuilder. He soon mastered the science of navigation by apprenticing himself on various whaling vessels.

Voyage to Sierra Leone

Only five years after his maiden voyage on a whaler, Paul Cuffe started to build his own ships. In six years he built one large ship, two brigs and several smaller boats.[11] From his real estate investments, he was able to fund his maritime interests. By 1810 he had amassed enough money to captain his own ship, with a black crew, to Philadelphia and ultimately to Sierra Leone where he would investigate the possibility of African resettlement and of commerce.[12] While in Sierra Leone he established cultural links with the Africans as well as instructed some of the people in the art of navigation. This was significant because for the first time in history, an African-American had successfully returned to Africa. Not only did he return, but he began to share many of the skills obtained in America with his brothers and sisters on the continent. He worked closely with both the indigenous and returned Africans in a spirit of cooperation and respect.[13] While motivated by a spirit of evangelism, he was also deeply concerned about the physical well-being of Africans both in Africa and America. The "Epistle of the Society of Sierra Leone," which he helped draft with the assistance of other Africans who had been returned from Britain, acknowledged a Pan-African kinship and a willingness to accept returning Africans to the continent:

"The Epistle of the Society of Sierra Leone in Africa"

> To the Saints and faithful Brethren in Christ; grace be unto you, and peace from God our Father and the Lord Jesus Christ, We desire to humble ourselves with that Thankful acknowledgement to the Father and Fountain of all our mercies, for the liberty and freedom we enjoy. And our prayer to God is, that our Brethren, who live in distant lands, and are held in bondage, and groan under the galling chain of Slavery, that they may be liberated, and enjoy the liberty that God has granted unto all his faithful Saints. Dearly Brethren in the Lord, may the power and peace of God rule in all your hearts, for we feel, from an awful experience, the distresses that many of our African brethren groan under; therefore we feel our minds engaged to desire all the Saints and Professors in Christ, to diligently consider our cause, and to put our cause to the Christian query; whether it is agreeable to the testimony of Jesus Christ, for one Professor to make merchandize of another? We are desirous, that this may be made manifest to all Professors of all Christian denominations, who have not abolished the holding of slaves. We salute you, beloved Brethren, in the Lord, with sincere desire that the works of regeneration may be more and more experienced. It would be a consolation to us, to hear from the Saints in distant lands, and we could receive all who are disposed to come unto us with open arms. Our dearly beloved African Brethren, we also salute you in the love of God, to be obedient unto your masters, with your prayers lifted up to God, whom we would recommend you

> to confide in, who is just as able in these days, to deliver you from the yoke of oppression, as he hath in time past brought your fore fathers, out of the Egyptian bondage; finally brethren, may the power and peace of God rule in all your hearts. Grace be unto you, and peace from God our Father, and the Lord Jesus Christ. Amen.[14]

Although this statement expressed a genuine concern for the welfare of Africans in America, it urged a gradualist approach to liberation. It was ironic that they could recognize the gravity of their people's oppression, yet urge obedience to the slave masters. Unlike radical abolitionists later in the century, such as David Walker and Nat Turner, Cuffe believed in the redemptive power of capitalism. In his personal life and in his dealings with Africa, he espoused the virtues of thrift, hard work and ownership of capital. When he returned to the States he brought African products that he sold both in the United States and Europe.[15] With the profits that accrued from his economic ventures, he planned to establish the "Friendly Society for American Negroes" in West Africa. On the domestic front, he used a large proportion of his wealth to build a small schoolhouse on his property to educate the black children of New Bedford. He hired the teacher and paid her salary.[16]

Cuffe's trip to Sierra Leone, West Africa, in 1811 signaled the beginning of a history of African repatriation. Not only was it a tremendous task for any African to contemplate, it was also extremely risky, given that the African slave trade continued, despite its illegality in 1808. Despite these perils, Cuffe equipped his brig *Traveller* for the voyage back to the section of the continent where his father originated. His crew consisted of nine men, all of whom were black, with the exception of an apprentice, Abraham Rodin, a Swede who in 1807 attached himself to Cuffe to learn "seamanship and other industry."[17] The fact that Cuffe allowed this young man to apprentice under him meant that, although Cuffe identified strongly with his people, he did not allow bitterness to color his perception of people.

On January 2, 1811, he sailed for West Africa, and arrived on March 1, at Bence Island which was a British outpost. His crew was enthusiastically greeted by the governor of Sierra Leone. On March 4, 1811, Paul Cuffe dined with Captain Edward Henry Columbine, governor of the island. This dinner and reception was a testimony to

Cuffe's diplomatic skills, given that the United States and Britain had been engaged in severe territorial disagreements that ultimately erupted into war. The discussion at the dinner table was frank and cordial. The governor spoke of the problems of trying to steer clear of slave traders and the great difficulty of life in Sierra Leone because he had recently lost both his wife and a child to tropical diseases.[18] This discussion was important to Cuffe because he did not want to paint an unrealistic picture of Sierra Leone to blacks in the United States. Repatriation would have its challenges, the most significant of which was disease.

While in Sierra Leone he visited some of the schools for the settlers and sold some of the products that he had brought from the United States. He sold most of the bread and meat and had to hire three Kru men at $3.00 per month to help him conduct the business. He also bartered cloth for ivory. When another brig arrived from the British West Indies on March 6, 1811, he learned that a Portuguese slaver was near the islands, and that Sierra Leone authorities had attempted to intercept it, but could not. However, the government had strong laws that prohibited the slave trade and severe penalties for those who violated them. On March 9, 1811, Cuffe had the great fortune to sit in on the trial of a Portuguese slaver who was being prosecuted before the Court of Admiralty. The captain was found guilty, the cargo and vessel were condemned and proceeds distributed to the slaves aboard the ship.[19] This experience was significant for Cuffe as well. He witnessed blacks and whites working cooperatively to confront a great scourge on free-market commercial activities. More important, he came face to face with pirates who roamed the seas and jeopardized the lives of himself and his crew.

Not only did Cuffe meet frequently with the governor, who was British, he also met with the key traditional rulers. This ability to interface with both the European and African world was a hallmark of Cuffe's abilities. On March 13, 1811, a traditional leader known to the British as King Tom came aboard the *Traveller*. His traditional name was Pa Kokelly and he ruled the Koya Temne ethnic group and much of Cape Sierra Leone. As was his custom when meeting with traditional leaders, Cuffe gave to King Tom a Bible, a book on the history of slavery and a book of essays on war.[20] On March 18, 1811, he met with King George of the Bullom people, and exchanged similar gifts.

After a little over two months in Sierra Leone, the Cuffe party decided to move on. While he had been treated with the utmost respect, the colony, nevertheless, was unwilling to engage in widespread commerce in American goods. In addition, the political leadership of the colony was unable to grant permission for the emigration of Africans from America. The permission for both of these endeavors had to be obtained in England. Cuffe therefore had two choices: He could either return to the United States without all of his preliminary goals accomplished, or he could sail to England and seek the requisite approvals there. Believing that he had come too far to turn around, Cuffe set sail for England on May 11, 1811. He felt assured that his powerful Quaker friends would assist him in getting the necessary permits and licenses for his work in Sierra Leone.

Arrival in Britain

On July 12, 1811, his crew arrived in Liverpool after sixty-two days at sea. Upon arriving in Liverpool Harbor, his ship was searched and an African, Aaron Richards, taken off board. The British claimed him as a British subject. This taking of Aaron Richards was the first major obstacle that confronted Cuffe upon his arrival in Liverpool. He tried to obtain the African's release, but was unsuccessful. He then consulted some Quaker friends, Richard Rathbone and Thomas Thompson, who were able to obtain agreement from authorities that Richards would not be removed from Liverpool. They then wrote to the Board of Admiralty in London.

Several days later Cuffe took a stagecoach to London, where he hoped to plead his case directly with authorities. On July 16, Cuffe arrived in London, obtained a room and prepared himself for the ordeal that was to follow. After eating breakfast, he went to court where he met his friend, William Allen. Allen was an extremely wealthy Englishman who had made his fortune in the chemical manufacturing business. He was a member of the African Institution and a benefactor for the poor. On July 18, Allen arranged a meeting with William Wilberforce, philanthropist and founder of the Anti-Slavery Society, who had led a crusade to abolish the African slave trade. After Wilberforce was told that Richards had been moved, he quickly dispatched a note to the Board of Admiralty. This high-ranking involvement in the Richards' case got immediate results. On July 23, Thomas Clarkson met with the Lord of Admiralty and was told that papers had been executed that ordered the discharge of Richards. Clarkson, a staunch abolitionist and one of the primary supporters of the Sierra Leone colony, wrote a book entitled *The History of the Rise, Progress, and Accomplishment of the Abolition of the African Slave Trade by the British Government*. His book, more than any other, had considerable impact upon English attitudes toward slavery.

After the ordeal with Richards had been concluded satisfactorily, Cuffe set out to obtain the necessary licenses for his return trip to Sierra Leone. Again his friends were extremely instrumental in helping him get through the bureaucratic redtape. John Clarkson, brother of Thomas, was particularly helpful. John had experience in resettlement efforts because in 1791, he recruited and transported Africans from Nova Scotia to Sierra Leone.[21]

While his petition for licenses was processed, Cuffe returned to Liverpool to inform his crew of his progress. The news of his ship being at harbor spread quickly throughout the City of Liverpool. Even a renowned slave dealer, William Bottell, invited Cuffe to dinner. Still other British subjects periodically approached Cuffe and his crew and inquired about conditions at Sierra Leone and expressed their interest in gaining passage.

Although Cuffe had many meetings with prominent individuals, a meeting on August 7, was particularly noteworthy. He dined with William and Richard Rathbone, William Thompson, William Roscoe and Lord John Russell. At this dinner the conversation turned to methods that the British government could adopt in order to stop the illegal slave trade. William Roscoe suggested that the British government commission its ships to seize all British vessels found to be engaged in the trade. It was significant that Cuffe was able to be engaged in such high-level discussions with the British while he was effectively precluded from similar discussions in America.

It is in these Liverpool meetings that we get a clear picture of Cuffe's ideas on commerce with Africa. Not only did he envision Africans returning to Sierra Leone, but he also believed that both Britain and America should engage in legitimate trade. At a meeting at the home of William Roscoe on September 4, Cuffe stated that there must be greater communication between England, America and Africa in order to civilize Africa. In his view, the two governments must trade with Africa, despite the conflict between the two countries. He saw trade with Africa as a neutral venture that even the French, who were hostile to England, should be encouraged to join.[22]

Return Trip to Sierra Leone

Finally, on September 20, 1811, the *Traveller* set sail for Sierra Leone with five additional passengers: four English Methodist missionaries and one African boy.[23] On shore, many of the Quaker dignitaries, who had helped Cuffe, stood by to wave farewell as the crew steered in the direction of the African continent.

On November 12, Cuffe went ashore at Sierra Leone. As a result of his trip to England and the critical positions that his Quaker friends occupied, his efforts progressed smoothly. Before sailing for America with renewed optimism, he reassured the leaders of Sierra Leone of his success in London. By the time he left for America on February 11, 1812, he received assurances from the governor of Sierra Leone that Africans from America could receive citizenship.

First Return to America

Despite Cuffe's attempts at diplomacy between England and America, he got caught up in the developing hostility between the two countries. Upon arriving in Westport on April 19, 1812, his ship and cargo were impounded because of these renewed hostilities. To his surprise on March 2, 1811, Congress had passed a bill prohibiting trade with the enemy, that is England.

Here again, Cuffe turned to his white Quaker friends for assistance, most notably Walter Channing and Moses Brown. Brown was the founder of the cotton-spinning industry, and Rhode Island College, which later was renamed Brown University. After intercession from these men and a journey to Washington by Cuffe, President James Madison and Secretary of the Treasury Albert Gallatin released his ship and cargo.

Cuffe continued to get information from his friends in England as he continued to prepare his repatriation scheme. He finally received a letter, dated July 1, 1812, from Thomas Clarkson and William Allen that set forth the terms of their cooperation. The African Institution, which administered the colony, agreed to grant land directly to Paul

Cuffe. Cuffe could, in turn, farm himself, let, divide or sell if he complied with certain conditions. The first condition was that the land had to be settled by the individual who would cultivate it. There was no limit on the amount of land that would be granted to Cuffe. The only requirement was that it be cultivated. If Cuffe successfully cultivated the first grant of land, he could apply for more. A further condition to the initial grant was that Cuffe had to become a resident of the colony. It was not required that he become a permanent resident, but that he become at least what was referred to as an occasional resident. The residency could be obtained if he maintained communications between England and Sierra Leone, between America and Sierra Leone or if he maintained a whaling business.[24]

The second condition related to the type of settlers Cuffe would bring to the colony. First, they had to be willing to become subjects of Britain. Clarkson and Allen described the desired settlers in the following manner: "The inhabitants are free; they enjoy religious toleration. All matters are decided by a jury; and they compose the jury themselves"[25] The settlers would be selected by Cuffe and they had to be free and of good known character. In addition, they had to be persons of some property. It was desired that they be acquainted with mechanical arts and the cultivation of tropical produce.[26] Finally, the colony expected that Cuffe would bring no more than eighteen settlers.

War of 1812

Cuffe's plan for repatriation was delayed because of the War of 1812 that waged between England and the United States. This conflict did not deter Cuffe in his efforts, however. In June 1813 he wrote a letter to the president, Senate and House of Representatives seeking assistance for his project. In this letter Cuffe stressed that the main object would be to end the slave trade and to civilize Africa through the efforts of free African-Americans. He wrote:

> One of these objects was to keep up an intercourse with the free people of color in the United States, in the expectation that some persons of reputation would feel sufficiently interested to visit Africa, and endeavor to promote habits of industry, sobriety and frugality, among the natives of that country.[27]

In this petition, Cuffe asked for assistance from the government in carrying out his project. He also envisioned Africans from Sierra Leone traveling to the United States as well. This novel idea was the first effort to institute an international exchange program between Africa and the United States. He never received a response from the government, so he continued to make provisions for the voyage that would represent the culmination of his work.

Repatriation to Africa

Despite the international conflicts between England and the United States, the assurances that he had personally received were sufficient motivations to go forward with his plans. He therefore outfitted his ship, carefully selected his passengers and crew and set sail for Africa. On December 4, 1815, he wrote William Allen in England that he had cleared customs with a small cargo and thirty-eight passengers, twenty of whom were children. Cuffe explained that many of them did not have property or knowledge of tropical produce, but that they were fit for the colony. The passengers were from New York City, Philadelphia and Boston and were transported at a cost of from $3,000 to $4,000 by Cuffe's brig, *Traveller.*

The individuals Cuffe took to Africa voluntarily left the United States. They were all common laborers, none were mechanically inclined as had been hoped for by the London African Institution. Two settlers could trace their lineage from the Congo and Senegal and therefore hoped to work with individuals from their ethnic group, who resided in Sierra Leone. They hoped to eventually reassimilate entirely with their traditional people. They, like most of the settlers, paid from $100 to $250 per person for their passage, which did not fully cover the cost of the voyage. A man of Congo extraction, Anthony Survance, made the voyage with his wife. Survance owned property in Philadelphia, and was once a slave in Santa Domingo. After the revolution he escaped to America, and learned to read and write. Some of the individuals on this maiden voyage were from Boston such as William Guin, Samuel Hughes and Robert Rigsbary.[28]

Second Return to America

On April 4, 1816, Cuffe set sail for America. Upon returning to the United States after a long journey of fifty-four days, he tried to interest other blacks in repatriation and business opportunities in Sierra Leone, but did not have much success.[29] In an effort to increase the number of black emigrants, he corresponded with his friend in Philadelphia, James Forten. In a letter to Forten dated May 29, 1816, Cuffe enthusiastically wrote that the governor of Sierra Leone had given the settlers land to farm. Forten, like Cuffe, was educated in a Quaker school, after which he worked with a sail-maker for many years. He invented a device for sails and became very wealthy. Cuffe did not, however, receive the type of encouragement that he had received in England and felt that he deserved in Philadelphia. In a letter to Peter Williams dated June 14, 1816, Cuffe wrote that he had heard from John James of Philadelphia that many "people of colour" had received unfavorable reports on the Sierra Leone settlement. The letter urged Cuffe to come to Philadelphia to clear up the negative rumors. Due to illness, however, Cuffe was unable to make the trip.

On January 25, 1817, James Forten wrote Paul Cuffe from Philadelphia explaining his failure to interest many blacks in repatriation. Part of the letter read:

> Esteemed friend... the *African Institution* met at the Reverend R. Allens the very day your letter came to hand. I red (sic) that part to them that wished them a happy New Year, for which they desired me to return you many thanks. I must now mention to you that the whole continent seems to be agitated concerning colonising the People of Colour. Indeed the People of Colour, here was very much fritened (sic) at first. They were afrade (sic) that all the free people would be compelled to go, particularly in the southern states. We had a large meets (sic) of Males at the Rev. R. Allens church the other evening three thousand at least attended, and there was not one sole (sic) that was in favor of going to Africa. They think, that the slave holders want to get rid of them so as to make their property more secure....My opinion is that they will never become a people until they com (sic) out from amongst the white people, but as the majority is decidedly against me I am determined to remain silent, accept as to my opinion which I freely give when asked.[30]

In the same year of this letter, Paul Cuffe died before he could make a personal appeal in Philadelphia. In some respects the decision by the

Africans of Philadelphia to reject Cuffe's emigration program was wise. With over half of the African population in America still enslaved on southern plantations, many believed that a retreat to Africa would have left a considerable political vacuum in America. Some argued that if militant free Africans emigrated to Africa, who would be available to agitate and protest against the cruel institution of slavery? In reality, the majority of the free Africans who did remain in America made no significant and revolutionary impacts upon the efforts to end slavery. As the plantations in the South became more efficient, and the threats of violent upheavals increased, the owners considered freedom and colonization as an option. As the population of free Africans increased, many became preoccupied with issues of survival and widespread discrimination such as in churches. Their protests over segregation in the European-American churches of Philadelphia led to the founding of the African-Methodist Episcopal Church by Absalom Jones and Richard Allen. This pattern of reaction against European-American institutions resulted in the formation of useless parallel organizations that contributed very little to the actual liberation of Africans from slavery.

Despite the less-than-enthusiastic reception to Cuffe's efforts among free Africans in Philadelphia, one cannot deny the importance of his pioneering work. As a Pan-Africanist, he established a clear paradigm for free Africans who acquired wealth in the nineteenth century. Central to his conceptualization of African people's role in the universe was Africa. He believed that Africans should compete with Europeans in the realm of economics in order to acquire a reasonable level of self-sufficiency. However, capitalism to Cuffe was no end in itself, but a vehicle to achieve independence on the African continent. He envisioned a strong Africa and recognized the potential impetus that the repatriated African could give to that development.

He was significant in two other respects. On the one hand he demonstrated to the heartless traders in human flesh that a person could engage in commerce and make an honorable living. He posed a striking contrast to the slavers who dealt in the oppression and murder of other human beings. Seen in the context of the early nineteenth century, when the slave trade was booming, Cuffe's accomplishments warrant the utmost praise.

Finally, the greatness of the man cannot be divorced from the vicissitudes of his convictions. Paul Cuffe was a Quaker and the Quakers were the first religious group in America to condemn slavery. Cuffe demonstrated to the world the depth of his convictions and the extent to which he was willing to sacrifice himself and his resources. Some will argue that he was merely an African-American missionary desiring to civilize the natives; or an African-American capitalist desiring to create great wealth through legitimate trade between nations. It is clear that he was both a religious person and a businessman. But his interest in commerce and loathing of the institution of slavery provided him a unique opportunity to offer a small number of Africans in America an alternative to despair and racism.

Even though Cuffe was unable to garner substantial support for repatriation, powerful European-American interests moved forward to fill the vacuum of leadership by establishing the American Colonization Society. Thus indecision on the part of African-American leadership, particularly in Philadelphia, meant that the repatriation efforts of Cuffe, with its reliance upon African control, would be compromised. This compromise had a profound effect upon repatriation efforts in the nineteenth century. First, it meant that it created an opportunity for northern industrialists and southern plantation owners to consolidate their resources for the further exploitation of Africa. Second, and more important, it meant that the future of Liberia would be integrally tied to American economic and racial interests, without free Africans having a substantial role in its early planning and development.

Notes

1. Sheldon H. Harris, *Paul Cuffe: Black America and the African Return* (New York: Simon and Schuster, 1972), page 15.
2. Carter G. Woodson and Charles H. Wesley, *The Story of the Negro Retold* (Washington, DC: The Associated Publishers, 1959), page 107.
3. E. Franklin Frazier, *The Negro in the United States,* rev. ed. (New York: Macmillan, 1961), page 67.
4. Woodson, page 108.
5. Frazier, page 68.
6. Frazier, page 68.
7. Frazier, page 60.

8. Free Public Library of New Bedford, *Cuffee Collection*, Reel 1.
9. Harris, page 36.
10. Cuffe cited in Harris, page 36.
11. George Padmore, *Pan-Africanism or Communism* (London: Dennis Dobson, 1965), page 45.
12. John Cuffe, in his letter dated January 5, 1811, indicated that Paul left home on November 15, setting off for Philadelphia, then for Africa. John indicated that it was "for a religious visit among the inhabitants" Free Public Library of New Bedford, *Cuffee Collection*, Reel 1.
13. Julie Winch, *Philadelphia's Black Elite:Activism, Accommodation, and the Struggle for Autonomy, 1787 to1848* (Philadelphia: Temple University Press, 1988), page 31. Professor Winch indicates that Cuffe organized the Friendly Society of Sierra Leone, but there is also evidence that he organized the Society of Sierra Leone in Africa as well.
14. Free Public Library of New Bedford, *Cuffee Collection*, Reel 1. Sixteen free men of color signed this statement in Sierra Leone on April 26, 1811. They were John Gordon; preacher, Warwick Francis, James Reed, Joseph Brown, Moses Wilkerson, S. Jones, John Ellis, Adam Jones, Geo Clark, Peter Francis, George Carrel, Edward Willoughley, Tho Richards, Eli Aikim, Jn Stevenson and Jas. Wise.
15. William Loren Katz, *Eyewitness: The Negro in American History* (New York: Pitman, 1967), page 139.
16. Mabel Morsbach, *The Negro in American Life* (Cincinnati: Cincinnati Lithographing, 1966), page 45.
17. Harris, page 77.
18. Harris, page 82.
19. Harris, page 83.
20. Harris, page 84.
21. Harris, page 95.
22. Harris, page 105.
23. Harris, page 108.
24. Harris, page 176.
25. Clarkson and Allen cited in Harris, page 176.
26. Harris, page 177.
27. Cuffe cited in Harris, page 184.
28. Harris, page 192.
29. Free Library of New Bedford, "Letter Book of Paul Cuffe," *Cuffee Collection*, Reel 1.
30. Free Library, "Letter Book," Reel 1.

Chapter Three

AFRO-BRITISH RESETTLEMENT: THE EARLIEST EUROPEAN EXPERIMENT

The British experience with African resettlement in Sierra Leone provided a rationale and plan of action for America's nascent resettlement efforts. While the southerners had initially viewed Africa as a repository for their unwanted blacks, they quickly recognized the potential for economic exploitation as well. Both the British and the Americans found that they had a common problem within their countries: unwanted African populations. For the British, slavery, which was primarily concentrated in the colonies, was becoming an economic drain, and a strong and vocal antislavery movement had begun to develop. The removal of Africans from British soil to the West African colony of Sierra Leone represented, in part, a solution to these pressing problems. Moreover, colonization presented more than the mere opportunity for removal of Africans, it opened up an opportunity to exploit the land and its natural resources.

The British experiment, therefore, provided the Americans with a model that went beyond mere resettlement but required a continuing presence and involvement with the continent. Colonization required the Americans to maintain a tutelage relationship with the returning Africans, which gave the Americans a valuable foothold on the continent that they had failed to establish during the slave-trade era. Therefore, slavery, and the social and economic challenges it engendered, represented the primary cause of America's look to colonization and the British experiment as an appropriate model.

American Controversy over Slavery

After over 300 years of importing Africans into the United States as articles of commerce, the founding fathers were faced with a pressing moral dilemma on the eve of the founding of the new republic. Opposition to the institution of slavery was mounting and more important, it was becoming unprofitable.

The question of whether the new republic would be free of slaves had been a raging political controversy in the eighteenth century. Throughout the Constitutional Convention, delegates debated whether to keep Africans in bondage or to free them. The question of resettlement received little attention, although the British experiment was known to most of the delegates. By the signing of the Declaration of Independence, which represented the cornerstone of American democracy, slavery existed in all of the American colonies.[1] It therefore represented an ignominious blot upon the American conscience; and was a result of both northern and southern economic policies. In 1637 the first slaves were brought into New England,[2] and even the liberal Quaker William Penn owned slaves in Pennsylvania.[3]

As a result of this early presence of slaves in the colonies, the respective delegates to the Constitutional Convention articulated positions that grew out of their particular state's policy on the slavery question. It was not uncommon for southerners to come out against slavery, while northerners advocated for its continuation. For instance, a representative from Maryland, Luther Martin, favored the suppression of the slave trade on the grounds that it made a mockery out of the principles of the American Revolution.[4] Furthermore, representatives from Virginia as well as Maryland opposed the slave trade on the grounds that it would interfere with their domestic slave-breeding industries.

Another important issue in the Convention, which threatened to tear it apart, concerned the political status to be given Africans under the Constitution. Would Africans be recognized as full human beings for political representation? In other words, would the owners of slaves be able to count each slave as a person for purposes of determining representation in Congress? This question foreshadowed the essential issue for Africans during the nineteenth century, that is would this nation recognize them as full human beings, not only for purposes of political representation, but also because it was right and just? Some of the states threatened to withdraw completely from the Convention if slaves were given full representation in Congress. These states, such as Georgia, felt that since slavery was a matter controlled by the local state governments, and since some states recognized slavery, full representation in

Congress would undermine their rights as states. After a heated debate, a compromise was reached whereby slaves were given three-fifths status in the House of Representatives.[5]

Many Americans, however, refused to accept the resolutions coming out of the Constitutional Convention and began to organize campaigns for the elimination of slavery. One such person was John Woolman (1720 to1772), a devoutly religious man, who feared that the evil of slavery would lead to further social evils and that the only way for America to cleanse itself of these evils was to free the slaves-in essence, to repent of its sins and adopt more humane values.[6] To advance this belief, in 1804 Woolman and some of his friends founded the "American Convention for Promoting the Abolition of Slavery and Improving the Condition of the African Race," a private organization dedicated to disseminating information on slavery throughout the country.

Although many private citizens campaigned against slavery, the country was still split as to when to grant freedom to Africans and under what conditions. Some states, such as Massachusetts and Rhode Island, liberalized their laws in regard to slavery, but did not outlaw the traffic outright. For instance, Rhode Island in 1652 passed a law that slaves should be freed at the age of twenty-four, which significantly limited the number of years a person would be in bondage. Some private citizens instituted sugar boycotts against cane raised by slave labor.[7] This form of protest, initiated by Quakers, gathered considerable momentum among the Quaker community, but failed to spread to other communities.

Resettlement as an Alternative

As these protests against slavery gathered momentum in the nineteenth century, and European-Americans began to realize that abolition would result in a substantial portion of the African population being freed, resettlement increasingly was cited as a way of controlling the increase of the free African population. In the northern states the proponents of resettlement envisioned the removal of Africans from the United States as aiding the northern abolitionist movements by serving as an incentive for slaveowners to free their slaves.

The South, on the other hand, saw resettlement as a way to protect its economic investments in slaves. Therefore, resettlement received widespread support from southerners as long as it did not interfere with the property rights of the slaveowners. It would be supported only if it led to the elimination of potentially volatile groups of Africans who, they felt, incited uprisings on the plantations and therefore placed their property in jeopardy.

In 1817 southerners and northerners were able to put their differences aside and combine their efforts through a new organization, the American Colonization Society. As the Society sought greater support among southern plantation owners, the need to articulate its purposes in a clearer manner became evident. The Society promised that it would increase the value of the slave property and help strengthen the system of slavery. Those Africans who were an economic drain upon the plantation system would be removed. Those who would be freed would not be allowed to remain in the country.[8] Many believed that it was particularly important that the Africans in the South be removed because they were increasingly becoming a threat to the system.

Eastern supporters of resettlement envisioned free Africans returning to Africa to Christianize the so-called heathens. Their plan saw the creation of a colony on the coast of Africa and the resultant colonization as part of America's obligation to the inhabitants of the "benighted" continent. These emigrants would carry culture, Christianity and civilization to the African masses and become teachers, preachers and politicians and work to end the slave trade.

Americans in the western part of the United States considered free Africans a public nuisance and saw resettlement as a means of abating the nuisance: "Neither humanity, nor legislation can relieve them here. Must remain forever a degraded caste. In one part of the country dull as a British beast, in the other, the wild stirrers up of insurrection."[9]

British Colonization Efforts

The Society provided an important option for whites struggling with the African presence in the United States. At last, a vehicle had been created that would aid in the removal of Africans as well as open up new opportunities for trade in Africa. Despite the different rationales for resettlement, many people in the United States joined together under the aegis of the American Colonization Society.

Afro-British Resettlement: The Earliest European Experiment

The idea of mass removal of Africans from the Western world was not new, because the British had already successfully developed and implemented a program to the west coast of Africa. The leadership of the American Colonization Society, therefore, looked to Britain for information on how to develop its colonization scheme.

Surprisingly enough, the concerns of the British populace, which prompted the development of its colonization efforts, closely paralleled those of America. As in America, philanthropists and abolitionists, such as Granville Sharp, argued throughout Britain that slavery violated the natural rights of every man to be free.[10] Granville Sharp was born in England in 1735 and by 1787 had founded an abolitionist movement. In the latter years of his life, Sharp began to embrace colonization as a means to solve the problem of unwanted Africans in England. He developed his thinking on colonization, in part, from the writings of the Frenchman Du Pont de Nemours who, as editor of *Ephemerides du Citoyen*, articulated an economic rationale for the abolition of slavery.[11] Du Pont advocated colonization in order to replace expensive slave labor with free labor that would engage in commerce on the west coast of Africa. Granville Sharp adopted these economic arguments as he attempted to gather financial and moral support from the British population. In order to learn some of Sharp's ideas on colonization, Dr. R. Hopkins of Rhode Island wrote Sharp in 1783 enquiring about the topography of west Africa.[12] In 1790, a few years after Hopkins corresponded with Sharp, a Virginian, Fernando Fairfax, published an article on colonization that stirred considerable interest in the South, particularly among the large plantation owners. Shortly after this correspondence, in 1816, the Virginia legislature passed a resolution supporting the removal of Africans from the United States. The resolution authorized the executive of the Commonwealth of Virginia to communicate with the president of the United States in order to obtain information concerning the removal of free Africans from Virginia to Africa.[13]

In the following year the "American Society for Colonizing the Free People of Colour in the United States" was formed. Many of the Virginian politicians, such as Bushrod Washington, the brother of George Washington, quickly learned about Britain's experience and became leaders of the new society. Other American notables who served as officers of the society were James Madison, Henry Clay and Daniel Webster as presidents; and Chief Justice John Marshall as vice president.[14] The founders of this society intended to relocate free Africans, with their consent, in Africa or in any other place that Congress approved.

Similarly, the Sierra Leone effort was initiated by an act of the British Parliament in 1791 that established the Sierra Leone Company. The aims of the Sierra Leone Company found a receptive audience in the United States: (1.) To settle and cultivate these lands; (2.) To open a trade with other countries in the products of the soil....[15]

The Company's experiment was not solely humanitarian, rather, it was both humanitarian and economic. The British realized that they could no longer actively participate in the slave trade due to mounting public outrage at home, but they could continue to reap economic windfalls by developing trade on the African continent. In addition, those Africans who had freely roamed the streets of London could be exploited now as free laborers in the new British colony.

Prior to the Sierra Leone Company, the British, as well as the Portuguese, had been engaged in the exploitation of Africa. The first Europeans to reach West Africa to trade in slaves and gold were the Portuguese who, in attempting to find a route to the Far East, landed at Sierra Leone in the fifteenth century. The Portuguese immediately established trade with the Temne and Bulom ethnic groups and gave the country the name: "Serra Lyoa."[16] The missionaries closely followed the traders into Sierra Leone and preached that the Africans were heathen and needed to be converted to Christianity. This Christian propaganda led to social disintegration as many Africans began to feel that their culture and religious practices were inferior and evil. Such feelings led to social discord among the Africans and a favorable climate for more extensive European penetration into the continent.

Following the Portuguese, the Dutch arrived on the west coast of Africa. France and England followed suit as competition with the Dutch over African exports became more intense. Furthermore, the stock of English gold and silver constantly decreased as the Dutch monopolized the trade on the west coast. Consequently, the British government set up trading companies in the seventeenth century to compete with Dutch enterprises. In addition, the demand for slaves in the southern plantations led the British deeper into the competitive slave trade in the west coast of Africa.

The British therefore had a long history in the exploitation of Africa before it developed its Sierra Leone Company. This history was set on course by the Royal African Company, which was chartered in 1679. The first company was the Royal Adventurers into Africa (1660), which was chartered to compete with other European companies involved in the slave trade. These companies imported guns, fabrics and other commodities into Africa and exchanged them for slaves who were taken to the West Indies and America.[17] In 1680 the Royal African Company monopoly was abolished once Britain realized that greater profits could be gained by opening up the trade to free enterprise. Slaves were brought to America and England for selfish reasons. Colonization, likewise, resulted from continuing economic and racial motives.

As pressure mounted to participate in the colonization program, many free Africans in England were faced with a nagging dilemma: should they endorse and participate in British colonization? Some Africans, who had sufficient means, had emigrated from the West Indies to England, while others, who had fought for the British in the American Revolution, obtained their freedom and settled there. By 1785 the African population of England numbered about 25,000.[18] Most of the Africans who settled in the large cities of England, such as London, found that they were not welcome. Unable to find jobs, many turned to the streets and engaged in begging, which became a familiar scene in London during the eighteenth century. In 1772 an Englishman, Edward Long, wrote a pamphlet urging the government to restrain the immigration of Africans into England because their numbers were rising faster than they were able to find meaningful employment. He was also alarmed at the increase in miscegenation. He argued that "blacks" were impregnating British women, which caused him to warn the British people in no uncertain terms:

> The lower class of women in England, are remarkably fond of the Blacks, for reasons too brutal to mention; they would connect themselves to horses and asses, if the laws permitted them. By these ladies they generally have a numerous brood. Thus in the course of a few generations more, the English blood will become so contaminated by mixture,

> and from the chancers, the ups and downs of life, this alloy may spread so extensively, as even to reach the middle, and then the higher orders of the people, till the whole nation resembles the Portuguese and Moriscos in complexion of skin and baseness of mind.[19]

As a result of writings such as Long's, British citizens were awakened to the growing presence of Africans in their societies. Some attempted to raise monies to educate the Africans and provide them with the necessities of life, but many believed that the problem was too vast for charity to handle alone. Furthermore, the problem of the increasing number of free Africans became more complicated in 1772 after the ruling of Lord Mansfield in a case involving James Somerset, an African slave. The case helped raise the consciousness of the British public about the condition of free Africans in the country. James Somerset was a slave who had been brought from Virginia to England by his master. After a brief stop, Somerset was scheduled to be taken to Jamaica, where he would resume his duties as a slave. To the master's surprise, prominent abolitionists, such as Sharp, convinced the British courts to issue temporary legal orders that prohibited the master from removing Somerset from England, and required that he be brought to court for a hearing to determine the lawfulness of his detention. The issue at trial was whether Somerset had become free as a result of being brought onto British soil. After a lengthy trial, Lord Mansfield ruled that slavery could exist in England only as a result of positive law, and that since there was no evidence that positive law authorized slavery on British soil, Somerset had to be set free. As a result of the case and the agitation of Granville Sharp, thousands of Africans were freed from slavery without any form of financial support or chance of competing with British workers.

Sierra Leone Colony

As public opinion mounted concerning unemployed Africans, who were frequenting London streets, Granville Sharp seized the opportunity to draft a proposal to send Africans to Sierra Leone. Since the British had a historical relationship with West Africa, it was the logical place to send the unwanted Africans. Consequently, in 1786 a private company, the "St. George's Bay Company" was formed and charged with the task of transporting Britain's African population to

Sierra Leone. On February 22, 1787, two naval vessels, commissioned by the British Treasury, transported 4,000 Africans and a number of British settlers to Sierra Leone. The British public donated £240,000 toward the colonization effort.[20] Despite the protracted negotiating of the terms for a site with Temne rulers, Granville Sharp was only able to guarantee that seventy prostitutes accompany the male settlers.

Four years later the "Sierra Leone Company" under the leadership of Granville Sharp was founded and charged with the responsibility of continuing to transport Africans to Sierra Leone. The company built schools for the missionaries to train the settlers and to teach them Christianity. All land in the settlement was entrusted to the company and the British directors had immediate jurisdiction over it. Furthermore, the settlers were required to sign a declaration of allegiance to the company and its administration.

This control of the colony was consistent with the initial intentions of the Sierra Leone Company: to open up trade. Not only were the British interested in getting rid of a "despicable" group from its population, but they were also interested in exploiting the natural resources of West Africa. The scheme worked, as England discovered numerous resources in Sierra Leone which justified their control of the colony. In 1850 British commerce with Sierra Leone amounted to at least five million pounds sterling or $25 million per year.[21] The British also capitalized upon the gold found in West Africa. By 1850 the British had received $200,000 in gold from Sierra Leone.[22] Although the Africans had ostensibly been returned to Africa so that they could be free, in reality they were not free. They had no political freedom; effective control of the colony remained in the hands of the company. Many of the Africans therefore felt betrayed as they found themselves second class citizens.

The African settlers, on the other hand, did not complacently accept this second-class status. Many rose in protest in the early years of the settlement when a quit rent was levied upon them. In 1800 the rebellions reached a crescendo as the settlers vowed to disobey the laws of the country. The protests, however, subsided soon thereafter as the Sierra Leone Company continued to rule the colony until 1808 when the British government declared the colony Crown property. When Paul Cuffe, the prominent African-American merchant, visited Sierra

Leone in 1811, the colony was governed according to British law, which indicated that the colony had completely become a British possession.

British Model for Americans

The US House of Representatives, investigating the feasibility of establishing trade between Liberia and the United States, frequently cited the Sierra Leone model as a paradigm that should be followed. The Commerce Committee of the House contemplated the establishment of a steamship fleet to carry mail but also recognized the commercial potential of West Africa. The report read:

> The establishment of prosperous colonies on the western coast of Africa will, doubtless, tend greatly, in the course of time, to the augmentation of the commerce of this country... the commerce of Africa is certainly capable of great extension, and it is worthy of observation, that the proposed steamers will open entirely new sources of trade.[23]

The committee pointed out that the demand for palm oil, which is produced from palm tree nuts, was mounting throughout Europe as a result of the trade instituted by the British in Sierra Leone. According to the report, the average annual import of palm oil into Liverpool was 15,000 tons. The report also noted a trade in ivory, which was a significant revenue item for the British.

Liberia, according to the committee, was the key to opening this profitable trade to the Americas. The colonists were to be mere agents for the furtherance of United States economic interests:

> The Liberians have constitutions adapted to the climate, and a similarity of colorwith the natives. They will penetrate the interior with safety, and prosecute their trade in the bays and rivers of the coast, without suffering from the diseases which are fated to the whiteman. Liberia is the door of Africa, and is destined to develope the agricultural and commercial resources of that continent, besides being the means of regenerating her benighted millions.[24]

Furthermore, the committee took particular pains to emphasize that the proposed scheme of establishing steamships to carry mail would not interfere with slavery. Such a remark was necessary to assure the political leadership in the federal government, which had a vested interest in slavery, that their property rights would not be violated. The steamships would have the narrow function of transporting mail only and would not engage in any form of regulating the commercial trade between Africa and America. On the contrary, the mail services would enable the businessmen to communicate more effectively between the two continents and consequently enhance their business activities.

The Americans followed the same path of the British in denying the returned Africans any political power, and in subjugating the indigenous Africans with force. In Liberia, the settlement of free Africans required the acquisition of land. Some of the indigenous Africans consented to the sale of land known as Monserado to Dr. Eli Ayres and Captain Stockton of the US Navy in December 1821. Some, on the other hand, rebelled against the settlers who came in June 1822. On November 8 of that year, approximately 800 indigenous Africans attacked the settlement. A second attack by close to 2,000 Africans was carried out against the fort on November 30, resulting in heavy casualties among the colonists.[25]

After taking the land by both force and negotiation, the American Colonization Society, with the aid of the US government, instituted its administrative mechanism in the colony. In order to insure that the colony remained under the control of the Society, the Board of Managers appointed a colonial agent who was European-American, while the lower officers were African-American.[26] The former were given nominal power while absolute power resided in the society. Chief Justice Marshall, in a letter to the secretary of the American Colonization Society on December 14, 1831, confirmed that the ownership of the colony was vested in European-Americans: "The lands are the property of the United States, and have heretofore been disposed of by the government under the idea of absolute ownership."[27] As in the case of Sierra Leone, the land did not belong to the repatriated Africans, but to the colonial government.

Sierra Leone had a profound effect, not only upon the thinking of European-American political figures, but also upon the thinking of prominent free blacks. Paul Cuffe, the New Bedford, Massachusetts, shipbuilder and Quaker saw Sierra Leone as serving an important role in the evangelization of the African continent. In an account written by Cuffe in 1812 he admitted that it was his interest in missionary work that induced him to visit the colony of Sierra Leone in 1811.[28] When Cuffe arrived in the colony, he was impressed by the hold Christianity had on the new settlers. Even Africans in the interior of the country had been exposed to Christianity and some were converts as a result of early missionary activity.

As with most Western visitors to Africa, Cuffe was impressed by the abundance of fertile land in Sierra Leone and recognized the enormous potential for commerce, which could also be utilized to aid him in his efforts to spread Christianity.

Finally, Sierra Leone served as inspiration for the American plantation owners who wished to rid themselves of a growing "public nuisance." Therefore, the cry of humanitarianism and evangelism, which formed the basis of much of Britain's activities in Sierra Leone, became the justification to hide racist and economic motives that underlay the colonization movement in America. Furthermore, Africa had to be described as a land of heathens and darkness waiting for Christianity to bring light. Therefore, Granville Sharp's humanitarian idealism became a tool for southern plantation owners and northern philanthropists to mask their racism and economic greed.

Notes

1. James Z. George, *The Political History of Slavery in the United States* (New York: Mnemosyne Publishing Co., 1915), page 5.
2. George, page 6.
3. George, page 6.
4. George, page 9.
5. George, page 9.
6. William Pease and Jane H. Pease, eds, *The Anti-Slavery Argument* (New York: Bobbs-Merrill, 1965), page 8.
7. David Brion Davis, *The Problem of Slavery in Western Culture* (Ithaca. NY: Cornell University Press, 1966), page 490.
8. August Meier and Elliott M. Rudwick, *From Plantation to Ghetto* (New York: Hill and Wang, 1968), page 29.
9. Stanley Elkins, *Slavery: A Problem in American Institutional and Intellectual Life,* 2nd ed. (Chicago: University of Chicago Press, 1969), page 48.
10. Davis, page 412.
11. Davis, page 431.

12. James C. Dunn, *Address of the Managers of the American Colonization Society to the People in the United States* (Washington, DC: 1832), page 9.
13. Dunn, page 9.
14. F. Freeman, *Yaradee: A Plea for Africa: Familiar Conversations on the Subject of Slavery and Colonization* (Philadelphia: J. Whetham, 1836), page 202.
15. Adelaide Hill and Martin Kilson, *Apropos of Africa: Sentiments of Negro American Leaders on Africa from the 1800's to the 1950's* (New York: Frank Cass, 1969), page 1.
16. Christopher Fyfe, *A Short History of Sierra Leone* (London: Longmans, Green, 1962), page 5.
17. Meier and Rudwick, page 29.
18. Richard West, *Back to Africa: A History of Sierra Leone and Liberia* (London: Jonathan Cape, 1970), page 15.
19. Long cited in West, page 14.
20. George Padmore, *Pan-Africanism or Communism* (London: Dennis Dobson, 1956), page 31.
21. U.S. House of Representatives, *Report of Naval Committee on Establishing a Line of Mail Steamships on the Western Coast of Africa, and Thence via the Mediterranean to London* (Washington, DC: Gideon and Company, 1850), page 21.
22. U.S. House, page 21.
23. U.S. House, page 21.
24. U.S. House, page 21.
25. Dunn, page 10.
26. Dunn, page 10.
27. Marshall cited at Dunn, page 16.
28. Hill and Kilson, page 14.
29. William Loren Katz, *Eyewitness: The Negro in American History* (New York: Pitman, 1967), page 139.

Chapter Four

AFRICAN-AMERICAN MILITANCY AND THE IMPETUS FOR COLONIZATION

While the British efforts in Sierra Leone provided a model for the Americans, African militancy precipitated revolutionary action in the United States. Several historical events led to the creation of the American Colonization Society in 1817. First, on March 2, 1808, the slave trade to America became unlawful at a time when the slave population had increased to a point where, many believed, further growth would lead to economic instability. Furthermore, the success of the Haitian Revolution sent shock waves throughout the South as many plantation owners realized that their efforts to pacify Africans might fail.

Second, the fear of African population explosion was reinforced by this heightened fear of slave uprisings. Rebellions had been common occurrences in the South. As early as 1663, Virginia residents uncovered a conspiracy to rebel against the plantation system. In 1687 another plan to kill all whites in the vicinity of a slave cemetery was discovered in the Northern Neck section of Virginia.[1] Conditions reached such a point in Virginia that the state passed a series of slave codes that significantly restricted the movement of slaves on and off the plantation. In order to travel off the plantation, slaves needed the written permission of their owners. Even for the slightest offenses slaves became subject to severe punishment. In some cases, incorrigible slaves were maimed or disfigured by having their ears cut off.[2] These procedures, though largely unsuccessful, were undoubtedly instituted to prevent communication between slave communities at different plantations. Despite these comprehensive efforts to stifle protest, Africans rose up and confronted their oppression with revolutionary violence.

Gabriel Prosser

The first major insurrection plot in the United States led by a slave, Gabriel Prosser, caused widespread fear to spread among Virginia plantation owners. Some observers estimated that Gabriel had amassed over 1,000 slaves for his plot.[3] The plan was well thought out and could have been successful, but for the torrential rains and a few informers. The group, which consisted of African men and a few European-Americans, had planned to capture Richmond, Virginia, and take Governor James Monroe hostage. They would then kill all whites with the exception of Methodists, Quakers, Frenchmen and poor whites. They had hoped that the Catawba Indians would join in the revolt as well. The insurrection began on August 30, 1800, but the rains were so torrential that the group was forced to postpone for another day, which allowed the authorities to organize and crush the efforts. Gabriel's brothers, Martin and Solomon, were captured, tried and hanged. On October 6, Gabriel was tried and on October 10, 1800, hanged. His hopes of seizing Richmond, Norfolk and Petersburg were not realized, but he and his followers sent a strong message to the country that they would prefer death to denial of liberty.

This militant uprising, in the spirit of the Haitian Revolution, caused most Europeans to doubt whether Africans could ever be integrated into America.[4] As a result, many plantation owners, who had never seriously entertained the question of colonization before, became strong supporters. In 1805 the governor of Virginia wrote to the president of the United States requesting cooperation in its colonization efforts.[5] In the same year, the Virginia legislature passed a resolution requesting the federal government to allocate plots of land in Louisiana for black people who were considered "dangerous to the public safety." All of these movements on the part of the majority population indicated their belief that separation was the most advantageous manner to address the increasingly volatile African-American presence.

These revolutionary struggles for freedom did not dissipate as the nineteenth century progressed. Rather, they intensified as both enslaved and free Africans lashed out at their oppressors and their institutions of exploitation. The struggle intensified and spread throughout the South, sparking a massive rebellion in 1822 in South Carolina.

Denmark Vesey

The 1822 plot of Denmark Vesey in Charleston, South Carolina, heightened the fear among the plantation owners. Vesey, unlike Gabriel, was a free black who had purchased his freedom and worked as a carpenter. While plantation owners constantly feared slaves and therefore developed sophisticated instruments for their repression, little had been done to control free Africans. Vesey drew upon the courageous spirit of the Africans in Santo Domingo to support his movement: "We must unite together as the Santo Domingo people did, never to betray one another, and to die before we would tell upon one another.... We were fully able to conquer the whites, if we were only unanimous and courageous, as the Santo Domingo people were."[6]

The Vesey plan awakened the South to the potential threat of free Africans organizing and leading rebellions. Although Vesey planned his uprising for months, the revolt that involved as many as 9,000 slaves, was thwarted by informers.[7] As a result, thirty-five men were tried and hanged, of which twenty-one were members of the African Methodist Episcopal Church in Charleston. Although the plot was aborted, it made plantation owners aware that slaves and free Africans would not peacefully accept slavery and their continued exploitation.

Harriet Tubman

The plantation owners had to also worry about fugitives from slavery who, through multiethnic coalitions, developed a massive mechanism that helped other slaves escape slavery. Leaders such as Harriet Tubman, a runaway from Maryland, helped keep the hope of freedom alive among slaves and put their own freedom in jeopardy in order to strike at the plantation system. Each time that the "Underground Railroad" succeeded in getting slaves to freedom, it represented an effective assault against the system.

Tubman fled Maryland in 1849 at the age of thirty. Her personal freedom was empty and without meaning, unless her brothers and sisters held in bondage were free as well. She explained:

> I had crossed the line of which I had so long been dreaming. I was free; but there was no one to welcome me to the land of freedom. I was a stranger in a strange land, and my home after all was down in the old cabin quarters, with the

> old folks, and my brothers and sisters. But to this solemn resolution I came; I was free, and they should be free also; I would make a home for them in the North, and the Lord helping me, I would bring them all there.[8]

She returned to lead her two brothers and parents to freedom. In all, it is estimated that she made twenty trips into the South and rescued over 200 slaves from bondage.[9]

Tubman could not rest until she had done all she could to cripple the slavery system. In this regard, she was an extraordinary individual in the nineteenth century. She was able to realize that coalition building was essential to her struggle for liberation. African people being held in captivity needed the assistance, not only of free Africans, but others as well. As a result, she formed and became part of a broad spectrum of European-Americans whose political persuasions ranged from gradual abolitionists to revolutionaries. It is reported that she carried a pistol in one hand and a Bible in the other and met with the greatest European-American revolutionary of the nineteenth century, John Brown, when he and other African-Americans met in St. Catherines, Ontario, to plan their raid on Harpers Ferry, Virginia, and to begin a militant assault that they believe would topple slavery.

David Walker's Appeal

Another African who used his freedom to advance that of his people was David Walker. The publication of *David Walker's Appeal to the Coloured Citizens of the World* in 1829 caused still further apprehension among plantation owners. As a freeman David Walker lashed out unsparingly at the motives of the American Colonization Society and the institution of slavery in the South. He unequivocally objected to the colonization of Africans in Liberia, seeing colonization as a deliberate attempt by southern slaveowners to remove those who represented a political threat to the plantation system.[10] In his book, Walker analyzes and delineates the causes of what he terms African "wretchedness": (1). slavery, (2). ignorance, (3). the preachers of the religion of Jesus Christ, and (4). the colonizing plan. Of these four causes, the longest and most developed is the treatise entitled "the colonizing plan." In Article IV of his book, Walker developed a clear and forceful condemnation of colonization. In the opening paragraph, he discussed a speech made by Henry Clay, former secretary of state and speaker of the House, in which Clay argued that "coloured" people should be settled on the coast of Africa. Clay points out that these settlers could then bring to Africa "the arts, civilization, and Christianity."

Walker quickly lashed out at this goal as profoundly hypocritical and paradoxical. First, Walker, in very strong terms, distinguished the God of African people from that of the European-Americans engaged in the slave trade. In fact, his God of African people would avenge the wrongs perpetrated against his people by the slaveowners. Walker quickly puts himself in the company of the Biblical prophets of old who predicted divine retribution for the wrongs visited upon God's people. He writes: "When God Almighty commences his battle on the continent of America, for the oppression of *his people* (emphasis added), tyrants will wish they never were born."[11]

Through this writing, Walker holds up the entire political and business leadership of America to a more universal Christian moral standard. Despite their trappings of respectability and wealth, Walker sees Henry Clay and others as mere "tyrants" and their teachings as "false Christianity." Consequently, Walker's essays represented a major broadside against so-called American honor and virtue. His cry called not only for repentance, but also for reparations:

> The Blood of our fathers who have been murdered by the whites, and the groans of our Brethren, who are now held in cruel ignorance, wretchedness and slavery by them, cry aloud to the Maker of Heaven and of earth, against the whole continent of America, for redresses.[12]

In distinction to Henry Clay, Elias B. Caldwell, John Roanoke and others, he applauds Bishop Richard Allen of the African Methodist Episcopal Church. Bishop Allen and his church symbolized true righteousness in America, not only because of their steadfast opposition to slavery, but because of their opposition to colonization. Walker saw Bishop Allen's name and his work as ranking with the most illustrious of individuals: "Suffice it for me to say, that the name of this very man (Richard Allen) though now in obscurity and degradation, will notwithstanding, stand on the pages of history among the greatest divines who have lived since the apostolic age, and among the Africans, Bishop Allen's will be entirely preeminent."[13]

Walker contrasted Bishop Allen with "some of our brethren" who joined with their oppressors in supporting colonization and criticizing leaders like Allen. While Walker never described these individuals in modern parlance as "Uncle Toms," he made it clear that these "poor ignorant creatures" have been manipulated by "whites." These misguided "coloureds," because they allied themselves with the "whites" were, by definition, in opposition to "God and Righteousness."[14] Therefore, Richard Allen, in Walker's view, was more than a man, but a symbol of righteousness, while those who opposed him, whether African or "white," represented the embodiment of evil.

In his reader's mind, Walker left no doubt of his position on colonization: "Will any of us leave our homes and go to Africa? I hope not."[15] For him, African-Americans had made a tremendous investment in America, "Our Country." He, more than any individual in the nineteenth century, expressed an unequivocal claim to America and its land. America belonged to Africans more than it did to the "whites." Africans, according to Walker, had a vested interest in America: "The greatest riches in all America have arisen from our blood and tears:- and will they drive us from our property and homes, which we have earned with *our blood?*"[16] Furthermore, he boldly claimed America as the home of Africans. He wrote: "This country is as much ours as it is the whites, whether they will admit it now or not, they will see and believe it by and by."[17]

Walker was concerned not only with the plight of slaves in the South, but also with the exploitation of black people around the world. Walker's advocacy of armed insurrection against the slave system alarmed plantation owners throughout the South and eventually led to his death in 1830, the year of publication of the third edition of his book.

Nat Turner Rebellion

The Nat Turner rebellion, however, did more than any other rebellion to awaken southern aristocrats to the real dangers created by slavery. In 1828 Nat Turner, a Southampton County, Virginia slave, revealed to close acquaintances that the "Spirit of his God" had instructed him to lead a revolt against slavery. On August 22 1831, Turner and about 60 men lashed out at every white household in the area, killing all that they came in contact with. Their ultimate goal was to reach Jerusalem and capture the arms stored in the town. Although Turner's campaign for freedom was relentless, his band of revolutionaries could not fight off the heavily armed plantation owners and their loyal slaves. Turner escaped to the woods where he remained in hiding for six weeks. On October 30, he was captured and on November 11, hanged. Some scholars estimated the number of Europeans killed at sixty and Africans at over a hundred. As these reports spread throughout the South, the number of whites killed was grossly exaggerated, which created widespread alarm among southern plantation owners. In response, the southern states strengthened Black Codes, which limited the movement of slaves even further.

As a result of these rebellions, agitation for the American Colonization Society to transport blacks to Africa increased. Those slaves who constituted political threats to the plantation system were immediately deported to Liberia: between 1820 and 1842, of the total number (4,454) of emigrants sent to the colony, 2,290 were emancipated specifically for deportation.[18] Furthermore, the emigrants from Virginia, where the Turner rebellion occurred, made up a large part of the population in Liberia, constituting 1,649 of the total population. North Carolina, followed by Maryland, sent the next highest number of emigrants to the colony.

In addition, during the first thirty years of the nineteenth century, the U.S. government became more significantly involved in colonization than at any other time. The great majority of the emigrants to Liberia were transported under the auspices of the American Colonization Society, but in July 1827 the U.S. government sent 141 blacks to Liberia on the ship *Norfolk*. Three years later, on the brig *Heroine*, the U.S. government transported ninety-one blacks to the colony.[19] This direct involvement by the federal government became necessary due to the highly charged atmosphere that prevailed in the South because of the slave revolts.

This forced resettlement had devastating effects upon the settlers. By 1842 only 32 of the 141 individuals who sailed on the ship *Norfolk* were alive in the colony. Those on the brig *Heroine* did not suffer as many casualties: of the original ninety-one, fifty-six remained alive.[20] Consequently, it became clear that colonization was not merely a form of removal, but also of extermination as many died from tropical diseases.

Despite these appalling statistics on black survival, prominent whites continued to support colonization. John Marshall, chief justice of the U.S. Supreme Court, supported the Colonization Society and acknowledged that slave rebellions created more support for the efforts:

> The great object of the society, I presume, is to obtain pecuniary aids. Application will undoubtedly be made, I hope successfully, to the several State Legislatures, by the societies formed within them respectively. It is extremely desirable that they should pass permanent laws on the subject, and the excitement produced by the late insurrection makes this a favorable moment for the friends of the colony to press for such acts.[21]

Chief Justice Marshall wrote this letter to the secretary of the Colonization Society on December 14, 1831, a few months after Nat Turner was hanged for his part in the rebellion. At the time of the letter, as many as fourteen state legislatures had passed resolutions supporting colonization.[22]

European-American supporters of colonization, such as Robert Goodloe Harper, believed that the free African population was a continuing threat to slavery because it encouraged slaves to rebel. In a letter written to Elias B. Caldwell in 1817, Harper, secretary of the American Colonization Society, explained the detrimental effects free Africans had upon the slave population:

> It is not in themselves merely that the free people of color are a nuisance and burden. They contribute greatly to the corruption of the slaves, and to aggravate the evils of their condition, by rendering them idle, discontented, and disobedient. This also arises from the necessity, under which the free blacks are, of remaining incorporated with the slaves, of associating habitually with them, and forming part of the same class in society. The slave, seeing his free companion live in idleness, or subsist, however scantily or precariously, by occasional and desultory employment, is apt to grow discontented with his own condition, and to regard as tyranny and injustice the authority which compels him to labor.[23]

In short, Robert Harper, an ex-senator and prominent citizen of Baltimore, viewed free Africans as a potential threat to the plantation system that could be eliminated. Harper also explained in his letter that Africans in the United States constituted a distinct "nation" of people who could never be integrated into American society. He feared that Africans would always be a political threat as long as they remained in the country.

A foreign observer of the situation in America, Clericus (George Smith) also recognized the potential threat of rebellious free Africans to the United States:

> ...a slave population, rapidly increasing, and at present amounting to more than two million, has awakened the fears, if it has not appealed to the justice, of the slave-holders, and the conviction has gradually attained possession of their minds, that the victims of their cupidity cannot long be retained in their present unnatural position with safety to the commonwealth.[24]

Although leaders and supporters of the Society, such as Harper, argued that colonization would bring about the dissolution of slavery, Clericus flatly refuted such statements. He supported his position by quoting from the *African Repository*, a publication of the Colonization Society:

> The object of the Colonization Society commends itself to every class of society; the landed proprietor may enhance the value of his property by assisting the enterprise. The tendency of the scheme and one of its objects is to secure slave-holders and the whole southern country; it will render the slave who remains in America more obedient, more faithful, more honest, and more useful to his master.[25]

Northern states were not immune from the anxiety created by the slave rebellion. In 1833 members of the Ohio Colonization Society expressed concern over the rising population of free blacks and the political threat they posed to the larger community: "And in the fearful event of a servile war, it would not be in the slave-holding states, and ruin would be laid and ripened into maturity, but here, where they enjoy enough freedom to feel their chains and to encourage them in an effort to break them off, and are not under the watchful restraints of a master."[26]

To justify the removal of blacks from the United States, European-Americans developed rationalizations for their racist schemes. Thus it was during the nineteenth century that theories concerning the racial inferiority of Africans received their widest circulation. Africa was projected as the land of barbarism that would be redeemed by African settlers who would bring civilization and enlightenment. Even though some colonization societies saw Africans in America returning to Africa to bring civilization, other societies, such as that in Ohio, made no such pretense, but rather advocated for removal because of their supposedly innate inferiority. In a publication of the Ohio Society for the Colonization of Free Persons of Colour, issued in 1827, a distinction was drawn between "Negro" slavery and slavery in Greece and Rome. According to the article, a slave in the ancient world could always elevate himself to a respectable position in society upon acquiring education, but a "Negro" would always remain inferior. His condition as a slave resulted from the inherent inferiority of his blood.[27]

This racist justification for colonization also echoed the feelings of many members of the American Colonization Society. From the speeches and reports of the members, it became clear that a great many European-Americans during the early nineteenth century saw very little human value in a slave. Africans, both free and in bondage, were characterized as "barbarians" and "savages." Europeans, on the other hand, were the blessed of God. They were the developers of culture, Christianity and civilization. Everything that enlightened the spirit of mankind sprang from their civilization. Africa was viewed as a place of darkness, cannibalism and idolatry. The supporters of the colonization society therefore propagandized that colonization would aid Africa by exposing it to Christianity. In other words, the redemption of Africa depended upon Africans returning from the United States to Liberia as emissaries of Christianity and light.[28]

This attitude toward Africans prevailed even before colonization became an issue in the nineteenth century. The founding fathers of the United States considered Africans to be subhuman. Furthermore, in the Constitutional Convention of 1787, the very question of whether slaves were property or human beings was discussed.[29] Although George Washington, the first president of the United States, attended the discussions on slavery, he never took a position in opposition to Africans being classified as property. This was understandable given that he came from a family of three generations of slaveowners. Although President Washington was acutely aware of the moral implications of his slaveholdings, he could not forsake the economic privilege that slavery provided. By the time of the Constitutional Convention, Washington pledged not to directly purchase any more slaves, but had no objections to someone purchasing for him:

> It is not my wish to be your competitor in the purchase of any of M. Hunter's tradesmen; especially as I am in a great degree principled against increasing my number of slaves by purchase. Yet if you are not disposed to buy the bricklayer which is advertised for sale, for your own use...and his price does not exceed one hundred, or a few more pounds, I should be glad if you should buy him for me.[30]

Slavery had become such an important component of the socioeconomic life of the South that it was all but impossible to subordinate economic values to human values. In the long run the economic necessities of the plantation system overruled any considerations of the humanity of the slaves. Had it not been for slavery, they argued, African-Americans would never have been introduced to Christianity: "While, then, we abhor the iniquity of the slave trade, we may piously rejoice that these degraded heathens were brought to our shores, where they have had the opportunity of knowing the Lord Jesus Christ."[31] These European-Americans envisioned free Africans, who had been exposed to Christianity and Western civilization in America, taking this religion and way of life to Africa in an effort to civilize the so-called natives: "Her exiled children in the midst of us, are waiting to return to her, not as they came, ignorant and enslaved barbarians, but free and instructed Christians, capable with the aid that we can give them, of founding upon her shores civilized institutions."[32]

However, there was no unanimity among the parent body and the state agencies over the effects colonization would have upon Africa. For the most part, the state organizations did not care whether Africa would be civilized or debased as long as they were able to get rid of a group that they considered a drain upon their economy. The leadership of the Ohio society in 1827 made their position clear on the subject. In their eyes a manumitted slave whether in America or Africa was inherently incapable of fostering civilization.[33] Other colonization societies justified the removal of blacks from this country on purely racist grounds, and by advocating that such removal was economically necessary for the preservation of the plantation system.

Slave Labor versus Free Labor Debate

Another important factor in the debate over the efficacy of colonization involved the nature of labor that would continue to be used on the plantations. Would the plantations run more efficiently with free labor, instead of slave labor? In the early part of the nineteenth century there was considerable debate among southern plantation owners over whether slave labor should be gradually replaced by free labor. Slave labor in many cases was becoming an economic liability as a result of the numerous insurrections. The insurrections meant that plantation owners had to hire and train more security personnel and purchase more material, which drove up the cost of running the system. These new employees came from the white working classes whose financial well-being was directly linked to the maintenance of slavery. The large plantations bought up many of the smaller ones, leaving the former small plantation owners with few options but to seek employment on larger plantations.

Leaders of the American Colonization Society, who for the most part came from the southern aristocracy, recognized the need to supplant slave labor with free labor gradually. Henry Clay, speaker of the House and secretary of the American Colonization Society, wrote in the procolonization paper, *The Christian Statesman*, that once the European population increased further, European laborers would replace slaves.[34] This point of view was also widely held by other plantation owners in the South. No one was of the opinion that slavery would exist forever. Besides, many felt that slavery was becoming an economic liability as slaves were becoming less productive.[35]

Colonization, its opponents argued, would siphon off the free African population so as to lessen competition with European workers and institute commerce between the United States and Africa that would undercut the slave-based economy in the South. The colony would therefore produce goods at a lower cost than the plantations and consequently drive southern plantation owners out of business. To many plantation owners the choice was between "universal emancipation or universal bankruptcy."[36] It was not a matter of freeing the slaves out of any altruistic concern for their welfare, but rather because the economic viability of the South depended upon it.

This point of view did not mean that American southern businessmen did not recognize the importance of African labor in their enterprises, but rather indicated their concern over the continued viability of economic interests in view of changing political conditions in the country. Very few southerners doubted the fundamental role that African labor played in their enterprises.[37] However, as the plantation system grew in the South, it required more land upon which to grow cotton. Furthermore, the plantation owners were unable to restore the vitality of the soil due to lack of fertilizers.[38] In addition, slaves in many cases refused to work to capacity or broke agricultural instruments in protest over working conditions. This, of course, led to a level of productivity that was well below what could be realized under optimum conditions.[39]

There was also the problem of maintaining productive soil conditions. As a result of the soil depletion caused by the cultivation of cotton, the plantations began to expand into territories where slavery had not existed, but where free labor was recognized. These expansionist tendencies of the slavery system invariably generated conflicts. The cultivation of cotton in the South had greatly benefited the entire country so that, by 1860, 75 percent of the cotton was shipped abroad through northern cities and ports.[40] Despite the advantageous effects slavery had on the country as a whole, some sections, such as the West, objected to the extension of the system on the grounds that it would upset the balance between free and slave states.[41] By 1860 the western section of the United States was mainly populated by free laborers who worried about the possible exodus of their laborers to northern states because of industry. They also concerned themselves over the encroachment of the southern plantation system upon their land.[42] This part of the country, therefore, favored a check on the expansion of slavery in order to protect its way of life.

Northern industrialists, on the other hand, supported slavery because it formed the foundation of their economic structure. These men of high birth, education and religious training realized the importance that the plantation played in the accumulation of profits.[43] Slave labor on the cotton plantation led to the development of manufacturing, marketing, financing and transportation industries in the north.[44] Eric Williams in his book *Capitalism and Slavery* (1966) developed this point even further by maintaining that profits from the slave trade led to the accumulation of capital worldwide and the creation of the Industrial Revolution, thus directly benefiting both England and the United States. The triangular trade, in which southern slavery played a key part, fostered the development of the shipbuilding, woolen and sugar refining industries, particularly in England. For example, between 1840 and 1861 England received 80 percent of its cotton from the southern states.[45]

The northern industrialists did not worry as much as the westerners about the competition between free and slave labor because their enterprises were run by white laborers. Nevertheless, they did support colonization schemes that were designed to remove from the country free Africans who agitated for the destruction of slavery and therefore for a change in northern economic conditions.

Some writers, such as Robert Goodloe Harper, believed that poor "whites" who had been driven to poverty by the collapse of their small farms as a result of the plantation system, would do a better job than the slaves. According to Harper, slaves were inefficient workers who did as little as possible and consumed as much food as they could. In 1817, Harper therefore recommended to Secretary Caldwell of the Society that slaves be gradually replaced by "white" laborers. He stressed in his letter that the transition must be gradual because a sudden withdrawal would be disastrous to the nation's economy. Harper maintained that such a precipitous move would impoverish a large part of the country and render it unable to function efficiently.[46] He envisioned colonization as a necessary part of the gradual change in the southern economy:

> But to accomplish this great and beneficial change gradually and imperceptibly, to substitute a free white class of cultivators for the slaves, with the consent of the owners, by a slow but steady and certain operation, I hold to be as practicable as it would be beneficial; and I regard this scheme of colonization as the first step in that great enterprise.[47]

Another individual who developed an emancipation plan that would promote colonization was Frances Wright, an English feminist, who attempted to run a settlement in Tennessee for the training of slaves. Wright built her settlement, the Nashoba, near Memphis in 1825. In the same year, she published a paper that explained her settlement: "A Plan for the Gradual Abolition of Slavery in the United States." In the opening paragraphs of the paper she explained that her plan for emancipation would not affect the "pecuniary interest" of the South, and that colonization was indispensable to emancipation.[48] To her dismay, the Nashoba project had become a failure by 1830, but was instrumental in demonstrating the extent to which southern plantation economics influenced emancipation and colonization policies. The object of all these colonization schemes was to secure the property interests of the southern plantation owners. Consequently, those individuals who took antislavery positions took them because it was in their best economic interests to do so.

Some plantation owners feared that slaves would unite with poor Europeans and form a united front against the slavery system. Some southern aristocrats contemplated the havoc that would reign throughout the South if the oppressed poor "whites" and unruly slaves recognized their common oppression and revolted. Francis P. Blair, Jr., a Missouri antislavery politician, succinctly expressed this southern apprehension:

> (Southerners) see and feel the ruin around them in the poverty and despair of their unemployed countrymen and in the wasted face of the country. They know that mischief must fall on their prosperity when the land is surcharged with hosts of slaves wielding the physical energy of the country, and an oppressed white race, which may at some time turn the hatred now nurtured against the instruments which deprive them of their bread, to those whose opulence and power is founded on the subjection of both classes.[49]

In his paper, delivered in Boston on January 26, 1859, Blair explained that emancipation of the slaves must be followed by colonization in order to prevent a large class of free Africans from becoming a competitive force against "white" labor. Blair explained in his speech that just as the federal government had aided in the removal of the Native American population, so could they help in colonization. Furthermore, he explained that colonization would enable the United States to erase the blot of slavery from its history and reward their former slaves by guaranteeing them a home in Africa. However, more important, he saw colonization contributing to the enrichment of the United States; it would be a profitable venture. The colony in Africa, according to Blair, would yield $300 million, enough money to purchase the island of Cuba.[50]

Blair's appeal did not fall upon deaf ears; the leadership of the American Colonization Society had been contemplating the commercial exploitation of West Africa from its inception. In 1818, in a report of the Society, the leadership stated that part of their goal in colonizing West Africa was to: "Open an honorable trade and teach them a better use of the natural resources of their country."[51] In the same report, the Society spoke highly of the rich soil of West Africa and the many crops that could be raised and exported. Rice, the staple crop of the region, could be produced in large quantities. The cotton shrubs, according to the report, grew wild and could be perfected for manufacture. Coffee was another product that could yield high revenue from importation.[52]

Even after the American Colonization Society was formed, and colonizers had set foot on African soil, the rationale for continued presence there was clear and compelling. By 1850 interest in Liberia among American entrepreneurs had reached such a peak that the U.S. House of Representatives debated a bill that would establish a steamship line between Africa and America to facilitate the removal of Africans and the commercial exploitation of the land. In 1851 *The Christian Statesman* carried an article on the congressional bill. According to the article, the steamers would sail from southern ports carrying Africans to Africa; but, more important to the American industrialist: "It would open to us the richest commercial relations with Africa. The vessels might take out the products of our factories, and the numerous articles of every description which are in demand in Liberia, for trade with the natives."[53] Crops for manufacture were plentiful: sugar, cotton, corn, hemp, oranges, coffee, wild honey, lemons, limes, mahogany, camwood, satinwood and rosewood.[54]

Colonization to the enterprising American businessman would mean the elimination of the unprofitable practice of slavery, the institutionalization of free labor and the exploitation of the agricultural harvests of Africa. The U.S. government had ample information on the commercial rewards to Great Britain that grew out of the colony of Sierra Leone, and was therefore determined to improve upon that experience. The article in *The Christian Statesman* clearly warned free Africans in America that if they did not seize the opportunity to become partners in trade with Americans, the colony would be utilized directly by "whites." The following statement clearly reflected the imperialist designs of the American colonists: "In fact, if the free negroes do not soon embrace this opportunity of advancing their fortunes, we shall not be surprised to see the white men establishing a colony on the African coast, and appropriating to themselves the spoils of the golden harvest."[55] Ironically these European-American colonizers openly solicited the support of free Africans in the economic exploitation of Africa. Free Africans, emigrating to the colony, would serve the interests of American capitalists, thus making indirect exploitation possible. More important, the sudden downturn in economic development that many envisioned resulting from the abrupt emancipation of slaves could be softened.

Emancipation for colonization was the means by which the American planters and industrialists secured their southern property interests from rebellious slaves and insured the peaceful introduction of European labor into the economy.

Notes

1. John Hope Franklin, *From Slavery to Freedom* (New York: Vintage Books, 1967), page 74.
2. Franklin, page 74.
3. Thomas Wentworth Higginson, *Black Rebellion: A Selection From Travellers and Outlaws* (New York: Arno Press and the New York Times, 1969), page 194.
4. Eddie S. Glaude, Jr. *Exodus: Religion, Race and Nation in Early Nineteenth-Century Black America* (Chicago: University of Chicago Press, 2000), page 68.
5. Higginson, page 205.
6. Vesey cited in Peter P. Hinks, *To Awaken My Afflicted Brethren:David Walker and the Problem of Antebellum Slave Resistance* (University Park: Pennsylvania State University Press, 1997), page 35.

7. David Robertson, *Denmark Vesey: The Buried Story of America's Largest Slave Rebellion and the Man Who Led It.* (New York: Vintage Books, 1999), page 71.
8. Tubman cited in Bert James Loewenberg and Ruth Bogin, eds. *Black Women in Nineteenth-Century American Life: Their Words, Their Thoughts, Their Feelings* (University Park: Pennsylvania State University Press, 1991), page 220. Harriet Tubman kept her pledge until her death in 1913. During the Civil War on June 2, 1863, she encouraged over 700 slaves along the Combahee River, South Carolina to abandon their plantations.
9. Loewenberg and Bogin page 219.
10. William Seraile, "David Walker and Malcolm X: Brothers in Radical Thought." *Black World,* October, 1973.
11. David Walker, *David Walker's Appeal, in Four Articles; together with A Preamble, to the Coloured Citizens of the World, but in Particular, and Very Expressly, to Those of the United States of America, Third and Last Edition, Revised and Published by David Walker, 1830* (Baltimore: Black Classic Press, 1830), page 66.
12. Walker, page 73.
13. Walker, page 78.
14. Walker, page 83.
15. Walker, page 84.
16. Walker, page 84.
17. Walker, page 75.
18. U.S. Government, *Tables Showing the Numbers of Emigrants and Recaptured Africans Sent to the Colony of Liberia by the Government of the United States* (Washington, DC: 1845), page 306.
19. U.S. Government, page 300.
20. U.S. Government, page 303.
21. Marshall cited in James C. Dunn, *Address of the Managers of the American Colonization Society to the People of the United States* (Washington, DC: 1832), page 16.
22. Dunn, page 14.
23. Harper cited in William Pease and Jane H. Pease, eds., *The Anti-Slavery Argument* (New York: Bobbs-Merrill, 1965), page 21.
24. Clericus (George Smith), *Facts Designed to Exhibit the Real Character and Tendency of the American Colonization Society* (Liverpool: Egerton Smith and Co., 1833), page 3.
25. Clericus, page 8.

26. Historical Society of Ohio, *The Ouarterly Publication of the Historical and Philosophical Society of Ohio, Vol. VII to IX,* "A Brief Exposition of the Views of the Society for the Colonization of Free Persons of Color in America" (Columbus, Ohio, 1827), page 85.
27. Historical Society of Ohio, page 82.
28. Robert J. Breckinridge, *An Address Delivered Before the Colonization Society of Kentucky on January 6, 1831* (Frankfort: A.G. Hodges Printer, 1831), page 24.
29. Matthew T. Mellon, *Early American Views on Negro Slavery* (Boston: Meador Publishing Co. 1934), page 73.
30. Washington cited in Mellon, page 72.
31. Archibald Alexander, *A History of Colonization on the Western Coast of Africa* (New York: William S. Martien, 1846), page 37.
32. Dunn, page 5.
33. Henry Noble Sherwood, "Movement in Ohio to Deport the Negro." *Quarterly Publication of the Historical and Philosophical Society of Ohio*, 1912 to 1914, Vols. VII to IX (Cincinnati: Jennings and Graham, 1914).
34. *The Christian Statesman,* Vol. 1, No. 2 for the week ending September 13, 1851.
35. American Colonization Society, *Condition of the American Colored Population and of the Colony at Liberia* (Boston: Pierce and Parker, 1833), page 15. This very important report issued by the Society stated that four states (Missouri, Kentucky, Virginia and Maryland) would abandon slavery for free labor if labor was available.
36. American Colonization Society, *Conditions*, page 15.
37. Kenneth Stamp, *The Peculiar Institution* (New York: Vintage Books, 1956), page 59.
38. Eugene D. Genovese, *The Political Economy of Slavery* (New York: Vintage Books, 1965), page 89.
39. Genovese, page 44.
40. Genovese, page 159.
41. Barrington Moore, Jr., *Social Origins of Dictatorship and Democracy* (Boston: Beacon Press, 1967), page 120.
42. Moore, page 127.
43. Allen Weinstein and Frank Otto Gatell, eds., *American Negro Slavery,* 2nd ed. (New York: Oxford University Press, 1973), page 67.
44. Moore, page 125.
45. Williams cited in Moore, page 116.

46. Harper cited in Pease and Pease, l, page 25.
47. Harper cited in Pease and Pease, page 25.
48. Wright cited in Pease and Pease, page 39.
49. Blair cited in Pease and Pease, page 50.
50. Blair cited in Pease and Pease, page 58.
51. Dunn, page 7.
52. Dunn, page 23.
53. Rev. R. Gurley and Daniel R. Goodloe, eds., *The Christian Statesman,* Vol. 1: "Dedicated to African Colonization and Civilization, to Literature and General Intelligence," (Washington, DC:), August 9, 1851.
54. Gurley and Goodloe, *The Christian Statesman.*
55. Gurley and Goodloe, *The Christian Statesman.*

Chapter Five

THE INTEGRATION-SEPARATION DEBATE

The majority of free African-Americans found themselves torn between the equally attractive alternatives of integration and separation. Therefore, throughout the nineteenth century, consensus on the question of whether to leave America or not was difficult to achieve. In practical terms, this indecision revolved around the question of whether to strive for integration into the larger society through gradual assimilation or to cooperate with the American Colonization Society and repatriate to Africa. The laurels of American society, as pronounced by the Declaration of Independence, continued to attract the attention of free Africans. Some believed that if they continued to struggle for equality within America, the conscience of the nation would be aroused and African people would be freed from slavery. Even the great abolitionist leader Frederick Douglass believed that African people, through agitation, education and hard work, could better their condition in America.

These abolitionists and integrationists, out of sincere love for their people, believed that Africa did not offer them an alternative that would substantially improve their condition. Wealthy businessman James Forten, like Bishop Richard Allen, represented this group of African leaders who bitterly opposed the colonization policies of the American Colonization Society.[1] Both Forten and Allen were deeply involved in community activities around the Philadelphia area and therefore felt that their duty was with those Africans in the United States who were fighting for quality citizenship and freedom from slavery.

On the other hand, though suspicious of the motives of the American Colonization Society, Daniel Coker, a founding member of the African Methodist Episcopal Church, resolved to use it as a vehicle for returning to Africa. Consequently, in 1820 he accompanied eighty-six free Africans to Sierra Leone under the auspices of the Society.[2] Although Coker was interested in establishing a viable nation in Africa, he, like others, felt a religious calling to evangelize the African population. He felt so strong about his calling to repatriate that although he was elected first bishop of the African Methodist Episcopal Church, he declined the position in deference to Richard Allen. A close reading of a letter Daniel Coker wrote from Africa on April 13, 1820, to Jeremiah Watts, a resident of Baltimore gives some insight into his views on Africa. He was appalled at the way the people lived and their complete preoccupation with religions other than Christianity.[3] In describing the condition of the people he writes: "What darkness has covered the minds of this people... and as ignorant of God as the brutes that perish"[4]

Yet, despite the cultural and religious shock experienced by Coker, he still believed that African people in America could build a better future for themselves in Africa. The land, according to his letter, was vast, rich and well suited for the development of a powerful nation.[5] As he called for more emigrants to come to West Africa, he urged that they be Christian and hard working because, far from seeing Africa as a paradise for returning Africans, he saw great potential that could only be realized through hard work.

Men like Coker and John Brown Russwurm, who supported the efforts of the Society, did so because they saw it as the most significant vehicle for achieving repatriation. Although these men worked under the auspices of the Society, they maintained close contact with the fledgling African community in America. These men of high professional standing in the African community could not be seen as acting out of ignorance or lack of ostensible choices. Rather, these decisions were calculated and designed to facilitate their leaving America for the continent of Africa.

Their roots were deeply engrained in the struggles of their communities before they repatriated. Coker was a founder of a pioneering African institution in America, the African Methodist Episcopal Church. Immediately after Russwurm graduated from Bowdoin College, he developed the first African-American newspaper in America, *Freedom's Journal*, which became a major source of communication for free Africans during this period. The motto of the paper, "Too Long Have

Africa, particularly the activities of the American Colonization Society, they pledged to continue as a forum for agitation against slavery which kept many of their people in the "iron fetters of bondage."[6]

While these men could effectively use the Society as a vehicle for repatriation, they knew they could not alter its momentum or purpose. As the population of Africans in the United States continued to increase, the leadership of the Society felt compelled to urge more colonization as a means of arresting this population increase. In 1833, a report was issued by the American Colonization Society, which laid the philosophical basis of colonization for many of the state auxiliaries of the parent body. It was entitled *Condition of the American Colored Population and the Colony at Liberia.* The first section of the study concerned itself with the condition of Africans (primarily slaves) in the United States: "(1.) their (slaves) population and increase, (2.) their civil disabilities, and (3.) their intellectual and moral condition."

The first table in the report clearly demonstrated the extent to which the African population in America was increasing. Furthermore, in the southern states where many of the leaders of the American Colonization Society lived, the rate of growth was highest. Table 5.1 illustrates the growth trend.[7]

Table 5.1 Growth of Slave/White Populations Over Ten Years

	Census of 1820	Census of 1830	Increase from 1820 to 1830	Rate % of slave increase	Rate % of the whites
Virginia	425,153	469,724	44,571	10.5	15
North Carolina	205,017	246,462	41,445	20	10.5
South Carolina	251,783	315,668	63,882	25	8.5
Georgia	149,656	217,407	67,761	45	56.5
Alabama	41,879	117,494	75,618	180	122.5
Mississippi	32,814	65,659	32,845	100	67
Louisiana	69,064	109,631	40,567	59	22
Tennessee	80,107	142,379	62,272	77	58
Kentucky	126,732	165,350	28,618	30	19
Missouri	10,232	24,986	14,754	144	104
Arkansas	1,616	4,578	2,978	271	104

In all the states mentioned in the table except Virginia and Georgia, the rate of increase of the slave population was greater than that of European-Americans. These figures caused such alarm among the European population that the Honorable Daniel Mayes of Kentucky calculated that if the current rate of growth among Africans living in slave states continued, then by the end of 1900 the relative population of "blacks" and "whites" would be as shown in Table 5.2.[8]

Table 5.2 Population of Whites and Blacks in Southern States, 1840

YEAR	WHITES	BLACKS
1840	4,523,248	3,041,456
1850	5,789,737	4,136,380
1860	7,131,863	6,625,476
1870	8,129,770	9,010,647
1880	11,696,110	12,434,451
1890	14,967,420	16,910,853
1900	18,158,297	22,898,700

According to Daniel Mayes, by 1880 Africans in slaveholding states would outnumber Europeans. This prediction caused apprehension among Europeans in the South as well as in the North. State colonization societies seized the statement and distributed it widely among its members. Many states for the first time took a close look at the increasing rate of the African population. Reports modeled on that of the American Colonization Society appeared throughout the nation. Shortly after the Society report, the State of Ohio initiated its own study, which also revealed that the African population was increasing at a higher rate than European-Americans. Ohio published facts that indicated that between 1800 and 1810 the African population in the state increased sixfold.[9] The state concluded that most of the African immigrants came from the slave states of Virginia and Kentucky. As a result of this increase in Ohio, the state sought the active support and advice of the American Colonization Society, which resulted in the establishment of approximately 100 of its branches throughout the state.[10] These branches actively sought legislation to curtail the entry of Africans into Ohio. In 1804 a statute was passed that required African immigrants to have a certificate from a U.S. court stating that the individual was indeed a free person. The validity of the statute was tested in the Ohio Supreme Court in 1829, where the court upheld its constitutionality.

Immediately the City of Cincinnati notified its free Africans that they had to leave within thirty days or post a bond of $500 as required by law.[11] Faced with such racism, the Africans of Cincinnati assembled and decided to pursue two courses of action. They would ask for a three-month delay in the order and appeal to the Canadian government for asylum. Shortly afterward Sir James Colebrock, governor of Upper Canada, agreed to allow them to settle in Canada. However, after extensive thought, the Africans rejected the Canadian offer and decided to cast their fate with their brethren in the United States as they resolved: "That we will never separate ourselves voluntarily from the slave population of this country; they are our brethren by the ties of consanguinity, of suffering and of wrong; and we feel that there is more virtue in suffering privations with them than in fancied advantage for a season."[12]

Living conditions for free Africans in other parts of the country were no better. Wherever Africans lived, they became the target of segregation and discrimination. Numerous laws were passed by the states to regulate their behavior. Because there was no uniformity among the laws, free Africans never knew what to expect as they traveled from state to state in search of employment. In Louisiana, laws prohibited the instruction of Africans in Sunday schools, while in Virginia an emancipated African over the age of twenty-one, who remained in the state more than twelve months after emancipation, could be put back into slavery.[13] In other states they could not be part of the militia, and in the states of Rhode Island, Connecticut, New Jersey, Delaware, Maryland, Virginia, South Carolina, Alabama, Mississippi, Louisiana, Kentucky, Ohio, Illinois and Missouri only "whites" were allowed to vote.[14] In some states, free Africans could not hold public office nor could they purchase property. In Missouri and Maryland free Africans could testify only in cases between "black" parties. No Africans could immigrate to Georgia unless they were former residents of the state. Segregation in schooling was widespread, in both the North and the South.

As a result of this blatant and widespread discrimination, free Africans were unable to procure meaningful employment and consequently came into conflict with the judicial process. As the Africans transgressed the criminal codes in greater numbers, racists seized the opportunity to proclaim the inferiority and depravity of the Africans. The following, from New York state, was a typical reaction:

> The fact, that out of 40,000 blacks in this state in 1825, but nine hundred and thirty-one were taxed, and but two hundred and ninety-eight were qualified to vote; and the further fact, that this population according to its amount, furnishes ten-fold more of the inmates of our prisons and alms-houses, than our white population does, testify conclusively to the general improvidence, indolence, and abounding viciousness and misery of this unhappy portion of our fellow men.[15]

The first report of the Prison Discipline Society in 1827 convinced many of the inferiority of Africans and the need to remove them from the American continent. The report linked crime in the country with this degraded condition: "The first cause existing in society, of the frequency and increase of crime, is the degraded character of the coloured population."[16] The report then presented facts from close to twenty-five states showing that Africans constituted the majority in their prison populations. Furthermore, it stated that the amount of money spent annually by the states of New York, Massachusetts and Connecticut as a result of crime would be enough to transport 420 Africans to Africa.[17]

It is clear, therefore, that the increasing population of the free Africans caused considerable discomfort to Europeans in America. As slaves became free there was no place for them to go where they would be accepted as equals, and the majority of European-Americans had no intention of integrating with their former slaves. Therefore, for many Europeans emancipation from slavery had to become conditioned upon removal from the United States.

Voluntary Repatriation

Paul Cuffe, however, did not believe that his people should wait to be ordered to leave. He demonstrated that free Africans of means could and should consider Africa as a haven from oppression. After his trip to Sierra Leone in 1811, Cuffe negotiated with the British anti-slavery African Institution in London concerning repatriation. When he returned to the United States he persuaded prominent free Africans such as Peter Williams, Daniel Coker, James Forten, Absalom Jones and Richard Allen to form branches of the African Institution.

These men of high standing gladly accepted Cuffe's invitation to form the organization, because many Africans felt there was a need for a strong organization to counter the policies of the American Colonization Society. Ironically the African Institution of London, upon which the Philadelphia organization was based, supported colonization for both philanthropic and commercial reasons.[18] The branch formed in Philadelphia, however, did not concern itself with the potential business undertakings in Africa but with the deplorable social conditions of Africans in the United States. For example, in 1787, a month after the Constitutional Convention, African worshippers were pulled from a white church because they refused to sit in segregated pews. The granddaughter of James Forten explained the climate of Philadelphia: "There was no Northern city in which colored people were so badly treated as in that 'City of Brotherly Love.' In some parts of the city their lives were in constant danger; they were mobbed, insults of all kinds were heaped upon them."[19] Furthermore, African families in Philadelphia lived in constant fear of kidnapping. Men from the slave states would falsify documents concerning the ownership of certain Africans and snatch them from the streets.

At first men like James Forten supported the scheme of colonization that was promulgated by Reverend Robert Finley, founder of the American Society for Colonizing the Free People of Color in the United States, as the American Colonization Society was initially called. Since conditions seemed to be deteriorating for his people in Philadelphia, colonization seemed a welcome alternative. As these leaders grew more aware of the motives of the colonization society, their support waned, culminating in a massive conference in September 1830 where the American Colonization Society was denounced. Nevertheless, favorable reports continued to stream from Liberia. In addition, several influential free Africans in the United States decided to repatriate, which made the debate more complex.

However, reports of hardships and discrimination began to leak back as well. Thomas C. Brown, an African who left Liberia to return to the United States, wrote an account of the conditions there that was published widely in the African-American community. In the book, Brown stated that his major reasons for returning to the United States were that he could not adequately support his family and could not ward off sicknesses.[20] The climate also adversely affected other settlers in the colony. Between 1820 and 1843, 4,454 immigrants arrived in the colony of Liberia, but by September 30, 1843, only 1,736 still resided there. Deaths were the result of a number of diseases: 874 people died of African fever; 280 died of consumption and pleurisy; 130 died of anasarca (a type of edema); 95 died of bug diseases; 55 died in childbirth and because of female diseases; 224 died of old age. A host of others died from accidents and unknown causes. By 1843 a total of 2,198 people had died, which was close to one half of the total number of settlers in the colony during the period of this study.[21]

Moreover, Thomas Brown, in his report, acknowledged that some men such as Russwurm, who engaged in commercial activities, continued to have positive attitudes toward the colonization effort. For instance, John Russwurm enjoyed considerable wealth in the colony and was regarded by many as one of its "principal merchants."[22] According to the report, discrimination against the indigenous Africans was a widespread practice. Commenting on the attitudes the colonists took towards the indigenous Africans, Mr. Brown explained: "Kings, coming to that place, and chief men are taken into their houses. The lower order are not. They are employed as servants for the purpose of toting burdens, as there are no animals there, or very few."[23] In the area of religious conversion, Mr. Brown saw very few positive changes in the lives of the settlers: "It has little or no effect. I know Mandingoes who are sober and temperate; professing the Mohammedan religion. Among those who have adopted the Christian mode intoxication is frequent."[24]

Washington-Douglass Debate

These conflicting reports on the conditions in the colony had a direct effect upon the thinking of the free Africans in the United States. Some men such as Frederick Douglass questioned the motives of the colonization society and therefore were not surprised to hear of the intolerable conditions in the colony. However, some continued to support the Society despite bad news from Liberia. One such man, who acted as an agent of the colonization society, was Augustus Washington, the author of an article supporting colonization that appeared in the *New York Tribune* in 1850. In an 1851 edition of the procolonization *Christian Statesman,* the responses of both Frederick Douglass and Augustus Washington were printed. The debate between the two exemplified the disunity that existed at the time on the subject.

Augustus C. Washington

Washington, born in Trenton, New Jersey, in 1820, believed that African people would never be accepted as equals in the United States and that Liberia represented an opportunity to build a national base. This belief was particularly extraordinary, given that Washington, more than any other individual, could have remained in America and made a relatively good living for himself. He had successfully confronted American racism that placed significant limitations upon a young African man's aspirations. No doubt, he and his family faced considerable odds, given that he had to contend with bigotry based upon both sides of his family tree. His stepmother had been a slave of mixed heritage. He described her as "an excellent Christian woman of Indian, white and negro extraction." His father, Christian Washington, had been a slave in Virginia as well.[25] Despite the obstacles placed in his path, he enrolled at Kimball Union Academy in Meriden, New Hampshire, and Dartmouth College in Hanover, New Hampshire, as the only African-American member of the class of 1847.[26]

Before moving to Hartford, Connecticut, he was a teacher at the African Public School in Brooklyn, New York, and while at Dartmouth learned daguerreotyping in order to help pay for his education. He took pictures of students, faculty and townspeople and developed a good reputation as a student and businessman. In 1844, when he arrived in Hartford, he established the Washington Daguerrean Gallery and in 1847 he opened a second gallery in his home. By the time he, his wife Cordelia, and his two children (Alonzo Seward and Helena Augusta) repatriated to Liberia, Washington had established himself in Hartford and beyond as an accomplished daguerreotypist and abolitionist. As an artist in Hartford his studio serviced the city's most successful European-American citizens. He also provided leadership to one of Hartford's schools for African-American children. The move to Hartford also provided him with a strong free African community where he could raise his children. Despite ever-present problems, the African community, under the leadership of Rev. James W.C. Pennington, attempted to protect the fledgling community and keep the struggle for abolition alive. Washington added his skills to the struggle by teaching in the North African School, which was located in the basement of Rev. Pennington's Talcott Street Congregational Church.[27]

In 1848 he sold his first gallery to Samuel Cooley, a European-American man. Washington continued to operate his second gallery in his home at 136 Main Street. The next few years were eventful for him. In 1850 he married and by December 18, 1853, had repatriated to Liberia. His motives were very clear as he stated: "only Africa could be the black man's home in the world."[28]

Many of the forty-nine other repatriates, aboard the *Isla de Cuba*, stayed up all night, the evening before the sighting of Africa. Washington captured the important moments before his family's reunification with the African continent: "Such was the desire to see this land of promise, hope, and mystery, that the noise and excitement drove from our couch and repose. Some I think remained up all night."[29] The next morning, he described the importance of Liberia to him and his family: "It was a beautiful sight to look for the first time in our life on the sunny hills and verdant plains of the only land in which we can feel ourselves truly free."[30]

Like many African abolitionists of the period, Washington formed coalitions with progressive European-American activists. Like Frederick Douglass and Harriet Tubman, he became friends with European-American abolitionists such as Garrison and the revolutionary John Brown. It is reputed that he made a daguerreotype of Brown in 1846.

Given the excellent work that he was doing as an artist, Washington never returned to Dartmouth to complete his studies. Rather, he turned his sights to Africa, which he saw as a necessary part of his future. By 1851 he had concluded that Africans in America could never be fully accepted in America. He wrote that it was: "Impossible for us to develop our moral and intellectual capacities as a distinct people, under our present social and political disabilities; and judging from the past and present state of things, there is no reason to hope that we can do it in this country in the future."[31]

After arriving in Liberia, he thrived in the colony. He became a sugarcane grower on Saint Paul River with sixty workers and was elected to the Liberian House of Representatives and the Senate.[32] He traveled extensively in West Africa to Gambia, Senegal and Sierra Leone where he continued to take pictures.[33] He became the most successful artist on the west coast of Africa, and took pictures of President Stephen Allen Benson and other prominent individuals. He continued to depart knowledge to the young, just as he had done in America. In Liberia he taught Greek and Latin to the senior class at Alexander High School.[34] He continued to be sensitive to the plight of the most disadvantaged in society.

In Hartford he was able to make an excellent living by taking the daguerreotypes of prominent European-Americans. In Liberia he continued to do well as an artist by controlling the market for the Liberian elite. Nevertheless, as his sugar plantation business expanded, Washington remained ever mindful of his responsibilities toward his workers, particularly the native workers. He became the owner and editor of *New Era* newspaper and he and his family never returned to the United States. On June 7, 1875, he died in Monrovia, which he called "the last refuge of the oppressed colored man."[35]

Frederick Douglass

Douglass, on the other hand, recognized the inhospitable environment that prevailed in Liberia and consequently urged Africans to remain in the United States and fight for political and social equality.[36] Douglass, more than any other African leader who opposed colonization, recognized the selfish motives of the Colonization Society. It was inconceivable to him that African people would leave America after struggling for a little over 200 years to build it.[37] In addition, he understood that the members of the colonization society wanted the free Africans removed from the United States in order to secure their property interest in slaves. He could not see going to Africa when the vast majority of Africans in America continued to live in slavery. For him slavery was too fresh in his mind. He had escaped only in 1838, and he committed himself to using all of his energy to eradicate the scourge of involuntary servitude from the American landscape. He could not envision a nation where slavery existed, and therefore he even supported revolutionary change if it meant the end of slavery. In a speech to the American Anti-Slavery Society in 1847, Douglass openly advocated the overthrow of the U.S. government:

> How can I love a country that dooms three million of my brethren, some of them my own kindred, my own brothers, my own sisters, who are now clanking the chains of slavery upon the plains of the South, whose warm blood is now making fat the soil of Maryland and of Alabama, and over whose crushed spirits rolls the dark shadow of oppression, shutting out and extinguishing forever, the cheering rays of that bright sun of liberty lighted in the soul of all God's children by the omnipotent hand of deity itself? How can I, and I say, love a country thus cursed, thus bedewed with the blood of my brethren? A country, the church of which, and the government of which, and the constitution of which, is in favour of supporting and perpetuating this monstrous system of injustice and blood? I have not, I cannot have, any love for this country; as such, or for its constitution. I desire to see its overthrow as speedily as possible, and its constitution shivered in a thousand fragments, rather than this foul curse should continue to remain as now.[38]

Douglass was not alone in his position against the Colonization Society. In the year that the Society was founded, free Africans in Philadelphia assembled and voiced their unequivocal opposition to it. Their statement, though of an apologetic tone, stated first that those of them who were free had no interest in colonization as long as they enjoyed the protection of the laws.[39] They realized, like Douglass, that if they left the United States, other Africans, still in slavery, would have no free Africans to advocate for abolition. They also recognized that the colony would serve as a place of banishment for slaves who, because of political agitation, were a threat to the plantation system.

This opposition found expression in Europe as well. In 1833 the Reverend Nathaniel Paul, a black clergyman, and other abolitionists gathered in London to deliver speeches exposing the true motives of the American Colonization Society. At the meeting, Reverend Paul severely attacked the Society for sending to Africa men and women of questionable character. In his speech he made it clear that if Africa was to be enlightened, Christian men and women had to be sent.[40]

European-American Opposition to Colonization

Not only did influential Africans oppose the colonization society but European-American abolitionists also mounted strong opposition. One of the most vociferous opponents of colonization was William Lloyd Garrison. Garrison recognized the irony of advocating humanitarianism through colonization in a society formed by southern slaveowners. Garrison, along with African abolitionists, realized the contradiction in a philosophy that essentially stated that it worked in the interests of Africans by supporting colonization while at the same time assuring their southern supporters that colonization would not affect slavery (property).[41] In his speech at the same meeting, William Lloyd Garrison echoed the sentiments of Reverend Paul: "I believe that colony will be a curse, an awful curse to Africa, especially if the American Colonization Society succeeded in its direful purpose of crowding her shores with a vicious and ignorant population."[42]

The most significant document, however, to come out of this 1833 meeting was a resolution that denounced the humanitarian rhetoric of the society. The resolution clearly stated that the true purpose of the American Colonization Society was to secure slave property.[43] This resolution of 1833, opposing colonization, closely resembled that promulgated by free Africans in Philadelphia in 1816. The Philadelphia resolution read:

> Resolved, that it is the decided opinion of this meeting, that African colonization is a scheme to drain the better informed part of the colored people out of these United States, so that the chain of slavery may be rivetted more tightly; but we are determined not to be cheated out of our rights by the colonization men, or any other set of intriguers. We believe there is no philosophy in the colonization plan towards the people of color, but that it is got up to delude us away from our country and home to the burning shores of Africa.[44]

African-Americans Who Repatriated

Those free Africans who opposed colonization did so not out of any love for America, but because they refused to support the underhanded scheme, developed by southern aristocrats, which benefited the landed southern aristocracy and did little to abolish slavery or insure a secure foothold for Africans in the United States. Many of those free Africans, who were able to secure a relatively prosperous existence in the United States, chose to repatriate. Their motives were mixed, but they all gave up what little status they had in order to establish themselves in Africa and work for African national improvement.

Nevertheless, the American Colonization Society during the nineteenth century did generate some procolonization sentiment among the African-American community. For the most part those African leaders who advocated colonization reflected the views of the Society, although some saw colonization as a means to nationalist or individual development in West Africa. Many were devout Christians and envisioned Christianity playing a role in the colonization process. Others fled to Africa because they believed that they should be reunited with their people. Many chose Africa because of the lack of opportunity for professional development in America, as compared to Africa. Consequently some of the most talented free Africans in the country repatriated. For example, two of the first three college graduates returned home to Africa.

Edward Jones

Edward Jones entered Amherst College in 1822 and graduated on August 23, 1826, the same year that John Brown Russwurm graduated from Bowdoin College. Unlike Russwurm, Jones devoted the bulk of his life to missionary work in Sierra Leone. Still, unlike Russwurm, Jones never developed a clear nationalist view of Africa and died in England, rather than in Africa. Unlike Russwurm, Jones came from a family of successful free Africans in America, who resided in Charleston, South Carolina. His father, Jehu Jones (1767 to1833), owned the hotel in town regarded by many to be the most exclusive and successful. His mother's name was Abigail. In addition, Jehu was a member of the exclusive Brown Fellowship Society.[45] Jones was the only African to attend Amherst College prior to the Civil War.[46] He apparently stayed on campus and had a pleasant stay.[47]

After graduating from Amherst, he attended Andover Theological Seminary where he studied from 1828 to 1830. After which he studied at Hartford's African Mission School and was ordained into the Episcopal Church and given an honorary degree by Trinity College in 1830. The next year he repatriated to Africa, where he worked as the head of a school in Kent, Sierra Leone and in the Banana Islands.

In January 1841 he became principal of Fourah Bay Christian Institution, a school founded by the British Church Missionary Society in 1827.[48] The timing of Rev. Jones's arrival in Sierra Leone was propitious for missionary efforts in West Africa. It was in that year that the missionaries decided to extend their influence into the interior of the colony. The search committee therefore believed that Rev. Jones, an "American Negro," could facilitate their goal of reaching Africans in the interior.

Soon after Jones arrived, Samuel Crowther, an African who had repatriated from England, accompanied a missionary expedition down the Niger River, which resulted in disaster for everyone but Crowther, who was one of the original students at Fourah School when it opened in 1827. Consequently, the British Church Missionary Society felt even more confident that Rev. Jones, rather than a European, would be able to lead them into the interior. In addition, he had to administer a school of thirty-seven students and a staff of two tutors.

The tasks for Rev. Jones were difficult. Not only did he have to help expand missionary activities into the interior, but he also had to contend with a building that needed major repairs. In June 1843 he received some relief when Rev. Samuel Crowther came back to the school as a tutor. When Rev. Jones went into the interior, Rev. Crowther served as acting principal.[49] It was in this capacity that Jones made his contribution to African development. By 1848 the school had become a "college" and offered courses in African languages, which was unique to educational institutions on the west coast of Africa. Jones had to cultivate and maintain congenial relations with England, which required him to travel frequently there to raise money. He was extremely successful in his fund-raising efforts, and was able to raise enough money to build a new school building and to open a grammar school. With its focus upon African languages, the college would become critically important in the evangelization of the west coast. The church had hoped that many returned Africans would travel back to their homelands and spread the gospel. For those who could not remember their native tongues, the language training was one way to solve that problem.

When the naturalization act was passed by Britain in 1845, Jones became a British subject. In May 1858 he was called to England to explain certain irregularities in the running of the college. By that year the number of students at the college had dropped to six.[50] The church decided to close the college and keep the grammar school open, which effectively ended Jones's involvement.

After returning to Sierra Leone, he became a pastor in Sierra Leone and helped edit *The African and Sierra Leone Weekly Adviser.* Later he became the editor of *Sierra Leone Weekly Times and West African.* As a result of a dispute with Governor Stephen John Hill, he was dismissed from the latter paper.[51]

While in Sierra Leone, he married the daughters of two German missionaries: Hannah, daughter of Gustavus Reinhold Nylander and, upon her death, the daughter of Frederick Bultmann. In 1862 he married a third time to a Miss Shuff. He had approximately five children from these women before he died in Chatham, England, in 1864.

Edward Garrison Draper

Many individuals who chose to repatriate came from prominent families and believed that true freedom was impossible to obtain in the United States. Some, who did obtain "free" status worked and saved to put their children through school in preparation for repatriation to Africa. One example of this determination was the Draper family of Baltimore, Maryland.

Garrison Draper, a successful tobacconist and cigar maker, was considered "a colored man of high respectability, and long resident of Old Town."[52] For Mr. Draper the choice had already been made for his only son, Edward (born on January 1, 1834). The child would learn about Africa, obtain a college education, then repatriate. Although he was a businessman, he involved himself with political issues affecting his community, particularly with issues of colonization. He became secretary of the Society of Enquiry, an organization of free individuals who conducted workshops on Africa and African affairs. He also became a correspondent to the *Maryland Colonization Journal.* In a letter to the *Journal*, he clearly articulated his general ambivalence on colonization:

> Within the last twenty years I have given much thought to the project of colonizing Africa with the free people of colour from the United States, and it appears to me that the

> right course is not pursued to induce them to emigrate, their fancy and senses are appealed to, and not their judgment. They are persuaded that by going to Africa they can enjoy a life of ease and luxury, instead of labour and hardships. The object appears, to persuade and coax them to go. I think the solution of one or two questions would go far towards settling the matter of our *rights* in this country. What were the motives which induced the English, Scotch, Irish, French and other European nations to emigrate to this country? Did they come of their own free will, and did they acquire according to the customs and usages of civilized nations, legal possession of the territory? Then I would ask, what was the condition and prospects of the Africans on coming to this country? Did they come of their own accord, and did they acquire legal possession of the territory?[53]

While the senior Draper supported the efforts of the Maryland Colonization Society, he did not want his only child to repatriate without first acquiring the best education that America could offer. Because he did not believe that the Baltimore schools offered quality education for Africans, he arranged for his son to attend a segregated public school in Philadelphia.[54] The decision to enroll his son paid off. Young Edward was later admitted to Dartmouth College in the class of 1855. At Dartmouth he maintained a respectable average and graduated with his class. (See Figure 5.3).

By the time Edward graduated from Dartmouth, his father was convinced that he should become an attorney and then repatriate. The only problem was that there was no law school in Maryland, and even if there was, Africans were prohibited from being admitted to its bar.[55] Garrison's involvement, however, with the Maryland Colonization Society proved helpful to his son in his efforts to obtain legal training. When Edward returned from Dartmouth, his father had arranged for him to work with James Hall, editor of the *Maryland Colonization Journal* and general agent for Maryland Colonization Society. Hall, a European-American physician and graduate of Bowdoin College had helped earlier African college graduates obtain positions in Liberia, most notably John Brown Russwurm (Bowdoin College, 1826). Through his assistance, Russwurm became governor of Cape Palmas Colony. Hall

Figure 5.3 Edward Draper, Graduate of Dartmouth College

wrote that Edward had "an amiable disposition, very modest and retiring, a good student, possessing a sound and discriminating mind."[56]

As he had done with Russwurm, Hall put Draper in contact with an individual who could help advance his legal career. Charles Gilman, a retired lawyer and member of the Board of Managers of the Maryland Colonization Society, agreed to assist. For the next two years, Draper "read" law with Attorney Gilman. However, he needed actual courtroom experience. Therefore, Gilman made arrangements for him to study for a few months in Boston with Attorney Charles W. Storey, who would arrange for him to attend court.

When he returned to Baltimore, Attorney Gilman felt that the young man was sufficiently qualified to practice law. He therefore petitioned Z. Collins Lee, judge of the Superior Court, to give Draper a certificate of good standing and fitness. On October 29, 1857, Judge Lee issued the following certificate:

> Upon application of Charles Gilman, Esq., of the Baltimore Bar, I have examined Edward G. Draper, a young man of

> color, who has been reading law under the direction of Mr. Gilman, with the view of pursuing its practice in Liberia, Africa. And I have found him most intelligent and well informed in his answers to the questions propounded by me, and qualified in all respects to be admitted to the Bar in Maryland, if he was a free white citizen of this State. Mr. Gilman, in whom I have the highest confidence, has also testified to his good moral character.
>
> This Certificate is therefore furnished to him by me, with a view to promote his establishment and success in Liberia at the Bar there.[57]

In the same year that he received his certificate, he married Jane Rebecca, daughter of John Jordan, and sailed for Liberia. Therefore, young Draper became the first African-American attorney in Monrovia, Liberia. More important, he represented a class of individuals who, with determination and hard work, succeeded in returning home to Africa. To men like Edward Draper, the choice was clear. America did not recognize their human potential. While a few colleges such as Oberlin, Dartmouth, Bowdoin and Amherst would admit some African students, employment opportunities were limited and there was always the ever-present threat of being snatched from the streets and forced into slavery, even though one may have never been a slave.

The future, it seemed, was much brighter in Africa. When Draper and his new wife arrived in Monrovia, they experienced none of the fear and uncertainty of America. He began to practice law in what appeared to be a promising profession. However, on December 20, 1858, he was struck by pulmonary consumption and died in Cape Palmas. The young Draper had realized his dream of returning home to Africa and though his sudden death was tragic, his body and soul had returned for eternal rest in Africa.

Dartmouth College would play a key role in educating physicians for Liberia as well.

Samuel F. McGill

Samuel McGill was another child of a family that had made clear decisions about where they would reside and raise a family. Samuel's mother and father, George R. and Angelina of Baltimore, arrived in Monrovia in February 1831. Samuel and his brothers Urias Africanus,

R.S. and sister Sarah, had never known slavery. Urias (1832 to1866) was eight years old when his family repatriated aboard the ship *Reaper*.

Samuel's mother died in the same month of their arrival, but George was determined to make their stay in Africa a success. The sons became successful businessmen and the daughter, by marrying John Brown Russwurm, became the wife of the governor of Cape Palmas.

Soon Samuel found his calling in Africa because the colony needed trained medical professionals. Although many repatriates had the requisite desire to reconnect with Africa, many had difficulty surviving the "African fever." Although the Maryland colony had been founded by a physician, James Hall, he could not adequately provide the medical care that was required. George McGill therefore decided to send Samuel to the United States for medical education.

Before Samuel set sail for America he was told what to expect. In Liberia his family had stature and respect, whereas in the United States, he had to be prepared to accept humility. European-Americans in the medical schools were not accustomed to treating Africans on equal terms, so young Samuel had to be told in no uncertain terms that he was not the social peer of the other students, even though he may be their intellectual equal. Moses Sheppard, a friend of the McGill family in Liberia, explained what would be required:

> You must not expect to hear the term Mr. McGill from a white man. In the College you must appear as a servant; there is not a medical school in the United States into which you could be admitted in any other character, but you will have all the means of improvement and the same instruction as the other students, and in proportion as you waive the claim of equality it will be conceded to you, in proportion as you claim it, it will be denied.[58]

After heeding the advice of Mr. Sheppard, Samuel set sail for Baltimore in 1836, where he entered Washington Medical College. His path of instruction was clearly explained to him. After completing two four-month sessions satisfactorily and writing a thesis, he would become a physician. Upon his return to Liberia, he would be the first African from Liberia to obtain a medical degree in the United States.

After only a month of study, European-American students protested over Samuel's presence in the classrooms. The board of the

Figure 5.4 Urias Africanus McGill, circa 1854 (Library of Congress)

Figure 5.5 Unidentified woman, (McGill family member), circa 1854 (Library of Congress)

Maryland Colonization Society interceded, but to no avail. The school was unwilling to challenge the students and was afraid that public attention to the fact that it had enrolled a "Negro" would hurt their reputation. Consequently Dr. James Hall interceded once again and made arrangements for Samuel to apprentice with Dr. Edward Elisha Phelps in Windsor, Vermont. After a period of time under Dr. Phelps's instruction, Samuel was admitted to Dartmouth College Medical Department. In order to avoid the student uproar that had occurred in Baltimore, Samuel was told to tell his fellow students at Dartmouth that he was a "native African."[59] The disguise worked as Samuel Draper successfully completed his studies at the school.

On November 22, 1838, he set sail for Liberia on the ship *Oberon.* By 1840 he had become the colonial physician. He enjoyed a tremendous career in medicine, business and government. In 1848 he became assistant agent of the Maryland colony and in 1851 governor upon the death of John Brown Russwurm. In 1854 he joined Urias and R.S. to create the trading partnership of McGill Brothers. They engaged in both trans-Atlantic and African trade and established themselves as the most successful business concerns in Liberia. Samuel died in Monrovia in August 1872. Another former Dartmouth College student, Augustus Washington, preserved daguerreotypes of Urias Africanus McGill and an unidentified woman.[60] (See Figures 5.4 and 5.5 from the Library of Congress.)

After Samuel McGill graduated from Dartmouth, a number of other individuals entered its halls to obtain an education and return to Liberia. Their stories await discovery and interpretation by future historians. Among those who had a Dartmouth connection were Daniel Laing, who graduated from medical college in 1849 and was a physician in Liberia before he died in 1869 in Charleston, South Carolina; Henry J. Roberts of Monrovia, who entered Dartmouth Medical School in 1846 and received an MD from Berkshire Medical College in 1847; Dempsey Rollo Fletcher, who was a member of Dartmouth Medical School class of 1847 and died in Monrovia in August 1878.[61]

An African-American Who Integrated: Alexander Lucious Twilight

On the other hand, there were some who were able to chart a path for themselves that steered clear of colonization as well as abolitionism. These individuals paved a third path where they neither identified with the overall "struggle" to abolish slavery, nor with the back-to-Africa movement. One man in particular who represented this political viewpoint was Alexander Lucious Twilight. Twilight was the first African-American to graduate from an American college, Middlebury in1823. He entered the college as a junior, at age 26, to comprise one of eight students. Before Middlebury, he enrolled at Randolph Academy in 1815 to 1821. He would pioneer not only as the first African-American to graduate from an American college, but as the first Vermonter of African descent to graduate from Middlebury in the nineteenth century. Martin Henry Freeman of Rutland graduated in 1849, and Mary Annette Anderson of Shoreham in 1899; Richard Greener completed his freshman year at Middlebury before graduating from Harvard in 1870.[62]

Twilight was a native Vermonter, born in Corinth on September 23, 1795, to Ichabod and Mary Twilight.[63] The Twilights had considerable mobility, as compared to the more than 4 million Africans held in bondage. They lived in Plattsburgh, New York, before moving to Bradford, Vermont and then to Corinth.[64] His father died when he was a child and Alexander worked his way through Middlebury College. After graduating, he taught for four years at Peru, New York, and one year at Vergennes, Vermont. His memory and accomplishments have been memorialized by the college through the construction of a building on its campus, which is called Twilight Hall.

On April 20, 1826, he married Mercy Merrill, who was born in Unity, New Hampshire, and was the daughter of Dudley and Polly (Mary) Conant Merrill.[65] Apparently, Miss Merrill had been recently widowed from a man name Ladd, whose family had connections to Middlebury College. It has been speculated that her brother-in-law, Daniel Ladd, graduated from the college in 1832. However, the connection to the Ladd family has not been documented in any definitive manner.

What is clear, however, is that immediately after the marriage to Mercy Merrill, a number of catastrophic events occurred in her family.

While it is impossible to determine whether the marriage to Twilight constituted a major contributing factor, it cannot be ruled out either. The couple was married on April 26, 1826, in Peru, New York. On June 9, Mrs. Polly Merrill, mother of Mercy, hanged herself to death. On June 16, 1826, Ebenezer Conant Merrill, brother of Mercy, hanged himself to death.[66]

Twilight moved in August 1829 to the Northeast Kingdom town of Brownington, Vermont, with Mercy. Despite the racial animosity of the time, the couple defied racial barriers and moved to this remote northern outpost. Vermont in the nineteenth century was a relatively safe place for free Africans. As both a republic and a state, it had never tolerated slavery. It agreed to enter the union as the 14th state, only if the union recognized it as a state free of slavery. In addition, Vermont was the first state to write into its state constitution that slavery could not exist within its borders.

The Twilights quickly absorbed themselves into the local community. Given the educational training that Twilight had obtained at Middlebury, it would make sense that he would devote the bulk of his life's work to education. Education had come to Vermont in a big way as the state legislature established funding for primary school education. Brownington grappled with this issue as did as many other towns. This state effort to establish public schools caused quite a stir among the northern Vermonters and Canadian neighbors. The town quickly placed the school in a wooden structure, which was totally inadequate for the number of students, particularly for those who did not live in the town.

Twilight, as the new headmaster demanded more. When it was clear that the town did not have the expertise or resources to solve the problem, he took the matter into his own hands. At the heart of his plan was a boarding house. When the town refused to appropriate funds for such a venture, he decided to raise the funds himself. With the assistance of friends and town farmers, he brought granite by oxen from Lake Memphremagog and built a four- story structure that he called "Athenian Hall," but later became known as the Stone House.[67] Legend has it that he built the structure single-handedly on the salary of a teacher and minister.[68] At the school, students learned "common English," Latin, Greek, Italian, Spanish, "higher English," French, music, chemistry, natural philosophy, geology, astronomy, botany and agriculture. Shortly after their arrival, they built a home, and Twilight served in the state legislature from 1836 to1838.[69] In 1835 he ran for the seat in order to work against legislation that would have split state funding for education between Brownington and Craftsbury. Twilight had already expended his personal resources and believed that the division of funds to the county would place his school in jeopardy.

Twilight quickly became involved in local real estate matters as well. Shortly after his arrival, he brought a 60-acre farm from Cyrus Eaton for $650. During his tenure in Brownington, he bought and sold real property an estimated thirty times. Scholars speculate that his wife may have inherited money from her deceased husband, which Twilight used for these ventures.[70]

Not only did Twilight become the principal of the school, but he also became the minister for the village Congregational Church. Only in the state of Vermont could an African person in the nineteenth century rise to such heights of leadership. The proximity to Canada, a land of freedom for Africans, no doubt contributed to the spirit of inclusiveness in Brownington during this century. Here, in the early part of the nineteenth century, a man of African descent ministered not only to the spiritual needs of his community, but also to the educational needs as well.

As the principal of the Orleans County Grammar School (Brownington Academy), Twilight maintained a stellar reputation. One student wrote of him:

> His peculiar gift was in the instruction and management of a school. He seldom failed to get the good will and high esteem of his pupils. His power to influence, stimulate and direct them in regards to their character, studies and future pursuits was very great. He governed them wholly by appeals to their honor and manliness, but could use sterner persuasives when they were called for. Sometimes, when the subject and occasion demanded it, and all other measures failed, his power of invective sarcasm, satire and ridicule were tremendous. No sensible rogue would wish to encounter it but once.[71]

By 1841 the school had 101 students, with some from as far as Albany, New York, and Boston. The school was governed by an eleven-man

Board of Trustees, with the honorable Portus Baxter as president. Eight of the members were lawyers, with one doctor, one reverend and a colonel. In addition to Rev. Twilight, the instructors consisted of a teacher in vocal music, lecturer on chemistry and a preceptress. The students had to purchase books in Latin, Greek, French and English.[72]

Apparently a dispute arose between Rev. Twilight and the board over staffing of the school. This controversy over governance resulted in an agreement between the parties, dated August 2, 1844, in which Rev. Twilight agreed to "procure a suitable female teacher ... and to advertize the school at suitable times in the public newspapers."[73] As of 1841, the school had no female teachers, but a strong contingent of female students: 42, out of 101. In 1846 the Prudential Committee, a subcommittee of the board, issued a report to the board in which it reported on Twilight's compliance with the agreement of August 2, 1844. With respect to hiring a female teacher, one was hired the second year of his term. However, the committee stated that Rev. Twilight had not complied with bylaws related to attendance at meetings on the Sabbath.[74] Indeed the catalogue of the school, dated November 1845, listed a Miss Harriet N. Verback as preceptress and Ms. Mary Jane Thrasher as teacher of instrumental music. In addition, the number of students had increased to 123, and a policy on religious worship had been adopted.[75]

These minutes of the Board of Trustees, beginning in 1844, indicated a concern about the financial condition of the school. Many of these financial problems were the result of competition between Brownington, Craftsbury and Derby for the same state funds. Soon the pressure of securing a firm financial base for the school forced Twilight to seek a reprieve. In 1847, he resigned as principal, and moved to Shipton, Canada, where he continued as a teacher. It is believed that he sold Athenian Hall to the trustees for $3,000. Shortly thereafter he moved to Richmond, Canada, where he opened Twilights' Academy. The school did not succeed, due in large part to lack of adequate space. The school was located above Job Adam's Tavern (St. Francis Hotel).[76]

Conditions at the Brownington school did not improve in his absence. Since Rev. Twilight held a mortgage on the Stone House, in February 1852 the board voted to give the house to Rev. Twilight.[77] On October 11, 1852, Rev. Twilight was rehired as principal where he remained until October 1855, when he suffered a stroke. On June 19,

1857, he died at the age of 61 and was buried in Brownington. Two years later his school closed.

Years later at class reunions, students made fond remarks about Mr.Twilight. On August 30, 1888, letters were read from his former pupils at a meeting of the Orleans County Historical Society. All of the responses praised Twilight as a disciplinarian, gifted teacher and exemplary Christian. James W. Strong from Northfield, Minnesota, wrote on August 23, 1889, the following: "In that old academy many young men were filled with lofty ambitions and stimulated to noble attainments, and in them he still lives, a mighty and an abiding power for good in the world"[78] H.H. Tarbell wrote from Winterport, Maine on August 25, 1888: "As I look back I can realize, what I did not then see, that Father Twilight was a hero, struggling manfully with ill health, hard labor, small reward, and many discouragements. But he was faithful. He did his best intellectually and morally by all his pupils."[79] Mr. Tarbell graduated from Wesleyan University in 1859 and at the time of the above writing was superintendent of schools in Providence, Rhode Island.

While the nation was grappling with the throes of racism and exploitation of human resources, in the backwoods of New England, Rev. Twilight utilized his personal skills to erect a Stone House, charter a school and administer religious advice to a rural Vermont community.

African-American Abolitionists: Harriet and Dred Scott

Those Africans who remained in the United States, and saw themselves as part of the abolitionist movement, had to confront the mounting public policies that were designed to maintain the status quo. With the passage of the Fugitive Slave Act in 1850, the federal government effectively controlled the movement of Africans throughout the country and gave slave masters extensive rights with respect to the reclamation of runaway slaves. Despite these Draconian laws, African activists engaged in both nonviolent and violent actions in order to secure their freedom.

Two of the most significant abolitionists of the century were Harriet and Dred Scott, who, unlike Harriet Tubman and others, resorted to the legal process in an attempt to gain freedom for their family. Their case, which was ultimately decided by the U.S. Supreme Court, represented the most devastating blow to African freedom of the nineteenth century. Because they, as slaves, had been taken by their master from Missouri into Illinois, a free state, the Scotts claimed through their lawsuit that they were free. The Scotts initially brought suit in the Missouri courts, but were unsuccessful. Their most significant challenge, however, was lodged in the federal courts, resulting in a decision by the Supreme Court on March 6, 1857. The decision, written by Chief Justice Roger B. Taney, (See Figure 5.9) and joined in by Justices Nelson of New York, Wayne of Georgia, Grier of Pennsylvania, Daniel of Virginia, Campbell of Alabama and Catron of Tennessee confirmed the racist nature of American institutions and denied Dred, Harriet and their two children their freedom. Several public policy pronouncements came out of the case that codified racism in American democracy. For example, the Court ruled that:

1. Negroes whose ancestors were imported into this country and sold as slaves were not intended to be members of the political community.
2. Negroes, at the time of the adoption of the U.S. Constitution, were considered a subordinate and inferior class of beings.
3. Simply because a Negro may have rights of a citizen in a particular state, does not mean that he is a citizen of the United States.
4. Negroes were not intended to be included under the definition of citizen of the United States in either the "legislation and histories of the times" or in the Declaration of Independence.
5. Negroes were "beings of an inferior order; and altogether unfit to associate with the white race, either in social or political relations; and so far inferior, that they had no rights which the whiteman was bound to respect; and that the negro might justly and lawfully be reduced to slavery for his benefit."
6. The Negro was lawfully bought and sold as an "ordinary article of merchandise and traffic."
7. A "perpetual and impassable barrier was intended to be erected between the white race and the one which they had reduced to slavery."
8. The "stigma, of the deepest degradation, was fixed upon the whole race."
9. The Scott family was not entitled to freedom in Missouri because of their stay in the State of Illinois or any other territory of the United States.

10. "The right of property in a slave is distinctly and expressly affirmed in the Constitution."[80]

The Dred Scott case accomplished several important tasks. First, it established the absolute and degraded nature of U.S. public policy toward Africans. Second, it exposed the racist and paradoxical thinking of the most highly educated and powerful "white"men in the country. Racism, therefore, was not merely a reflection of uneducated, "rednecked," rural European-Americans, but rather an institutionalized system of dehumanization that was woven into the fabric of the nation by the highly educated and privileged.

The chief justice of the Court best represented this paradox in racial thinking. Here was a man who held slaves, along with four other justices in the majority opinion. In addition, he married into a prominent American family that symbolized the ideals of American freedom. In 1806 Taney married Anne Key, the sister of Francis Scott Key and later became a law partner with Francis, the author of the "Star Spangled Banner." Both men owned slaves, and Key in 1816 became one of the organizers of the American Colonization Society. From 1816 to1821, Taney served as a member of the Maryland Senate, then as attorney general of Maryland, attorney general of the United States, secretary of war, and secretary of the Treasury. In 1836 he was appointed chief justice of the U.S. Supreme Court by President Andrew Jackson and served until his death in 1864. It is ironic that the man most responsible for institutionalizing racism in the legal and moral fabric of America would be remembered in his hometown as a hero, rather than a despot and murderer. Yet, on his tombstone in Frederick, Maryland, is written:

HE WAS A PROFOUND AND ABLE
LAWYER
AN UPRIGHT AND FEARLESS
JUDGE
A PIOUS AND EXEMPLARY
CHRISTIAN

In the chief justice's slave quarters hangs a revealing picture of his house slave, Rose. One can sense from this picture her utter helplessness

Figure 5.6 Rose, Taney's House Slave. Photo by Robert Johnson, Jr.

as the property of the public servant most responsible for preserving "white" supremacy and insuring that the blessings of liberty and freedom accrue solely to "white" people. (See Figures 5.6 and Figure 5.7).

Chief Justice Taney, more than any other racist thinker of the period, provided the impetus to militant abolitionists to strike out by force against slavery and institutional racism.

European-American Abolitionists: John Brown

Because not all European-American people shared Taney's racist view of Africans, several took militant steps to confront slavery. John Brown was such a person who reached out to the African-American community, learned their plight and organized a militant resistance to slavery (See Figure 5.8). He was born in Torrington, Connecticut, on May 9, 1800, later moving to Ohio. In 1854 he and his sons went to Kansas where they fought to secure Kansas as a free state. Before engaging in his bold attempt to free slaves, he consulted with some of his close African-American friends, such as Frederick Douglass and Thomas Thomas. Before moving on to Canada for the convention that would decide on a provisional government for a new nation, Brown

Figure 5.7 Bust of Chief Justice Roger Brooke Taney. Photo by Robert Johnson, Jr.

consulted with Henry Highland Garnet, Martin Delany, Harriet Tubman and many other prominent Africans in America.[81]

On May 8, 1858, a convention was held in Chatham, Canada, to discuss and adopt a Provisional Constitution for a nonracist government in the United States. The convention was intended only for "colored men" but was attended by both Africans and Europeans, and declared in the preamble of its constitution that U.S. slavery was "a most barbarous and unprovoked war by one portion of the citizens against another, the only conditions of which are perpetual imprisonment and servitude or absolute extermination."[82] The decision to hold the convention in Canada was wise. In Canada they would find approximately 50,000 Africans, some of whom had monetary resources.

Attendance at the convention was a success. Thirty-two Africans attended, including Martin R. Delaney and James M. Jones, a graduate of Oberlin College's class of 1849.[83] Twelve European-American men

Figure 5.8 John Brown

were in attendance, which included John Brown and his son Owen. The group adopted a constitution with forty-eight articles and ended its "declaration of independence" with the following words: "Nature is mourning for its murdered and afflicted children. Hung be the Heavens in scarlet!"[84] This movement, whose goal was to totally reorganize American society, was multiracial and under the leadership of John Brown.

In the summer of 1859, Brown rented the Kennedy Farm in Maryland, five miles from Harpers Ferry, which was located where the Shenandoah and Potomac rivers intersect between the Blue Ridge Mountains and Loudoun Heights. At the farm, he and his men stored 200 rifles, 200 pistols and 1000 to 1500 spikes. On October 16, 1859, Brown attacked the U.S. Armory at Harpers Ferry with sixteen European-Americans and five Africans. The assault was well executed as the men took three guards captive, cut telegraph wires and tore up railroad tracks. As was planned, Brown and his men attacked the surrounding plantations, captured the slave masters and freed the slaves, who joined in the revolt.

By October 17, Brown and his party had taken about sixty prisoners. These prisoners, though hostages, were allowed to visit their homes in order to allay any fears relatives might have. Quickly a militia group formed and began to fight Brown and his men. Soon Colonel Robert E. Lee arrived with 90 U.S. Marines and two pieces of artillery. Colonel Lee sent a flag of truce to Brown, demanding unconditional surrender. Brown refused such offer, the flag was withdrawn and his men were marched upon. Brown was wounded and captured.

The raid's significance was both of a military and strategic nature. For the first time in American history, a multiethnic movement for social change confronted the powers of the U. S. government. Several Africans in America served in the raid on Harpers Ferry. All of them were under thirty years of age and many were well educated. They included Osborne Perry Anderson, Shields Green (executed), Dangerfield Newby (killed), John A. Copeland, and Lewis Sherrard Leary (executed).[85] Anderson escaped after the assault, wrote an account of the raid and served in the Civil War. Green was an escaped slave, who met Brown at the home of Frederick Douglass. Newby was free and from the Harpers Ferry area. He served as a spy for Brown, since he lived in the community where the raid was to take place. Copeland was educated at Oberlin College and was a second-generation free African-American. Leary was from Oberlin, Ohio, and an escaped slave.

John Brown led the raid with three sons: Oliver, Watson and Owen. On December 2, 1859, John Brown was hanged for believing in and fighting for African-American freedom. His last written statement was: "I, John Brown am now quite certain that the crimes of this guilty land: will never be purged away; but with Blood. I had as I now think: vainly flattered myself that without very much bloodshed; it might be done."[86]

After Brown's death, his body was removed to North Elba, New York, where he was laid to rest among his friends, most of whom were African-Americans. He was buried in a colony known at various times as Blackville and Timbucto. The colony was established by a philanthropist and abolitionist by the name of Gerrit Smith, who also financially supported Brown's raid. In the 1840s, Smith donated over 100,000 acres of land to African-Americans in New York State. The settlements were spread through eight counties. In Franklin County, 17,000 acres were distributed in 40-acre panels.[87] In 1849 Brown, his wife and seven children leased farmland from Smith and helped the African colonists till their land and grow crops. Later that year Brown and two of his sons bought 244 acres from Smith.

It was in this land that the greatest European-American fighter for African-American freedom was laid to rest. Many of the Africans he had helped in Timbucto attended and one, in particular, Lyman E. Epps, Sr., sang hymns as part of the services. The friendship and solidarity among Brown, his family and the African-Americans he worked with continued long after his death in 1859. On July 18, 1938, Ella Thompson Towne from West Hollywood, California, whose mother was the eldest daughter of John Brown, wrote to friends in North Elba that she was pleased to learn that Lyman Epps, Jr. was alive at age 96 (See Figure 5.9). Ms. Towne wrote that Mr. Epps, Sr. supported the abolitionist goals of John Brown and helped move their family to California. He played a key role in his local church and helped found the first library in Lake Placid.[88] Despite the years, the descendants kept in touch with each other. In 1885 Lyman Epps, Jr. wrote to Mrs. Towne and her husband the following:

> When you were at North Elba in 1882 I promised to write to you, a promise I confess to have needlessly neglected, an offence for which I humbly ask forgiveness. How are you and family and how do you like California? I suppose it is very different from New York State. Where is Miss Sarah, I have written to her and shall send it in your care and request you to remail it to her. Please send me her address. We have had a very severe winter but our healths have been very good. Please don't fail to answer this soon. I very often think of you and hope we may some day meet again if it is God's will. Give my respects to your husband and believe me ever your true friend.[89]

Free African men and women in the nineteenth century did not have many political and economic options. Those who remained in the United States and gave their lives in the struggle for freedom deserved no less respect than those who decided to leave. The choice was excru-

Figure 5.9 Lyman E. Epps, Jr., son of free African who sang at John Brown's funeral

ciating. The decision to repatriate, however, recognized that the evil American system could not be changed without massive bloodshed, and that a more humane alternative existed in Africa. There, through peaceful but militant efforts, one could attain the personal dignity that most, both African and European, were denied in America.

Notes

1. John H. Bracey, Jr., August Meir and Elliott Rudwick, eds., *Black Nationalism in America* (New York: Bobbs-Merrill, 1970), page 40.
2. Bracey et al., page 40.
3. Bracey et al., page 47.
4. Bracey et al., page 47.
5. Bracey et al., page 47.
6. Bracey et al., page 26.
7. American Colonization Society, *Condition of the American Colored Population and the Colony at Liberia* (Boston: Pierce and Parker, 1833), page 1.
8. American Colonization Society, *Condition,* page 4.

9. Henry Noble Sherwood, "Movement in Ohio to Deport the Negro."*Quarterly Publication of the Historical and Philosophical Society of Ohio, 1912 to1914*, Volumes VII-IX, (Cincinnati: Jennings and Graham, 1914), page 54.
10. Sherwood, page 60.
11. Sherwood, page 60.
12. Sherwood, page 72.
13. American Colonization Society, *Condition*, page 5.
14. American Colonization Society, *Condition*, page 7.
15. American Colonization Society, *Condition*, page 10.
16. Sherwood, page 83.
17. Sherwood, page 85.
18. William Lloyd Garrison, *Thoughts on African Colonization* (New York: Arno-New York Times, 1968), page IV.
19. Garrison, page V.
20. *Examination of Mr. Thomas C. Brown, A Free Colored Citizen of South Carolina, As to the Actual State of Things in Liberia* (New York: S.W. Benedict and Company Printers, 1834), page 8.
21. American Colonization Society, *Condition*, Table 306.
22. *Examination of Mr. Thomas C. Brown*, page 30.
23. *Examination of Mr. Thomas C. Brown*, page 30.
24. *Examination of Mr. Thomas C. Brown*, page 30.
25. Dartmouth College Library, Special Collections, Augustus Washington, N1847, Ann Shumard, Smithsonian Institute.
26. Dartmouth College Library, Augustus Washington. His mother was apparently from South Asia, rather than a native American. In 1837 he attended Oneida Institute for a year.
27. Ann M. Shumard, *A Durable Memento: Portraits by Augustus Washington, African-American Daguerreotypist,* (Washington, D.C.: National Portrait Gallery, Smithsonian Institution, 2000), page 3.
28. Shumard, page 3. Other sources of information on his life are the Connecticut Historical Society in Hartford and the Schomburg Center for Research in Black Culture. The sources are conflicting as to whether he had two or three children.
29. Shumard, page 11.
30. Shumard, page 11.
31. Shumard, page 8.

32. Margaret Loke, "In a John Brown Portrait, the Essence of a Militant," *New York Times,* July 7, 2000.
33. Dartmouth College Library, Special Collections, Augustus Washington
34. Shumard, page 13.
35. Shumard, page 18.
36. Rev. R.R. Gurley and Daniel R. Goodloe, eds., *The Christian Statesman,* Vol. I "Dedicated to African Colonization and Civilization, to Literature and General Intelligence" (Washington, DC: August 9, 1851).
37. Adelaide Hill and Martin Kilson, *Apropos of Africa: Sentiments of Negro American Leaders on Africa from the 1800's to the 1850's,* (New York: Frank and Cass, 1969), page 39.
38. Douglass cited in Hill and Kilson, page 39.
39. William Pease and Jane H. Pease, eds., *The Anti-slavery Argument* (New York: Bobbs-Merrill, 1965) page 33. This statement by free Africans is ironic because many were not enjoying the protection of the laws, but were victims of discrimination and kidnapping.
40. James Cropper, William Lloyd Garrison, Reverend Nathaniel Paul, Daniel O. Connell and George Thompson, *Speeches Delivered at the Anti-Colonization Meeting in Exeter Hall, London* (Boston: Garrison and Knapp, 1833), page 11.
41. Cropper et al., page 15.
42. Garrison cited in Cropper et al, page 13.
43. Cropper et al, page 24.
44. Pease and Pease, page 37.
45. Logan, Rayford W. and Michael R. Winston, *Dictionary of American Negro Biography* (New York: Norton Press, 1983), page 364.
46. Hugh Hawkins, "Edward Jones: First American Negro College Graduate?" *School and Society,* November 4, 1961, page 376.
47. Hawkins, page 375.
48. Hawkins, page 364.
49. Thomas Josiah Thompson, *The Jubilee and Centenary Volume of Fourah Bay College, Freetown, Sierra Leone* (Freetown: The Elsiemay Printing Works, 1930), page 16.
50. Thompson, page 25.
51. Thompson, page 364.
52. Dartmouth College Library, Special Collections, *The African Repository,* Vol. 34 (American Colonization Society, 1855). The Dartmouth College records state that Edward Draper's parents were Jamison and Charlotte

(Gilburg) Draper, but *The African Repository* indicates that his father was Garrison Draper.

53. Dartmouth College Library, Special Collections, Edward Garrison Draper, 1855, "Edward Garrison Draper, A Lawyer for Liberia," page 2.
54. Dartmouth College Library, "Draper," Philadelphia set up public schools for Africans in 1822.
55. Dartmouth College Library, "Draper," Only "white" males could be admitted. Laws of Maryland 1831 ch. 268 s2. The first African-American admitted to any bar in the United States was Macon B. Allen (Maine, 1844).
56. Hall cited in Dartmouth College Library, "Draper," page 4.
57. Dartmouth College Library "Draper," 1855, *The African Repository,* page 27.
58. Sheppard cited in Dartmouth College Library, Special Collections, Samuel F. McGill, M1839; Penelope Campbell, "Medical Education for an African Colonist," *Maryland Historical Magazine,* Summer, 1970, page 131.
59. Dartmouth College Library, "McGill," page 135. Additional information on colonization in general and the Maryland colony in particular can be found in Archibald Alexander, *A History of Colonization on the Western Coast of Africa* (Philadelphia: William S. Martien, 1846).
60. Shumard, page 14.
61. Dartmouth College Library, Special Collections, "Dartmouth Medical School Graduates."
62. "The Iron-willed Black Schoolmaster and his Granite Academy," *Middlebury*, Spring 1974, page 6.
63. E.A. Stewart, *Early History of Brownington Academy,* "Proceedings of the Orleans County Historical Society," August 30, 1888, page 326. Some researchers have written that he was born in Bradford, Vermont. See John M. Lovejoy, "The Life of Ichabod Twilight and the Early Life of Alexander Twilight, 1765 to 1821" (unpublished), Starr Library, Middlebury College, page 16. Scholars have debated the ethnic background of Twilight's parents, but the weight of the evidence indicates that Ichabod and his wife were mulatto. See John M. Lovejoy's genealogy of "Ichabod Twilight," Starr Library, Middlebury College page 1. Also see Philip M. Bowler, Sr. "The Twilight Mystery Solved?" (unpublished), page 2, Starr Library, Middlebury College, in which the author argues that Ichabod Twilight was the off-spring of Ann Ichabod (white woman) and Cesar (black man). Nantucket Court Records indicate that they were married

on December 8, 1763. Reference is made in Nantucket Court Records page 542.

64. Stewart, page 326.
65. Stewart, page 326.
66. Bowler, page 19.
67. *Boston Evening Transcript*, June 5, 1935, Courtesy of Middlebury College Library.
68. The Orleans County Historical Society, *A Walking Tour of Brownington Village Historic District*, Orleans, Vermont.
69. *Orleans County Historical Society.* The next African-American who served in the Vermont legislature was William Anderson (elected in 1948) from Shoreham.
70. Vincent Nicolosi, "Twilight Mystery," Starr Library, Middlebury College.
71. Stewart, page 328.
72. *Catalogue of the Officers and Students of Orleans County Grammar School,* (St. Johnsbury: A.G. Chadwick, 1841).
73. The Orleans County Historical Society, Brownington, Vermont, "Agreement between Twilight and Orleans County Grammar School Board of Trustees," August 2, 1844.
74. The Orleans County Historical Society, Brownington, Vermont, "1846 Followup re: Agreement between Twilight + OCGS Trustees, dated August 2, 1844, July 2, 1846."
75. *Catalogue of the Corporation, Officers of the Orleans County Grammar School, Brownington, Vermont*, November 1845 (Stanstead: L.R. Robinson, 1845).
76. Bernard Epps, "Pioneer Teachers in the Townships: Twilights' Academy in Richmond," *The Record,* Friday, September 9, 1988; Starr Library, Middlebury College.
77. Carroll E. Jenkins, "The Purge of 1851," *Newport Express,* May 23, 1939.
78. Stewart, page 342.
79. Stewart, page 342.
80. Robert Johnson, Jr., *Race, Law and Public Policy* (Baltimore: Black Classic Press, 1998), page 50.
81. W.E.B. Du Bois, *John Brown* (New York: International, 1963), page 249.
82. James McPherson and William Loren Katz, *The Anti-Slavery History of John Brown*, page 76.

83. Du Bois, page 258.
84. Du Bois, page 272.
85. Richard J. Hinton, *John Brown and His Men* (New York: Funk and Wagnalls, 1894), page 504.
86. Louis Ruchames, *John Brown: The Making of a Revolutionary* (New York: Grosset and Dunlap, 1969), page 167.
87. Edwin N. Cotter, Jr., "John Brown in the Adirondacks," *Adirondack Life*, Summer 1972.
88. Lake Placid-North Elba Historical Society, "Lake Placid Publication," July 18, 1938.
89. Lake Placid Publication.

Chapter Six

RESETTLEMENT OPTIONS IN THE AMERICAS

The tumultuous period of 1815 to 1865 was a time of great mobility and uncertainty for the African in America. During this period the institution of slavery reached its peak and became even more entrenched. It was also a time when free Africans and those emancipated for colonization experienced some modicum of national independence. Liberia was the situs for this national fervor that African-Americans controlled only in part. Were they merely the beneficiaries of self-centered African removal schemes? Was it possible for the returning Africans to fully integrate into Africa, given their forced separation, both culturally and physically? The freedom experienced by those who returned to Africa under the auspices of the American Colonization Society was preferred to slavery in America. In letters sent to America, many spoke of their increased ability to move about freely. Though still in relative bondage, most appreciated being free of slavery and in a place where they could envision becoming a part of a self-governing nation. Consequently, for those free Africans who voluntarily returned to Africa, the decision was deliberate and manifested a considered choice of liberty over slavery. For the vast majority, who were manumitted specifically for colonization, it represented a fundamental change from dependency and exploitation to self-governance.

In no other period in the history of America did Africans, on such a large scale, uproot themselves to journey to another country. The closest parallel was the movement to the northern states during the two world wars. These fifty years of repatriation constituted a time when those free Africans assessed very critically their position in America. Essentially those who voluntarily left had to decide whether to leave America or try to aid their people who continued to live under bondage. Many of these individuals understood that southern politicians and planters encouraged colonization as a means of removing potential political opposition. Nevertheless, for a substantial number of them the choice was the difference between life and death.

Life as a free person in the United States presented even greater obstacles. Even though they possessed legal documents, such as manumission papers, they did not automatically share in the fruits of American citizenship. Discrimination in housing and employment, both in the North and the South, drove many to the brink of starvation, poverty and crime.

Sojourn among Native-Americans

Some Africans fled to the Midwest to join friendly Native Americans where they were welcomed into a supportive community. Some married into tribes, such as the Cherokees and Seminoles, and fought in their wars. In Arkansas a large settlement of Africans joined the Cherokee tribe and owned vast farms and livestock. Still others were reenslaved by the Cherokee, Chickasaw, Choctaw and Creek nations where they worked in agriculture and the trades.[1] The Cherokees, for example, did not abolish slavery until July 19, 1866, as required by Article IX of a treaty with the United States:

> The Cherokee Nation having, voluntarily, in February, eighteen hundred and sixty-three, by an act of their national council, forever abolished slavery, hereby covenant and agree that never hereafter shall either slavery or involuntary servitude exist in their nation otherwise than in the punishment of crime, whereof the party shall have been duly convicted, in accordance with laws applicable to all the members of said tribe alike. They further agree that all freedmen who have been liberated by voluntary act of their former owners or by law, as well as all free colored persons who were in the country at the commencement of the rebellion, and are now residents therein, or who may return within six months, and their descendants, shall have all the rights of native Cherokees: Provided, That owners of slaves so emancipated in the Cherokee Nation shall never receive any compensation or pay for the slaves so emancipated.[2]

Despite some of these Natives having slaves, escaped Africans continued to find refuge among the Native populations.[3] Furthermore, it was not uncommon for Africans to obtain their freedom through litigation by claiming that they were in fact Natives.[4]

In the southeastern portion of Tennessee near the Georgia border, the Cherokees had their last council before the "Trail of Tears," the forced march to Oklahoma. Before this march Africans and Cherokees lived together, married and fought the European invaders together. Consequently, in this area of the country it is not unusual to hear African-Americans tell stories of their Cherokee relatives and many continue to this day to have resemblance to their Cherokee ancestors.

This popular folklore has been supported by scholarly research. The *Nineteenth Annual Report* for the Bureau of American Ethnology supported the popular notions by stating: "a considerable proportion of the blood of the southern Negroes (of the U.S.) is unquestionably Indian."[5] Another scholar, James Hugo Johnston, wrote: "where the negro was brought into contact with the American Indian the blood of the two races intermingled, the Indian has not disappeared from the land, but is now part of the Negro population of the United States."[6] Jack Forbes in his important book states that many of the federal censuses listed "free colored" people as including Indians.[7]

The capital of the Cherokee Nation once existed in New Echota, which is less than forty miles from Chattanooga in northwest Georgia. It was there that the Cherokee Nation established the first newspaper among American Indians, *The Cherokee Phoenix*. In the early 1800s they were scattered as far west as Alabama and as far east as North Carolina. Between 1817, the date New Echota was established, and 1826 the Cherokees translated the Bible, novels and other newspapers into their language. In 1827 they adopted a constitution that was based upon the U.S. Constitution.[8]

The Cherokees had lived peacefully among the European-Americans until 1828, when gold was discovered in the middle of the Cherokee Nation. In January 1830 Georgia seized Indian land and pursuant to the Treaty of New Echota of December 29, 1835, required the removal of the Cherokees. By 1838, 7000 federal troops came into Georgia, Tennessee and North Carolina to place the Cherokees into camps, prior to taking them to Oklahoma. More than 4,000 Cherokees died on the march from their nation to Oklahoma. The trip through bitter cold and unfamiliar territory has been referred to as the "Trail of Tears." Some of the Cherokees escaped to the Smoky Mountains and were never captured by the Americans. Today they form what is called the Cherokee Nation of the Eastern Band. These Natives, who refused to be taken west, roamed the countryside and occasionally engaged in "insurrections."[9]

This new Indian removal policy of the U.S. government created an even more precarious existence for the African who had run away from the plantation. As a result, no longer did Native communities provide the type of haven the Africans had hoped for, particularly among the Cherokee Nation. By 1868 Congress had authorized the secretary of the interior to take direct supervision of the Eastern Band of Cherokees.[10] The state of North Carolina passed ch. 54 of the Laws of 1868 to protect the Cherokee, but it was invalidated by the U.S. Supreme Court.[11]

One of the longest and most enduring relationships between Natives and Africans occurred in the Seminole Nation. As early as 1790 when George Washington signed a treaty with the Creek Nation, Africans had been living with Native people. As part of the treaty, the United States required the Creeks to capture Black Seminoles and turn them over for re-enslavement.[12]

Many Africans in the seventeenth century fled the slave states for refuge in Spanish territory known as Florida. A great many had lived there long enough to have descendants who had never known slavery. They were referred to as "Maroons."[13] Once in Florida they were granted freedom by the Spanish Crown. The integration of Africans with the Native population in Florida became so complete over time that a federal court in contemporary times issued a clear definition of the Seminole Nation:

> The Seminole Nation is an Indian tribe formed after the European conquest of America and composed of both Native American and African peoples. Some members of the Seminole Nation are descended from escaped African slaves who resided among several Native American groups living in what is now Florida. These Native American groups,

> together with the Africans living among them, became known as the Seminoles.[14]

In 1811 the United States invaded Florida in violation of its treaty with Spain, for the purpose of capturing Africans and bringing them back to servitude. The invaders were repelled by a force of approximately 400 Spaniards and 500 Africans.[15] Another invasion was attempted in 1813 to prevent what Secretary of State James Monroe thought would be an African revolt against slavery: "the whole province [of Florida] will be the refuge of fugitive slaves; and [will] ... bring about a revolt of the black population in the United States."[16]

In 1816 General Andrew Jackson attacked a fort on the Apalachicola River that housed hundreds of black Seminoles. The force killed or injured over 300 Seminole women and children. Soon thereafter a series of wars began against the United States referred to as the Seminole Wars. After 1819, when Spain sold Florida to the United States, the Seminoles began to lose ground in their war against the aggressors from the north. Once the United States obtained title to the land, it began to plan the removal of the Seminoles from Florida to the West.[17]

By 1823 the United States had beaten down the Seminoles so thoroughly that they were forced to enter into a treaty with the United States that required them to deliver runaways to U.S. authorities. It required the Seminoles to be "active and vigilant in preventing the retreating to, or passing through, of the district assigned them, of any absconding slaves, or fugitives from justice, and to deliver all such people to the agent."[18]

Many black Seminoles who escaped to the West found themselves enslaved by the Creeks who had a loose federation with the Seminoles. Facing this kind of oppression, now by once-friendly Creeks, forced many black Seminoles to escape to Mexico:

> They had witnessed the duplicity, the treachery of our Government often repeated.... They had, most of them, been born in freedom - they had grown to manhood, had become aged amidst persecutions, dangers and death - they had experienced the constant and repeated violations of our national faith: its perfidy was no longer disguised; if they remained, death or slavery would constitute their only alternative. One, and only one, mode of avoiding such a fate remained -

> that was, to leave the territory, the jurisdiction of the United States, and flee beyond its power and influence.[19]

By 1866, at the end of the Civil War, the United States signed a treaty with the Seminoles that required that black Seminoles receive equal treatment:

> Inasmuch as there are among the Seminoles many persons of African descent and blood, who have no interest or property in the soil, and no recognized civil rights, it is stipulated that hereafter these persons and their descendants, and such other of the same race as shall be permitted by said nation to settle there, shall have and enjoy all the rights of native citizens, and the laws of said nation shall be equally binding upon all persons of whatever race or color who may be adopted as citizens or members of said tribe.[20]

In conclusion, the relationship between Natives and Africans in the nineteenth century varied considerably, depending upon the degree to which the United States involved itself in the relationship. What is certain, however, is that Native populations represented an ever-present alternative to slavery and repatriation.

A Nation within a Nation

Many free Africans rejected Liberia as an option for resettlement. For some, the notion of Africa was too removed. Because they had to confront racism in America on a daily basis, many believed that the solution was to acquire land and remove themselves from "whites." If they could acquire land and build their independent communities, they would be free of racism and "white" domination. Therefore, the concept of a nation within the American nation increasingly became an option that was debated among free Africans. First, it was believed that remaining in America would be cheaper than repatriating to Africa. Second, they would not face the problem of assimilating into a foreign African culture that most in America had lost contact with. Third, they would not have to struggle with understanding African languages and dialects. Fourth, there would be no problem of cultural integration and development.

The arguments in support of remaining in the Americas and building a nation within America seemed compelling. The greatest urge to emigrate to other parts of the United States developed after the Civil

War and emancipation. Emancipation led to a sharp decrease in emigrants to Canada and caused many Africans to look to favorable locales, like Kansas and Oklahoma. During Reconstruction Africans felt that they would be accepted as full citizens in the United States, but with the end of Reconstruction and the rise in lynching by right-wing hate groups, they turned to the West as a place of refuge. As with those who settled in Canada and Liberia, these were movements of an oppressed national minority who could not depend on the American government to protect them. One author recognized the same reasons for emigrating to Kansas as to Liberia. He saw an "interconnection between it and the movement to Liberia... it is best not to see the attempt to settle in Liberia and the attempt to settle in Kansas as separate enterprises. The two can be understood as dimensions of a larger political impulse whose focus was on escaping from racism and poverty rather than on reaching a particular destination."[21]

This oppression caused Africans to bond together and seek collective solutions to their problems. As a collective, they had experienced racial oppression and it was only through collective action that they could hope to find a meaningful solution to the problem. The experiences of Reconstruction were still in their minds as well. During that period, they were able to experience a modicum of freedom as the American government protected them with both military and financial resources. Some Africans believed that the government would ultimately provide similar support in Kansas.[22]

It is interesting that the first major movements to Kansas occurred soon after Confederate colonels, plantation owners and religious leaders formed the Ku Klux Klan in Pulaski, Tennessee, in April 1867.[23] In 1869, Randall Brown of Nashville, Tennessee, organized a group to explore resettlement of Africans in Kansas, Nebraska and among Native American groups. In 1871, ninety-eight African farmers established The Alabama Negro Labor Union and dispatched its president, George Marlowe, to Kansas to explore opportunities for resettlement. Marlowe returned and reported that Africans could buy land for $1.25 per acre.[24]

The Great Exodus of 1879

Despite experiencing freedom from slavery and being afforded the rights of citizenship, Africans were still subject to dehumanizing indignities caused by white supremacy. The Old South continued to struggle to maintain its oppressive ways, at the heart of which was the debasement of Africans. The Western states, which did not have the experience of slavery and its virulent racism, therefore became attractive places for resettlement. Initially the resettlement movements sprang from the western parts of Kentucky, Missouri and Tennessee. However, in 1879, Africans from the Deep South began to look toward Kansas.

One of the organizers of this movement was Benjamin "Pap" Singleton, often called the "Moses of the Colored Exodus."[25] Singleton was born in 1809 as a slave, but escaped to Chatham, Ontario. By 1846 he had moved to Detroit where he became active in the Underground Railroad and used his home to shelter fugitive slaves on their way to Canada. In 1869 he moved to Tennessee where he formed the Tennessee Real Estate and Homestead Association. He fervently believed that the key to independence for Africans was the ownership of land. His organization therefore explored ways that Africans could acquire real property.

It was in Kansas that Singleton had the greatest success. His first colony of 300 settlers was established in 1873. Two years later a second colony of 300 settlers was established. By 1879 Singleton had resettled 7,432 Africans.[26] He personally established a colony called Nicodemus on the Solomon River and the Dunlap Colony in Morris County. The latter colony consisted of 7,500 acres of land and 200 families who were carefully selected and trained before their arrival in Kansas. Many had saved their money and brought with them skills, cattle and other personal property.

Other groups that came to Kansas were not as prepared. For example, in 1879, a group of 200 Africans on board the *Colorado* arrived in St. Louis where many of the Africans arrived before going to Kansas. Several days later another group of 1,400 arrived. They all had been misinformed by individuals working with them at their places of origin. Many had been told that the federal government would give each of them 40 acres and a mule once they arrived in Kansas. These false claims caused both African and European-American people in St. Louis to have concern. Many of the arrivals were destitute and unable to purchase land and care for their families. To assist the settlers, the Colored Immigration Aid Society was formed on April 14, 1879.[27] Through the efforts of the entire community, all the Africans immigrants were ultimately resettled in Kansas.

During the 1890s another proposal to establish an African state in America was advanced by Edwin McCabe, a Kansas politician who urged free persons to emigrate to Oklahoma.[28] Through his newspaper, *Langston City Herald,* he promised them land and political independence in their own state. During the first year of his appeal, over 7,000 blacks flocked to the Oklahoma settlement.

These resettlement schemes began to develop in other parts of the country as well. In 1839 the Young Men's Union Society developed an organization in Cleveland, Ohio, with the aim of establishing a colony for Africans within continental America. The project's chief architect was the young James Whitfield, a reporter for the *Coloured American.*[29] While there was general support among liberal whites for resettlement of Africans in the West, others rejected such schemes.

More conservative advocates of colonization, such as William Thornton, denounced outright any proposal to develop a colony within the United States. Thornton had spent considerable time in England during the nineteenth century and was thoroughly impressed by the British decision to send their unwanted "blacks" to West Africa. He wrote: "Could they, the free Blacks, ever be treated with an equality, in a country where many of their colour were still held in slavery?"[30]

On the other end of the spectrum, African men like Henry Highland Garnet (1815 to 1881) realized that all of the free Africans could not go to Africa because of the vast amount of money required: "There are those who, either from good or evil motives, plead for the Utopian plan of the colonization of a whole race to the shores of Africa. We are now colonized. We are planted here, and we cannot as a whole people, be re-colonized back to our fatherland."[31]

The Canadian Alternative

To most free Africans, Canada was the most realistic alternative to America's discrimination and plantation system. The Canadian government extended its welcome to fugitive slaves in the South, and freedom fighters such as Harriet Tubman and Sojourner Truth operated an underground organization that led slaves from the plantations to Canada.

This African grassroots support could not have been successful, however, without enlightened governmental policies in Canada. If the escaping slaves had been turned away at the Canadian borders, the efforts of Harriet Tubman and others would have been of no value. These emigration policies were particularly inviting in Upper Canada. Lieutenant Governor John Graves Simcoe took a militant stand against slavery in Upper Canada and openly welcomed runaways from the United States. By 1800 the Canadian courts had placed severe limitations upon the expansion of slavery.[32] The attorney general of Upper Canada issued the following exhortation and warning in 1819: "since freedom of the person was the most important civil right protected by the law of England which the province had adopted, the Negroes were entitled to personal freedom through residence in the country; and any attempt to infringe their rights would be resisted by the courts."[33]

The U.S. government at several points warned the Canadian government that amnesty for fugitive slaves would damage their relationship, but the Canadian government refused to change its policy.[34] Instead the government issued a greater appeal to free and enslaved Africans to come to Canada and settle. Throughout the South the word spread that Canada was the "Promised Land," and many slaves attempted to escape. Throughout the North many Africans, rather than continue to endure segregation and discrimination, left for Canada. In the Wilberforce settlement of 1831, a group from Cincinnati settled and bought land and cattle.

After the passage of the more expanded Fugitive Slave Law in 1850, the emigration of Africans to Canada increased significantly. To aid the refugees, the Anti-Slavery Society of Canada was formed in 1851. The society provided refugees with room and board and gave them advice on settlement in their country. John Hope Franklin, emeritus historian at the University of Chicago, estimated that the number of "blacks" in Canada by 1860 totaled 50,000. Near the end of the nineteenth century the number had dwindled slightly as many decided to return to the United States after the end of slavery in 1865. An 1881 census set the "coloured" population at 42,407.[35] After the end of the Civil War the number of yearly emigrants had trickled to practically zero.[36]

While it is important that Canada extended a welcome to runaways slaves, the country had not always been a haven for freedom. The first Africans to be brought into Canada were slaves. In 1628 an Englishman, David Kirke, brought the first slave into the country. During the period when slavery was legal in the country, many Africans fled south to northern states in an effort to escape Canadian slavery.

This movement to the south from Canada was meager compared to the African exodus from the states to Canada. In fact, the bulk of the population in Canada by the nineteenth century was a result of migration from the United States, rather than from slavery. The influx was especially strong after 1850:

> Those Canadians who have made it their special mission to find, to define, or to create a sense of Canadian identity often point with pride to the fact that, when the Negro slaves were seeking escape from his servitude after 1850, he sought out freedom "under the lion's paw" in the British provinces....There the monument proclaims, the fugitives "found in Canada friends, freedom, protection under the British flag."[37]

In the late 1820s substantial numbers emigrated to Canada. Some were free Africans who decided to form an organization of individuals in the United States to plan the transition to Canada. For example in 1830 a group of Africans arrived from Cincinnati, Ohio. During the same decade the National Convention of Blacks in the United States urged Africans who were seeking a better national affiliation to consider Canada, rather than Haiti or Sierra Leone. During the 1840s the Canadian government became less receptive to African emigration, largely due to the increased emigration of the Irish into Canada.

While the Canadian policies allowed Africans to come to Canada, they could do very little to prevent Canadians from distancing themselves from the new arrivals. Segregation and discrimination confronted the Africans throughout Canada, particularly in Nova Scotia.[38] Though free from the exploitation of slavery, the Africans faced tremendous hardship in fighting against the cold weather and the lack of meaningful employment. The Africans, however, joined together in efforts to foster a community and therefore insure their collective survival.

Although some became destitute in Canada, the vast majority established African organizations that were designed to better prepare the people to survive. For example, in 1842, Africans established a settlement in Canada West called Dawn. Under the leadership of Josiah Henson the settlers established a school that addressed the mental, moral and physical needs of the people.[39] The laws were silent on the question of segregated schools, which left wide discretion for communities to decide whether to integrate or not. Halifax in 1818 set up special classes for Africans, while Granville set up separate schools. Baptist churches sprang up in Nova Scotia between 1824 and 1891 and the African Baptist Association was formed in 1854.[40]

A number of houses of worship developed throughout the country. Like the schools, the churches encouraged the Africans to practice temperance and hard work as necessary ingredients for social advancement. In addition, the church leadership incorporated abolitionist principles into their weekly sermons as they prayed for the eventual end of slavery in the United States. Even though they were removed from the States, they still maintained spiritual connections with relatives and friends still held in bondage.[41]

As in the United States, Africans in Canada created their own press in order to tell their story. Among the papers that developed in the African community were *Provincial Freeman* (1853 to 1858), *The British American* (1845), *The Best* (1853), and *The Notes on Canada West* (1852).[42] All of these papers attacked slavery, drunkenness, and social and political inequality in Canada.

The options of Canada or the western sections of the United States offered Africans a more tolerable alternative to slavery in the South and blatant discrimination in the North. The movement to Canada was significant because it represented an international response to gross oppression and destruction of human lives. Most important, however, these movements proved that Africans would not quietly acquiesce to economic exploitation and racial subjugation without taking radical steps such as the mass removal of a people to a more humane environment.

Notes

1. Peter Kolchin, *American Slavery, 1619 to 1877* (New York: Hill and Wang, 1993), page 99.
2. *Stephens v. Cherokee Nation*, 174 U.S. 445 (1899).
3. John Hope Franklin and Loren Schweninger, *Runaway Slaves: Rebels on the Plantation* (Oxford: Oxford University Press, 1999), page 115. Some Africans who had taken refuge among Natives subsequently sued for their freedom. See *Jennie Johnson et al v. The Creek Nation* decided August 10, 1896, in North Carolina.

4. Jack D. Forbes, *Africans and Native Americans: The Language of Race and the Evolution of Red-Black Peoples,* 2nd ed., (Chicago: University of Illinois Press, 1933), page 218. Professor Forbes cites a North Carolina case (*Gobu v. Gobu*) to support his statement.
5. Forbes, page 191.
6. Johnson cited in Forbes, page 191.
7. Forbes, page 199. Professor Forbes states that entire counties in North Carolina (Robeson, Rockingham) and Georgia (Carroll) consisted of free colored Cherokee populations.
8. Fergus M. Bordewich, *Killing the White Man's Indian* (New York: Doubleday, 1996), page 40.
9. Franklin and Schweninger, page 87. The authors write that in 1821 a riot broke out in Onslow County, North Carolina.
10. Acts 40 Cong. 2d. Sess. ch. 259. This takeover by the federal government created confusion over land rights that resulted in a number of major lawsuits. *Rollins v. Eastern Band of Cherokee Indians*, 87 N.C. 229 (1882) and *W.W.W. Frazier v. Eastern Band of Cherokee Nation*, 146 N.C. 477 (1907).
11. *Eastern Band of Cherokee Indians v. United States and Cherokee Nation, West*, 117 U.S. 288.
12. Natsu Taylor Saito, "From Slavery and Seminoles to Aids in South Africa: An Essay on Race and Property in International Law," *Villanova University Law Review*, 45 Vill. L. Rev. 1135 (2000), page 1137.
13. Saito, page 1140. In 1858 Congressman Joshua Giddings wrote an important book that documented the presence of black Seminoles in Florida. The book was entitled: *The Exiles of Florida: Or, The Crimes Committed By Our Government against the Maroons, Who Fled from South Carolina and Other Slaves States, Seeking Protection Under Spanish Law, (*Baltimore: Black Classic Press, Imprints, 1997).
14. Saito, page 1144.
15. Saito, page 1148.
16. Saito, page 1149.
17. *Goat v. United States*, 224 U.S. 458, 461 (1912). The treaty that required removal was signed in 1832.
18. Saito, page 1153.
19. Saito, pages 1158 to 1159.
20. *Davis v. United States,* 343 F.3d 1282, 1286 (2003). Another case that is related to the Seminole's fight for equal rights is *Seminole Nation v. United States*, 78 Ct. Cl. 445, 458 (1933).

21. William Cohen, *At Freedom's Edge: Black Mobility and the Southern White Quest for Racial Control 1861 to 1951* (Baton Rouge: Louisiana State University, 1991), page 184.
22. Randall Bennett Woods, *A Black Odyssey: John Lewis Waller and the Promise of American Life, 1878 to 1900* (Lawrence: The Regents Press of Kansas, 1981), page 23.
23. Lerone Bennett, Jr., *Before the Mayflower: A History of Black America, 6th. ed.* (New York: Penguin Books, 1988), page 231.
24. Robert G. Athearn, *In Search of Canaan: Black Migration to Kansas 1879 to1880* , (Lawrence: The Regents Press of Kansas, 1978), page 77.
25. Athearn, page 6.
26. Norman L. Crockett, *The Black Towns*, (Lawrence: The Regents Press of Kansas, 1979), page 6.
27. Athearn, page 29.
28. Edwin S. Redkey, *Black Exodus: Black Nationalist and Back to Africa Movements, 1890-1910* (New Haven, Ct.: Yale University Press, 1969) page 100.
29. Martin R. Delany and Robert Campbell, *Search for a Place: Black Separatism and Africa* (Ann Arbor: University of Michigan Press, 1969), page 6.
30. Thornton cited in Richard West, *Back to Africa: A History of Sierra Leone and Liberia* (London: Jonathan Cape, 1970), page 92.
31. Garnet cited in Howard Brotz, *Negro Social and Political Thought 1850 to 1920, Representative Texts* (New York: Basic Books, 1966), page 201.
32. Robin W. Winks, *The Blacks in Canada: A History* (New Haven, Ct.: Yale University Press, 1971), page 96.
33. Franklin and Schweninger, p. 367.
34. Benjamin Drew, *The Refugee: A North Side View of Slavery* (New York: Addison-Wesley, 1969), page xiii.
35. Winks, page 486.
36. Franklin and Schweninger, page 377.
37. Winks, page x.
38. Winks, page 127.
39. Winks, page 180.
40. Peggy Bristow, et al., *Essays in African Canadian Women's History* (Toronto: University of Toronto Press, 1994), page 35.
41. Winks, page 340.
42. Winks, page 395.

Chapter Seven

LIBERIA, RACISM AND ECONOMIC DEPENDENCY

Throughout the nineteenth century Liberia represented a strange hybrid of African nationalism and American racism. During the century, Africans who earnestly desired to settle in Africa and to escape their precarious existence in America looked to its shores as a haven. Ironically, their nationalistic ideals found support among some of the most reactionary and racist individuals in the United States at the time. In fact, Liberia owed its existence as much to African nationalism as to racism. Despite this symbiotic relationship between nationalism and racism, nationalism survived in the face of American financial control of the colony and nation. Consequently those African nationalists who ultimately repatriated to Liberia due to the highest nationalist ideals, had to compromise with racism and become agents for American economic interests.

Racism and the Colony of Liberia

The American colony of Liberia was a direct creation of the American Colonization Society and its chief supporters: American industrialists, missionaries and plantation owners. All of these early supporters of the colony believed that African people were incapable of living among them as equals. Nevertheless, the Society attracted many free and highly educated Africans, who planted the seeds of nationalism on the African continent. Such an accomplishment was no small matter, given the extent to which the continent fell increasingly under European control.

One year after Paul Cuffe made his maiden voyage to Sierra Leone, the American Colonization Society was formed in 1817 to transport Africans back to Africa. The first president of the United States, George Washington, and his brother Bushrod Washington, supported the goals of this new Society, which was the removal of Africans.[1] These politicians acquiesced to slavery as long as Africans were an economic asset to the plantation system, but as soon as the slaves were freed, they advocated for the removal of Africans from America. The number of politicians who favored colonization was vast: Senator Daniel Webster, Francis Scott Key, Presidents Thomas Jefferson, James Madison and James Monroe and Speaker of the House Henry Clay. At one point Henry Clay advocated the extermination of Native Americans and had the following to say about Africans: "Can there be a nobler cause than that which, whilst it proposed to rid our country of a useless and pernicious, if not dangerous portion of its population, contemplates the spreading of civilized life, and the possible redemption from ignorance and barbarism of a benighted quarter of the globe."[2]

Thomas Jefferson, another supporter of colonization, owned over 150 slaves and said the following about Africans:

> They secrete less by the kidnies, and more by the glands of the skin, which gives them a very strong and disagreeable odour.... They seem to require less sleep.... They are more ardent after their females: but love seems with them to be more of an eager desire than a tender delicate mixture of sentiment and sensation. Their griefs are transient.... I advance it therefore as a suspicion only, that the blacks, whether originally a distinct race, or made distinct by time and circumstances, are inferior to the whites in endowment both of body and mind.[3]

It is clear, therefore, that the American Colonization Society was a creation of racist politicians. Governmental officials and private individuals collaborated in developing and implementing the scheme for the removal of African people from the United States to Liberia. Even before the founding of the Society, the U.S. government debated ways to rid the country of Africans. For instance, Congress thoroughly investigated the feasibility of building a military post on the west coast of Africa for Africans who were captured by the U.S. Navy on high seas. When the Congress blocked the plan, President Monroe approached the leadership of the American Colonization Society to see if he could get their support. He reached an agreement with the Society whereby the governmental agents in charge of recaptured slaves would work with the Society in returning the illegally seized Africans. This cooperation became particularly necessary after 1808, when the slave trade was declared illegal and the U.S. Navy was instructed to intercept all U.S. ships carrying slaves and return them to Africa.

It is no accident, however, that the birth of the American Colonization Society closely coincided with the ban on the slave trade. When the ban was placed, the United States had residing within its southern states more than enough slaves to enable the plantations to operate efficiently. The continued importation of slaves into the South would cause the already disproportionate number of slaves to increase and therefore become a liability, a potential threat to the status quo.

The clergy quickly supported the scheme. The church in America had always held an ambivalent posture toward slavery. Many so-called Christians allowed the nation's desire for capital accumulation through exploitation of African labor to overshadow any moral requirements of their faith. Others, however, believed that the government-sponsored resettlement efforts through the Colonization Society provided an easy solution to slavery and would open up an entire new land for missionary activities. Consequently, after the American Colonization Society was launched, two ministers, Rev. Samuel J. Mills and Rev. Ebenezer Burgess, were dispatched to West Africa to negotiate for land with the African chiefs and with British settlers in Sierra Leone. Because of the governmental interest, their voyage was paid for, in part, by the U.S. government. Once land was secured off Sherbro Island, Samuel Bacon was appointed agent for both the government and the Society. Rapidly, auxiliaries to the parent body developed throughout the United States as funds flowed into its coffers from both government and philanthropy.[4] Therefore from the beginning of the American Colonization Society, government, clergy and business worked together to develop and implement a plan for the removal of Africans from the United States. Government saw the removal as a means of eliminating from the American population a group that constituted a potential threat to those in power, while the business community saw the removal of free Africans as the elimination of competitive labor and a threat to the plantation system.

Life in the Colony and its Leaders

Liberia therefore served American governmental and plantation interests. Africans participated only marginally in the management of the colony; for the most part Liberian policies reflected the racism, paternalism and hypocrisy of its American founders. Free Africans, who emigrated under the aegis of the American Colonization Society, had to acquiesce to these policies. Africa, many Americans believed, was a natural and more suitable home for Africans. Consequently, politicians like Henry Clay publicly opposed laws that would give Africans equal rights and opportunities in America.[5] In addition, slaveowners in the South freed their slaves on the condition that they emigrate to Liberia, especially those who were incorrigible.

Jehudi Ashmun and Lott Cary

In Liberia, the Africans who returned from America seeking freedom ironically found themselves under the control of their former slave masters or misguided missionaries who administered the colony. Jehudi Ashmun, more than any other European-American, represented this group of Christian missionaries who opposed slavery and fervently believed that Africans should be returned to their homeland. On August 9, 1822, he and his wife, C.L. Gray, arrived in Cape Monserado aboard the *Strong* with a cargo of thirty-seven Africans who were being returned by the U.S. government.

Ashmun had been born to humble beginnings in Champlain, New York, on April 21, 1794. He graduated from the University of Vermont after spending his first three years at Middlebury College. While at Middlebury, he developed a strong interest and devotion to the Christian faith and on October 7, 1818, became a minister of the Congregational Church soon after graduation and marriage. It was in Washington, D.C., however, that he turned his religious interests and journalism skills toward the issue of African colonization, by becoming editor of the *Theological Review* and writing articles that praised the work of the Colonization Society. Furthermore, he wrote a well-respected biography of another American preacher, Rev. Samuel Bacon, who had taken the very first group of Africans back to the continent under the auspices of the Society.

These writings and missionary activities made Ashmun a prime candidate for a leadership position in Liberia, despite the difficult conditions early settlers encountered. Rev. Samuel J. Mills had died from the African fever and Rev. Ebenezer Burgess had fled to a West Indian island to recuperate from his illness. The settlers, it was believed, were floundering in despair. Although he had intended to stay only a day, he remained, largely due to the deplorable conditions that he discovered. He found that many of the settlers were sick and that the colony was not well received by the native Africans. In fact, he learned that an attack on the colony had been planned and was imminent. To make matters even worse, he had to contend with pressing personal matters because his wife suddenly died of the fever on September 15. Upon her death, Ashmun became the only European-American in the colony. Therefore he and Rev. Lott Cary, an African settler, became the leaders of the colony as they prepared to defend the settlement from attack.

On November 11, 1822, the settlement was attacked by between 800 and 900 native Africans, which was successfully repelled.[6] On November 30, 1822, the native Africans renewed their attack, which was again repelled by the settlers under the able leadership of Rev. Cary, since Ashmun had succumbed to the African fever. Another settler, Matilda Newport, a free African from Georgia, played a key role in securing the settlement. On December 1, 1822, she ignited several cannons near her house, thus causing the advancing Africans to flee in confusion.[7]

The postage stamp in figure 7.1 stands as a memorial to Lott Cary and Jehudi Ashmun who successfully organized and led the settlers against a hostile indigenous African population. Although returning Africans, like Lott Cary, played key roles in organizing the colony, they shared the paternalistic views of European-Americans and therefore failed to establish, through diplomatic channels, a smooth integration of the returning Africans. The British experience and that of Paul Cuffe could have served as a model, but due to inexperience and arrogance, the Americans resorted to the use of the sword and the Bible in order to "pacify" the Africans. Despite the involvement of Cary, Newport and other returned Africans, major government decisions were made by European-Americans before the colony became a republic in 1847.

Figure 7.1 Liberian Postage Stamp Commemorating Carey and Ashmun

Life for Repatriates in Liberia

The American managers adopted a constitution for Liberia, named the country and developed a plan for the capital city of Monrovia. The Society controlled every facet of the colony and decided who was brought there and how much land was allotted to each settler. Between 1821 and 1860, the Society allowed an estimated 13,000 Africans to resettle in Liberia.[8]

The Americans told the repatriates what to expect when they arrived in Liberia. Because these repatriates had minimum control over their lives, many developed antagonistic relationships with the indigenous Africans. The Society separated the repatriates from the larger community and over time many began to feel that they were superior to the African majority.[9] Many internalized, to a large extent, the rhetoric of the American Colonization Society, which viewed Africa as a land of barbarism and heathenism. Furthermore, these repatriates had little prior knowledge about Africa and relied upon information from the Society; information that many times was distorted. The settlers had no firsthand information about the living conditions, the climate and the land. For example, the first shipload of eighty-eight repatriates transported by the *Elizabeth* on January 31, 1820, which landed on Sherbro Island, was unprepared for the severe climate of the west coast. This resulted in the death of many and the eventual flight to Sierra Leone of the few survivors.[10]

The repatriates were at the mercy of the Society. The majority of the settlers, who were former slaves, had no real control over whether they even wanted to emigrate in the first place. The decisions were made for them by their owners. For example, 63 percent of the Africans deported to Liberia either had been emancipated specifically for the colony or recaptured by government agents and sent to Liberia. The next largest category consisted of those who were born free and volunteered to repatriate.[11]

In Sierra Leone, the situation was the same. In Freetown, Africans recaptured from slave ships formed a large percentage of the population. In the early nineteenth century, 74,000 of the 77,000 African settlers in Freetown had been captured from slave ships.[12] This policy created severe problems for the returned African because he or she would be placed with Africans from different ethnic groups, which resulted in language and cultural differences. Those brought directly from the United States and England had a significant advantage because they could speak English and were familiar with the cultural background of the colonizers.

As time passed, the repatriates grew more aware of the paradoxical nature of their situation in Liberia. The dilemma grew clearer as they reflected on the fact that they had been brought to Africa to escape white domination, yet found themselves under the control of the same group of people they supposedly left in America. Therefore, the first ten years of Liberia's history reflected these internal contradictions as civil disobedience increased. Many repatriates believed that they had been transported to Liberia to die of malaria and other tropical diseases. Such fears resulted in frequent workstoppages as they refused to clear the land for crops, roads and houses. The crisis reached the point where

Governor Jehudi Ashmun, warned that each person had to work at least two days per week in order to get food. In 1824 the frustration felt by the repatriates culminated in an armed insurrection by the settlers against the agents of the Society. This confrontation, led by Lott Cary, forced Ashmun to adopt a more liberal land grant policy.[13] After the settlers were able to get more land, the mood changed considerably as is evidenced by this letter of 1827 sent to friends in the United States:

> The first consideration which caused our voluntary removal to this country, and the object which we still regard with the deepest concern, is liberty, liberty, in the sober, simple, but complete sense of the word: not a licentious liberty, nor a liberty without government... but that liberty of speech, action and conscience, which distinguishes the free enfranchised citizens of a free state. We did not enjoy that freedom in our native country.... Our constitution secures to us, so far as our condition allows "all the rights and privileges enjoyed by the citizens of the United States" and these rights and privileges are ours. We are proprietors of the soil we live on, and possess the rights of freeholders. Our suffrages, and, what is of more importance, our sentiments and our opinions have their due weight in the government we live under.[14]

From this initial confrontation between the repatriates and the Society, more opportunities opened up as the repatriates began to participate more fully in the affairs of the colony. They began to serve in the courts as jurors. Some even grew wealthy by engaging in commerce. A case in point is J.J. Roberts, who made a fortune and later became the first president of Liberia. By 1823 the repatriates had constructed four small ships and seven years later carried on trade with neighboring territories that yielded over $50,000 annually.[15]

The repatriates continued to chart the political and economic course of the colony, despite the restraints imposed by the Society. In 1829, John Brown Russwurm, the most highly educated settler, arrived in Monrovia as superintendent of education. Russwurm had graduated from Bowdoin College in 1826 and published the first African newspaper in America, *Freedom's Journal* in New York City. While in the colony, he resurrected and edited *The Liberia Herald,* married and had two children.

However, these gains did not completely allay the dissatisfaction that lodged in the hearts and minds of many. In 1838, after Russwurm had gone south to become governor of Cape Palmas Colony, the political stability of the colony grew precarious as the settlers asked for more political power. This quest for authority and influence became more complicated as a result of the growing differences in language among the settlers. Some of the settlers, particularly from New Orleans, spoke only French, and felt that the agents of the Society favored those who spoke English. The language problem subsided in time, but the political authority question remained a heated issue. Many of the new colonies, such as "Mississippi in Africa," faced critical financial problems as well and did not know how to address them.

In the early days of the colony, questions of this type could be easily answered since it was clear that a bulk of the revenue came from the U.S. government. The federal government provided funds to the agents of the Society for the construction of buildings and the Monrovia Harbor. In addition, the colony received food supplies from the United States. However, with the proliferation of settlements, the federal government changed its policy of outright grants since it was losing more money than it was taking in from the venture. This situation was aggravated by such colonies such as Louisiana and Mississippi that failed to raise sufficient food crops for their settlers due to frequent raids from indigenous Africans, and the steady growth of these settlements. These financial difficulties forced some settlements in 1839 to form the Commonwealth of Liberia, consisting of Pennsylvania, New York, Mississippi and Louisiana. One colony, "Maryland in Africa," under the leadership of Russwurm, refused to join the commonwealth, but joined the republic in 1856 after Russwurm died.

Racism and the Republic of Liberia

Racism and the economic imperatives that precipitated the formation of the colony continued to affect Liberia, even after it became a republic. Despite the formation of the commonwealth, settlers were unable to wrestle funds from the parent body in Washington, which consistently turned a deaf ear to the pleas of the repatriates. In 1847 the national office of the Society severed all formal ties with its colony and Liberia became a republic. After twenty-seven years of a troubling tutelage by the Americans, the Africans found themselves faced with the ominous task of administering their nation, and resolving many pressing problems left by the Society. The American agents had never managed to develop a viable communications network with the indigenous Africans, which resulted in frequent raids and disputes. In order to alter this poor relationship, the settlers needed to integrate all of the local Africans into the governmental apparatus. In addition, the new nation would have to seek diplomatic recognition from the other nations of the world. More important, it would have to harness the potential of the land to produce crops for its people.

Upon independence, Liberia faced considerably greater difficulties consolidating its people than gaining diplomatic recognition. While the involvement of Americans in drafting the independence documents was considerable, some of the original settlers of 1820 were signatories to the declaration, most notably Elijah Johnson.[16] Britain, France and the other European countries recognized the new republic immediately, while the United States did not do so until 1862. However, the major problem remained that of caste discrimination perpetrated against the indigenous Africans and dark-skinned repatriates. The paradoxical position of Liberia was reflected in its Declaration of Independence, which was replete with the contradictions of the Thomas Jefferson model on which it was patterned:

> We recognize in all men, certain natural and inalienable rights: among these are life, liberty and the right to acquire, possess, enjoy, and defend property. In coming to the shores of Africa, we indulged the pleasing hope that we would be permitted to exercise and improve those faculties which impart to man his dignity- to nourish in our hearts the flame of honorable ambition, to cherish and indulge those aspirations, which a beneficent Creator had implanted to all who despise, ridicule and oppress our race, that we possess with them a common nature, one with them susceptible of equal refinement, and capable of equal advancement in all that adorns and dignifies man.[17]

Despite the declaration, the color issue reached threatening dimensions and received lashing criticism from African nationalists such as Edward Blyden, one of the early critics of the Republic's racial problems. As in the United States, skin color became a measure of social worth as lighter-skinned individuals occupied the pinnacle of the social hierarchy in Liberia, followed by the educated dark Africans, the returned slaves and the indigenous Africans. The republic's two political parties unofficially represented the different color groups. Those in the mulatto group were members of the Republican Party, while the educated Africans joined the Whig Party. The returned slaves and indigenous Africans were not recognized by either party. It was not until 1870 that the republic had its first pure African president, Edward Roye, a successful businessman, former Speaker of the Liberian House of Representatives and chief justice. Even after men like Roye reached high levels of political power, the basic discriminatory nature of the nation did not change. This sad state of affairs existed despite the efforts of enlightened leaders who worked diligently to create an African nationalist ideology in the republic.

Martin H. Freeman as Promoter of the Colony

Despite this discrimination toward the indigenous Africans, the colony and subsequent nation attracted men and women who held favorable views towards the African community. One such person was Martin H. Freeman of Rutland, Vermont. On September 13, 1864, Freeman, his wife Louisa , daughter Cora, and son John P. set sail for Liberia aboard the trader *Thomas Pope*. They would make the journey across the Atlantic to freedom just as 11,696 earlier Africans had done under the auspices of the Society.[18] Freeman was no ordinary repatriate, however. He had never known slavery. While his grandfather, Pearson Freeman, had been born into slavery on January 9, 1761, in Waterbury, Connecticut, he obtained his freedom after serving in the American Revolution. After obtaining his freedom, he settled in Rutland, Vermont, where he established a successful potash business.

Young Freeman, the child of Charles and Patience Freeman, grew up in a community where his family commanded respect and where well-meaning individuals freely gave him assistance and encouragement. He was born on May 11, 1826, and by 1838 had become a member of the all European East Parish Church. The pastor of the church, Rev. William Mitchell, took an interest in him and personally tutored and ultimately recommended him for admission to Middlebury College. In 1849 he graduated from the college and became a professor at Avery College in Pittsburgh.[19] While in Pittsburgh, a thriving African community unlike anything Freeman had ever experienced before, he came into contact with one of the most committed activists of the century, Martin R. Delany. Moreover, in Pittsburgh, Freeman would meet his wife, Louisa, a graduate of Oberlin College and the daughter of John Peck, an African trustee of Avery College.[20] In Pittsburgh, Freeman came into contact with other prominent free Africans, such as George B. Vashon, the first African-American graduate of Oberlin College.

Delany, however, had the greatest impact upon the thinking of Freeman. Prior to his meeting Delany, Freeman had never considered repatriation as an option for himself, his family and African people in general. For Delany, it was clear that African people would never get the respect that they deserved if they remained in America. Their return to Africa, for him, was the only sensible alternative. In order to get more free Africans interested in repatriation, Delany organized the National Emigration Convention that was held in Cleveland on August 24 to 26, 1854. He ran ads for the convention in two African-American newspapers, *The Alienated American* and *Frederick Douglass' Paper* for a full year in order to stimulate interest. At the conclusion of the convention he formed the Niger Valley Exploring Party.[21]

This convention had a transforming effect upon Freeman. For the first time he was in the company of a cadre of African intellectuals whose life work was developing strategies that would lead to the liberation of African people. Their focus, however, was not just upon Africans in the United States, but upon those in Africa as well. The convention touched something deep in the psyche of Freeman. He finally felt that he could become part of a national movement that could have a long-lasting impact upon Africans. Therefore, he gladly became an officer of the Niger Valley Exploring Party, with the title of special foreign secretary, while his mentor Delany became president.

By 1857 Freeman had set his sights firmly on emigration from America. Heeding the call given by Delany at the Cleveland convention to purchase land in Canada, Freeman bought fifty acres in Canada for $400. A year later he focused his attention upon Africa as the ultimate home of Africans in America. His letter to Delany on April 14, 1858, clearly indicated that Africa had to be the source of return:

> I am more and more convinced that Africa is the country to which all coloured men who wish to attain the full stature

> of manhood, and bring up their children to be men and not creeping things, should turn their steps; and I feel more and more every day, that I made a great mistake in not going there, when I was untrammelled by family ties, and had the opportunity.[22]

It was clear to Freeman that slavery had a debilitating effect upon the minds of African people and that the "slave mentality" had to be changed before any true liberation could occur. In an article published in the *Anglo-African* magazine in April 1859, Freeman articulated an educational paradigm that would lead to this transformation. He maintained that education does not begin in the schoolroom, but rather in the community and with parents. He explained that it was the "outdoor educational influences" that retarded African progress. "Our oppressed condition in this country has rendered us deficient in the first essentials of true manhood, self-respect and self-reliance."[23]

He recognized that oppression affected the African's sense of himself, his humanity, thereby making the ability to control his own destiny questionable. This oppression, he explained, is not limited to the slave states, but was also present in the North and had the same negative impact upon the African mind. "Thus in early childhood the circumstances that surround his parents, and the treatment they receive from community all tend to diminish his respect and reverence for them, hence to depreciate his respect for himself."[24] This lack of proper education leads to self-hatred and the distain for African features and self:

> Hence flat noses must be pinched up. Kinky hair must be subjected to a straightening process—oiled and pulled, twisted up, tied down, sleeked over and pressed under, or cut off so short that it can't curl, sometimes the natural hair is shaved off, and its place supplied by a straight wig, thus presenting the ludicrous anomaly of Indian hair over negro features. Thick lips are puckered up, and drawn in until the mouth no longer resembles the opening designed by nature for the admission of food, and the omission of sound. Beautiful black and brown faces by the application of rouge and lily white are made to assume unnatural tints, like the livid hue of painted corpses.[25]

In his article he urged African parents to teach their children about the nature of American wealth and slavery's role in its creation:

> Teach your child that slavery is a sin—that it is robbery in the highest degree, that it is the meanest as well as the wickedest of crimes, that those who practice it or in any way sustain or fellowship it, are the meanest of the mean and the vilest of the vile; in a word teach your child to look upon slavery and prejudice, in the light of reason and revelation, and you at once strip this boasted land and its lauded institutions of its grandeur and true character. Its vaunted freedom and equality, a stupid failure—its high sounding republicanism, a pitiful oligarchy of men-stealers and women-whippers, its religion a shameless inconsistency and an arrant hypocrisy, lifting its hand red with a brother's blood to Heaven, and mouthing its impious prayers in the face of the great Jehovah, while it tramples on God's image, and traffics in the souls of men. Let children learn from the lips of their parents the true character of this country and its institutions, and you need not fear, that their self-respect will be greatly diminished by all the wealth, splendour and seeming superiority of the oppressor.[26]

By the time Freeman left for Africa in October 1864, he had developed a clear African nationalist philosophy. On the eve of his departure, a number of people asked why he was leaving. His answers were unequivocal:

> because I am fully persuaded that emigration to Liberia is the quickest, the surest, the best—and I had almost said—the only way by which the Negro of the U.S. can rise to the full status of manhood...and last, though not least, the earnest conviction that I am a man, and by consequence, that it is not only my privilege but my duty to endeavor to secure for myself and my children all the rights, privileges and immunities that pertain to humanity.[27]

In Liberia he would continue his teaching as a professor of mathematics and natural philosophy. At Liberia College he would join colleagues who shared his visions for Liberia and Africa as a whole. On the faculty he would join Rev. Alexander Crummell, professor of intellectual and moral philosophy, and of English language and literature, and Rev. Edward W. Blyden, professor of Greek and Latin languages and literature.[28]

This type of Afrocentric view of his world certainly prepared Freeman to understand the social contradictions within Liberia. He therefore would go there with an understanding of the class distinctions and the need to integrate the indigenous Africans into the newly created society.

Even though Freeman had firmly set his mind upon Africa as the source of his return, he still pondered the question of Haiti. Why not go there? It was an African republic in the Caribbean that had obtained its freedom from France through revolutionary struggle, so why go all the way to Africa? He put this question to his mentor, Martin Delany, who chose to respond through a public letter published on February 1, 1862, in the *Weekly Anglo-American*. In a well-constructed article, Delany stated that he had no objections to Haitian "emigration." However, he did not believe that Haiti would ever become a great nation, because of its limited population and territorial size. Furthermore, he pointed out that "The international policy of the ruling powers of Europe" were "opposed to the self-government of the black races." He pointed to the seizure of two-thirds of Haiti by Spain as an example of this imperialist policy. In addition, he believed that Faber Jeffrard, president of Haiti, had essentially given to the French the island's sovereignty by signing a treaty with the pontiff of Rome, Pio Nuno.

Delany saw the treaty as the first step in Europe's plan to physically seize and control the Caribbean islands. This design would be particularly important after slavery came to an end, and the European powers sought to "extinguish the blacks." For Delany, Africa would be the one land mass where African people would be safe from such genocidal actions. Delany explained:

> To these general unfavorable contingencies Africa can never be subject, being a vast continent, peopled by one of the great enduring, fixed, reproducing, absorbing races of the earth, which must continue throughout all coming time—as it has time past-only ceasing when the world shall pass away.[29]

Despite the presence of this type of enlightened thinking, many of the dark-skinned politicians continued in the traditions of their light-skinned predecessors. Personal greed continued to play a significant part in the political life of the country. Even the successful Edward Roye remained in office only for a year after a special committee found that he had conspired with British officials to embezzle a loan of £100,000 from the British government.[30] Furthermore, the same committee discovered corruption in the administrations of Presidents Stephen Benson and Joseph J. Roberts. Such practices on the part of the Liberian officials did very little to give hope to indigenous Africans and dark settlers. George Brown, an African-American who wrote an economic history of Liberia in 1930, described the psychology of the settlers:

> As the psychology of many of the settlers closely resembled that of their former Virginia and cotton-belt masters, the Africans were regarded as a peon class. Such settlers immediately planned to dominate Africans as the white planters in America had dominated them.... Having come to Africa to escape the strictures of slavery, many of the colonists did not want to engage in the manual labour with which they had been so closely associated.[31]

Many of the repatriates wore American clothing in order to distinguish themselves from the indigenous Africans, even though the tropical heat made them extremely uncomfortable. Still other settlers built large homes that resembled those owned by southern plantation owners.

Western Economic Investments

A change for the worst occurred for the indigenous Africans when Liberia granted a concession to Firestone Rubber Company in 1926. Conditions for the indigenous Africans deteriorated to such an extent that an international commission had to be set up in 1930 by the League of Nations to inquire into the nation's labor conditions. Although the commission did not find slavery in the technical sense as defined by the League of Nations resolutions, it did find that domestic slavery existed. The commission found forced unpaid labor practices to be rampant. Indigenous Africans were recruited at random to perform services for governmental officials without compensation. The commission made the following recommendations to the Liberian government:

1. That Liberia abandon the policy of the "closed door."
2. Reestablish the authority of the chiefs.

3. Appoint Africans to administrative positions in government.
4. Declare domestic slavery and pawning illegal.
5. Stop the shipment of labourers to Fernando Po and other places outside Liberia.
6. Increase discipline over the military.
7. Encourage emigration from the United States.[32]

The warnings from the League of Nations had little effect upon the policies of the country. Color prejudice remained an integral part of de facto governmental policy. Africans from the interior not only found discrimination in governmental employment, but also in the churches. Africans from the hinterlands would seldom frequent the churches in the towns for fear of stares and occasional ejections.

Minor protests soon escalated into widespread revolts. The Kru people besieged the Province of Sinoe in protest over the treatment they received from district officials. Unable to bring the revolt under control, the Liberian government called for aid from the United States. The U.S. cruiser *Chester* was dispatched immediately with military supplies for the Liberian forces fighting to retake Sinoe. After the uprising was subdued, the United States sent the highest ranking African-American officer, Charles Young, to Liberia to advise the country's military. However, this military presence could not stifle the discontent among the Kru people. One Kru expressed his cynicism toward the Liberian government:

> Independence? We got no independence. The people on the France side, the Gold Coast people, they got it. The Americo-Liberians, they got it. We can't say anything, if we do, they put us in the B.T.C. (jail). Some of our people now get jobs in Government. But we poor people, we never get anywhere... ten years ago, stevedores 40 cents, now 55 cents. In Gold Coast they have new ships, men being sent overseas. We don't get anywhere.[33]

Although this state of affairs in Liberia can be explained by caste-class discrimination, to a certain extent, it cannot be divorced from the economic history of the country. In many cases, oppression of indigenous ethnic groups in Liberia varied directly with foreign economic penetration. Before 1908, the country had been heavily dependent upon economic aid from Great Britain, which came mainly in the form of longterm loans. In 1908 this parasitic relationship with Britain came to an end when President Arthur Barclay of Liberia sought aid from the United States.[34]

In 1910 Liberia entered into an agreement with the United States that placed the United States in direct control of Liberia's financial and military establishments. Other European countries, realizing that there was profit to be made in the country, consented to the agreement by sharing in the financial aid package to Liberia. In 1912 the multilateral loan agreement with the United States, Britain, France and Germany was completed. The function of collecting Liberia's revenue was placed in the hands of an American receiver-general. After all the paperwork was completed, Liberia received a loan of $1.7 million at 5 percent interest.[35] In 1917 Liberia severed all diplomatic relations with Germany as a result of pressure from the United States. Before the break, the Germans exercised considerable influence in Liberia's economy. After the break, the United States had virtual control over the republic's economy.

As Liberia became more dependent upon American economic aid, it became less autonomous and thus more subject to having its domestic and foreign policies dictated by the United States. A striking example of this occurred in the early 1920's when Liberia succumbed to American pressure and barred the Marcus Garvey settlement. In 1923 Garvey had sent several members of his Universal Negro Improvement Association (UNIA) to Liberia to discuss with President Charles King the possibility of acquiring land for settlers. The Republic of Liberia granted a tract of land, but before Garvey could get the first settlers to the continent, the president of Liberia revoked his offer and expelled the UNIA technicians.[36]

Immediately following this expulsion, the government entered into an agreement with Harvey S. Firestone, the American millionaire, for the construction of a deep-water harbor at Monrovia, and for a loan from the Firestone subsidiary, Finance Corporation of America. In return Liberia agreed to allow Firestone to lease up to 1 million acres of land for a period of ninety-nine years at an interest rate of 6 percent.

The Firestone Company would have to pay a nominal usage tax, but on the gross value of exported rubber it would pay no taxes.[37]

Two essential factors led to the expulsion of the Garvey technicians. The first was of a military nature. From 1912 to 1925 France had been trying to expand its west African colony, Ivory Coast, into the Zinta region of Liberia. In April 1925 the United States had to send its military to Liberia in order to repel the French. Nevertheless, the French invaded Liberia shortly after American withdrawal and occupied ten Liberian villages. When Liberia applied to the United States for further aid, President King was granted it on the condition that Liberia give rubber concessions to the Firestone Company.[38] The U.S. government, as part of the deal between Firestone and Liberia, urged President King to reject the Garvey scheme, which he did.

The other factor that persuaded President King to reject the Garvey scheme was the British monopoly of the world's rubber production. At the time, Britain controlled 75 percent of the world's rubber, while the United States was the largest consumer. Clearly the United States government would be able to break the economic deadlock with Britain if it could import its rubber needs from Liberia. Harry Firestone pressed the State Department to facilitate the deal with President King. In 1926 the agreement, which gave Firestone Company 1 million acres of land for six cents an acre annually, was signed.[39]

Since Liberia was the only West African country free of European colonial control, Garvey had to be kept out of the continent at all costs. The concession to Firestone, however, meant that the country became more dependent upon American economic controls. On the surface, the arrival of big business meant some improvements such as stores, roads and banking institutions; but it also ushered in a period of forced exploitation of African labor. In the year of the agreement with Firestone, the Liberian government established a Labour Bureau, the commissioner of which received orders directly from the U.S. secretary of the interior and was charged with supplying 10,000 men to the Firestone plantations each year.

After the expulsion of the Garvey technicians the posture of Liberia in international affairs became clear. The leaders of the republic were satisfied to exist as an economic colony of the United States. In 1942 Liberia signed an agreement that gave the United States the right to set up military bases in Liberia. The United States built Monrovia's Robertsfield Airport as a military base. For the strategic privilege of establishing a military presence in West Africa, the U.S. government gave the Liberians a loan of $20 million under the Mutual Aid Agreement. The United States also constructed a seaplane base at Fisherman Lake under the agreement.[40] In addition, an airfield was built in cooperation with Pan-American Airways and a garrison of 5,000 American troops was stationed nearby.[41] In 1946 the Liberian government granted 25,000 acres to Lansdell K. Christie, a New York financier, to extract iron deposits. The Christie contract was for eighty years.[42] In 1954 the Goodrich Rubber Company acquired 600,000 acres of land.[43] This capital infusion meant that the Liberian ruling class further entrenched its economic control of the nation. In 1969, 95 percent of the Liberian population received 25 percent of the national income, while the remaining 5 percent of the population received an incredible 75 percent.[44]

When Mr. William Tubman came to office in 1943, he promised the country reconciliation. But instead of opening the country to active participation by all elements of the society, he consolidated his own power. His term ran for eight years and he was reelected for another term of four years in 1955. In 1951 a Kru leader, Duhdwe Twe, formed a political party and challenged President Tubman at the polls. Twe had widespread support among the ethnic groups of the country, but he was charged with treason by the Tubman administration and had to leave the country.[45]

The situation deteriorated significantly as the country plunged into civil war. The ethnic conflicts that were spawned in the early nineteenth century and nurtured by American investments continued to plague the country. In 1997 Charles Taylor was elected resident of the republic after an election that many foreign observers felt was free and fair. The test for the future, however, will be whether Liberia can resolve many of the caste conflicts that were borne out of the racial contradictions and economic concessions of the nineteenth century.

Notes

1. Stanley Elkins, *Slavery: A Problem in American Institutional and Intellectual Life,* 2nd ed. (Chicago: University of Chicago Press, 1969), page 179.

2. Clay cited in Robert I. Rotberg, *A Political History of Tropical Africa* (New York: Harcourt, Brace and World, 1965), page 210.
3. Jefferson cited in Richard West, *Back to Africa: A History of Sierra Leone and Liberia* (London: Jonathan Cape, Ltd., 1970), page 95.
4. Henry S. Wilson, *The Origins of West African Nationalism* (New York: Macmillan, 1969), page 55.
5. Eli Ginzberg and Alfred S. Eichner, *The Troublesome Presence* (New York: Mentor Books, 1964), page 90.
6. Leonard Bacon, *A Discourse at the Funeral of Jehudi Ashmun* (New Haven, Ct: Hezekiah Howe, 1828), page 11, Middlebury College Archives.
7. David Stratton, *Liberia: The Love of Liberty Brought us Here,* Middlebury College Archives.
8. Edwin S. Redkey, *Black Exodus: Black Nationalism and Back to Africa Movements: 1890 to 1910* (New Haven, Ct: Yale University Press, 1969), page 21.
9. J. Gus Liebenow, *Liberia: The Evolution of Privilege*, (Ithaca, NY: Cornell University Press, 1969), page 12.
10. Redkey, page 35.
11. Merran Fraenkel, *Tribe and Class in Monrovia* (London: Oxford University Press, 1965), page 4.
12. Fraenkel, page 11.
13. Liebenow, page 11.
14. William Loren Katz, *Eyewitness: The Negro in American History* (New York: Pitman, 1967), page 148.
15. Fraenkel, page 11.
16. Stratton, page 2. Hiliary Johnson, the son of Elijah later would become the seventh president.
17. Howard Brotz, *Negro Social and Political Thought 1850 to 1920, Representative Texts* (New York: Basic Books, 1966), page 137.
18. "Departure of Emigrants," *The African Repository*, October 1864, Vol. 40, No. 10, page 314, Middlebury College Archives.
19. Dawn D. Hance, ed., *Early Families of Rutland, Vermont* (Rutland: The Rutland Historical Society), page 142, Middlebury College Archives.
20. Russell W. Irvine, "Martin H. Freeman of Rutland, America's First Black College Professor and Pioneering Black Social Activist," *Rutland Historical Society Quarterly*, Volume XXVI, No. 3, 1996, page 75.
21. Irvine, page 76.
22. "Freeman, M.H. to Martin Delany," Middlebury College Archives, A9 File.

23. M.H. Freeman, "The Educational Wants of the Free Colored People," Middlebury College Archives.
24. Freeman, "Educational Wants."
25. Freeman, "Educational Wants."
26. Freeman, "Educational Wants."
27. "Newspaper Items re: Martin H. Freeman, Middlebury College Class of 1849, From the Liberator Oct. 15, 1864" Middlebury College Archives.
28. Forty-Sixth Annual Report of the American Colonization Society, January 20, 1863, page 10, Middlebury College Archives.
29. *Weekly Anglo-African*, February 1, 1862, Middlebury College Archives.
30. George Padmore, *Pan-Africanism or Communism* (London: Dennis Dobson, 1965), page 57.
31. Brown cited in Fraenkel, page 13.
32. Padmore, page 69.
33. Fraenkel, page 225.
34. Liebenow, page 6.
35. Padmore, page 62.
36. John Henrik Clarke, ed., *Marcus Garvey: And the Vision of Africa* (New York: Vintage Books, 1974), page 106.
37. Fraenkel, page 23.
38. Padmore, page 61.
39. Padmore, page 67.
40. Padmore, page 70.
41. Fraenkel, page 28.
42. Padmore, page 61.
43. Padmore, page 68.
44. Liebenow, page 187.
45. Fraenkel, page 225.

Chapter Eight

JOHN BROWN RUSSWURM: COMPROMISE AND POLITICAL POWER

The decision of John Brown Russwurm on February 14, 1829 to repatriate to Liberia under the auspices of the American Colonization Society caused tremendous uproar among the free African population in America. This outcry echoed from the predominantly African five corners section of New York City, where Russwurm was burned in effigy, to African strongholds such as Boston and Philadelphia. Despite this outcry, Russwurm remained committed to joining the Colonization Society because he saw it as the most effective vehicle he could utilize to achieve his repatriation goals. Such a compromise would have been unthinkable for leaders such as Frederick Douglass and David Walker, but Russwurm's interracial and academic backgrounds enabled him to both accept and cross racial barriers that most Africans would never dream of challenging. Moreover, by 1829, John Russwurm had evolved into a pragmatist who would seek whatever alliances would help him achieve his ultimate goal of African political power on the continent of Africa.

Jamaican Birth

Russwurm was born into a mixed family on October 1, 1799. His father, John Russwurm, the senior, was born to a wealthy Virginian family in 1761. The patriarch and matriarch of the family are unknown, yet we do know that two sons resulted from the union: William Alexander Russwurm and John Russwurm, the father of John Brown. William, in 1781, married into a prominent southern family, the Sumners. His wife, Elenor Sumner (1763-1850) was a descendent of William Sumner, who settled in Nansemond, West Virginia in 1690. Her brother, named after her father Jethro, was a Revolutionary War General from Tennessee, who, after his death was honored by having

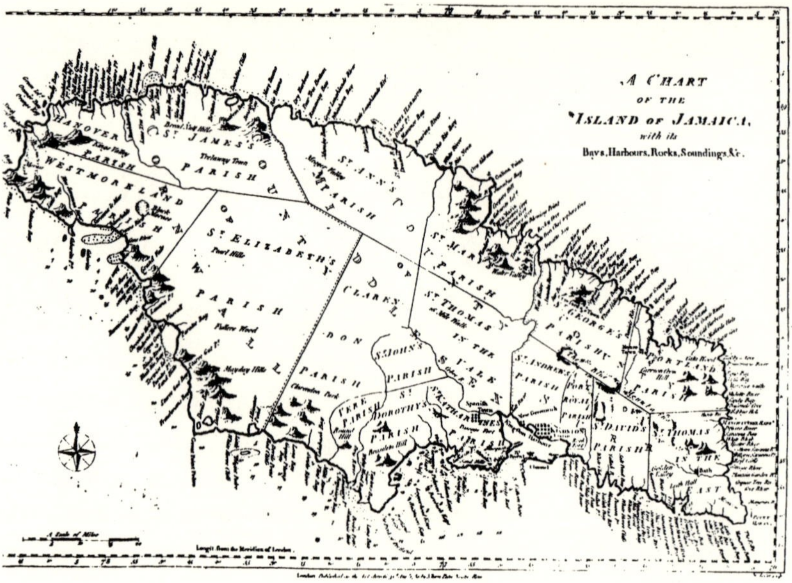

Courtesy of the National Library of Jamaica

Sumner County named after him. William Russwurm and Elenor had three children: William Alexander born in 1839, John Sumner (1793-1860, married Sarah (Sally), Martin Clark on December 25, 1817) and Mary, who married John Keyser. After completing his education in England, he traveled to Port Antonio, Jamaica where he engaged in agricultural production of sugar, and served his community as a judge. He, like most planters, used both free Africans and slaves in the production of his crops. By 1810 he and a partner owned over fifty-four (54) slaves in Jamaica.[1]

It is unclear at this point why he settled in Jamaica and the circumstances under which he met John Brown's mother. It is undisputed, however, that he fathered an African child in Jamaica and then made provisions for his travel and study in Canada and America. It was in Port Antonio, Portland Parish, Jamaica that the young child was first exposed to "racial" classifications. When John Brown was born in 1799, the Parish of Portland had been in existence for 76 years. At the time of its formation Jamaica was under the ultimate control of the British Government and the immediate administration of the Governor of Jamaica, who was also Duke of Portland. Jamaica's main economic value to Britain was its sugar industry. By 1768 twenty-nine sugar estates existed on the Island. These estates proliferated after the British signed a peace accord with the Maroons in 1739. The Maroons were Jamaicans who refused to be enslaved or colonized by the British and therefore ran into the mountains, where they waged a military struggle against the intruders. Despite this struggle, the British were able to hold the majority of Africans in slavery. By 1824, 8,800 slaves and 165 proprietors lived in Portland Parish.[2] The largest estates were Snow Hill, Passley Gardens, Norwich, Prospect, Williamsfield, Red Hazel, Bog Estate, Stanton-Harcourt, Tom's Hope, Newington, Windsor, Seaman's Valley, Comfort Castle, Golden Vale, Cold Harbour, Fairy Hill, Boston, Egg Hill and Fair Prospect.[3] By the 1820's the price of sugar fell precipitously, causing many farmers to abandon the industry. Those estates situated furthest from the coast gave up the trade the earliest because of the increased cost of transportation and increased political agitation by Africans. Throughout the 1820's there was a steady decline in production so that by 1854 only four estates existed.[4] To a large extent the main cause of this decline was emancipation of slaves throughout the British West Indies in 1834. John senior, however, left the Island on or about 1813, long before the decline and may have protected his financial well-being by withdrawing his investments at this early point.

Very little is known about John's mother, except that she was an African woman, who was most likely the concubine of his father. A number of free colored individuals by the name of Brown lived in Port Antonio in the early eighteen hundreds. An examination of baptismal records for the Parish of Portland, beginning in 1804, reveals both evidence of Browns as well as a woman by the name of Russwurm. For example, the following entries reveal the presence of a number of individuals by the name of Brown in the "Register of Baptisms, Parish of Portland":

1. William Brown, a slave belonging to Ms. Mary Brown, aged about 20 baptized.
2. Sarah Brown, Negroe property of Elizabeth Brown and Doctor Brown, baptized April 12, 1804.
3. John Brown, about 18 years, property of Dr. Brown.
4. Jane Brown, about 40 years, property of Dr. Brown.

5. William Brown about 30 years of age, a Negro slave, the property of Ms.(unintelligible), can't read, April 12, 1804.
6. John George Brown, son of John George Brown and Rebecca his wife, born November, 1802, baptized April 5, 1806.
7. Sarah Catherine Brown, daughter of John G. Brown and Rebecca his wife, born May 5, 1805, baptized April 5, 1806
8. Henry Sherwood Brown, son of Nicholas Brown and Barbara, his wife, born July 28, 1805, baptized April 4,1806.
9. Mary Brown, a free Sambo, aged 33 years, baptized May 8, 1844.
10. Richard Brown, a Negro, aged 35 years, the property of John Brown, baptized 1815.
11. Lucy Brown, aged about 35, Negro, the property of Richard King, baptized September, 1815.
12. Lambert Brown, Negro. Property of John Miller and Sarah Duncan, baptized August 18, 1810.
13. William Brown, a Sambo, age 15, property of Henry R. Brown, baptized 1816.
14. Bell Marina Brown, aged (unintelligible) years, a free woman of colour, baptized November 14, 1819.
15. Christiana Brown Bartlett, daughter of William Bartlett and Florence his wife, free.
16. Rosanna Brown (no age given) property of Seaman's Valley Estate, baptized January 25, 1818.
17. Elizabeth Brown, slave property of Henry Capley baptized February 2, 1818.
18. Thomas Brown, James Brown, Sarah Brown, Fanny Gadge, Elizabeth Moore, Mary Joseph—(no ages given) slave property of Twickenham Estate, baptized 1818.
19. Group of children of J. Deans, Esq. and Jane Brown, his wife (born 1800-1822) omitted from registry, baptized June 9, 1822.

It is clear from these records that both slave and free persons of colour held the name of Brown. In fact, the Vestry records indicate that on August 1, 1822, a G. Brown, who had served in local government, died. A special vestry was held at the Port Antonio Court House in her honor.

Furthermore, in the National Archives in Spanish Town, Jamaica, the following entry was made in the baptismal records:

> John Brown, a free child of color, born April 1, 1804, baptized 20 of June, 1804.

Earlier works on John Brown Russwurm, particularly of Mary Sagarin, indicated his birth as October 1, 1799. The National Archives contain no corroborating information for 1799, therefore, it is likely he may have been born five years later. Furthermore, in the above entry, there is no mention of the name of the mother of John Brown. However, the very next entry adds more clarity to this question:

> Rebecca Ann Russwurm, a free child of color, of Eliza Brown, born 2 of June 1810, baptized 24th of December, 1810.

In this entry we find the name of Russwurm for the first time. The father is not specifically mentioned, but it is highly unlikely that it was the name of anyone but John Russwurm, the father of John Brown Russwurm. It is undisputed that on June 2, 1810, John Russwurm was still in Jamaica, because all indication is that he did not leave until 1813. More importantly, what this most likely means is that the name of John Brown's mother was Eliza Brown, and he had a sister by the name of Rebecca Ann Russwurm.

Moreover, there is evidence that Eliza Brown continued to have children after John Brown left Jamaica in 1807 and his father in 1813. The following entries indicate that Eliza Brown married John George Brown and gave birth to several offspring:

- William Zachary Brown son of John George Brown and Eliza Brown, his wife born 16 Feb. 1814, baptized 4 of April, 1814.
- Margaret Ann Brown, daughter of John George Brown and Eliza Brown his wife born 10/18/1815 baptized 12/25/18.
- Henry James Brown son of John George Brown and Eliza his wife born July 1819 baptized August 1819 [5]

It would appear that after John Russwurm left Jamaica in 1813, Eliza married John George Brown and had three additional children, giving John Brown, two half brothers and one half sister who were born in

Jamaica. Furthermore, there is a reference to an Elizabeth Russwurm, "…a free woman of color…" who was baptized April 21, 1822. It is unlikely that John Russwurm was the father of this child, (assuming that she is not an adult), since he died much earlier.

John undoubtedly held a special place in his father's world. He was ultimately given his father's name and sent to Quebec, Canada for his education. The young Russwurm lived the first eight years of his life in Jamaica. Since John senior had no wife, John and his mother served as a surrogate family.[6] Jamaican law prohibited marriage between planters and slaves. Therefore it was highly unlikely that John's mother was lawfully married to his father. Slavery continued in Jamaica until August 1, 1834. Had John remained in the country his life would have been quite different. His father, however, envisioned a better life for the young boy and therefore made preparations for John to travel to Quebec for an education. This submersion into Canadian society helped further develop young Russwurm's understanding and appreciation of western culture and values.

Education in Quebec

In 1807, John traveled to Canada with his father, who was looking for land to buy in America. While there, the father enrolled John in a school. It is most likely that the school was in one of three cities: Montreal, Quebec City or Three Rivers. As he looked for places to settle in America, the choices were limited. He could not return to his native Virginia, the most brutal and prolific of the slave states, and risk his son being placed into slavery. Rather, Canada's more favorable governmental policies toward slavery made it an acceptable place to settle temporarily and to place his son in school. Canada, like America, had a history of slavery, but abolished it in 1793.[7] John senior could, therefore, leave young John in Canada without fear that he would be captured and sold into slavery. For five years, John attended school with Canada's elite and left only when his father acquired seventy-five acres of farm land in Back Cove, the District of Maine, which was at that time a part of the Commonwealth of Massachusetts.

Quebec was viewed internationally as a seat of abolitionist activity and a haven for runaway slaves. The United States, on the other hand, was not safe for an African person, even if he was free. Although federal constitutional law prohibited the importation of slaves into the

United States as of 1808, the illegal trade continued to proceed, as West Indians and Africans continued to be smuggled into the country, and sold into slavery.

Although slavery was not an issue that young Russwurm had to confront, Canada, nevertheless, was undergoing transition. The educational system of Quebec reflected this fundamental change. Although it is not known precisely when Russwurm arrived in Quebec, or the school he attended, it is clear that the approximate date was 1807. This educational experience in an English speaking school gave him the necessary foundation for later educational development.

The state of education in Quebec reflected the political changes that were occurring in the country as the British seized control from the French. Quebec, from 1608 to 1759, was under French control, and as a result, the schools were under the control of the Catholic church. The French, however, began to loosen this control gradually. Despite the Quebec Act of 1774, which re-established French control over culture and religion, by 1791 very few Catholic clergy were active in Quebec education.[8] The new Constitution of May 18, 1791, led to further complications as Canada was divided into two provinces, Lower Canada and Upper Canada. These changes would have profound impacts upon education in the country. Immediately, the new English Government established bans upon the recruitment of Jesuits, Recollects and Sulpcians, which almost led to the disappearance of secondary schools in Quebec. Even though the British was victorious over the French politically, they were unable to provide sufficient numbers of schools for the country's children. For example, in the three areas of Quebec, Three Rivers and Montreal, there were only seventeen primary schools (eleven for boys) for a population of 33,200.[9]

It is most likely that Russwurm attended one of these primary schools, or was taught by a private tutor, which was not unusual for children of the upper class. On the other hand, he may have been advanced enough to be placed in one of the secondary schools. His choices would have been between Seminaire de Quebec founded in 1765 by Mgr. de Laval; College de Montreal (College Saint-Raphael founded in 1767, later to become College de Montreal in 1806) established by the Sulpicians; and Seminaire de Nicolet founded by Mgr. J.O. Plessis in 1803.[10]

The College of Montreal was founded in 1767, and soon developed a lower level division known as Le Petite Seminaire de Montreal (1806). Information is available on these schools from the Archives du Seminaire de Quebec, among the papers of Jacques Viger, located at the Library of the Public Archives. Although a review of records for the school reveal the enrollment of Edward Brown (1809-1809), Matthew Brown (1816-1817) and John Joseph Brown (1818-1820), none appear to be John Brown. It is unlikely, therefore, that he attended the College of Montreal.

The Petite Seminaire of Montreal, however, would have offered young Russwurm the type of preparation that would have enabled him to successfully gain admission to Hebron Academy in Maine. The Little Seminary had both French and English institution. The students were taught from eight to eleven in the morning and from one to four in the afternoon. Their subjects consisted of reading, writing, geography, bookkeeping and arithmetic. As students progressed in their studies, they took French and Latin. In addition, the school accepted both borders and non-borders. If young Russwurm did not attend one of the above schools, it is possible that he received private instruction from several highly qualified men.

Many English gentlemen established small private schools out of their homes. John Pulliman opened the first such school in 1773. In 1799 the Classical and Mathematical School was opened at 43 Little St. James Street and remained open for eighteen years under the leadership of Alexander Skakel.[11] Regardless of which school young Russwurm attended, by the time he enrolled in school in Maine, he had received excellent academic preparation and invaluable experience in living and competing in a competitive environment.

While we may be unable to precisely determine which school John attended, we can safely conclude that it was one that was reserved for the privileged class. It is highly unlikely that he attended any of the schools reserved for runaway slaves or children of the lower economic classes.

Life in Portland, Maine

It was in Maine that John Brown Russwurm had to make another significant adjustment in his life: adapting to a family of step-brothers. On May 4, 1813, John's father, who was fifty-two, married Susanna

Blanchard, a young woman of approximately twenty-five years of age. Susan, a widow, had three children from a previous marriage, and young John immediately found himself, at the age of thirteen (13), in a strange and challenging culture. What was Maine life like in 1813? Were any African-Americans living in the Portland area during this time? Professor Randolph Stakeman of Bowdoin College has written a significant article analyzing the presence of "Blacks" in Maine from 1764 through 1900. He maintains that the African-American population in Maine has always remained under one percent. Much of his data is derived from statistical analysis of census data, but important conclusions can be drawn from his study. Nevertheless, he recognizes the problems inherent in trying to arrive at a reliable count of African-American in the state. For example, he argues that the first United States Census in 1790 undercounted "Blacks" because the government only counted those who were in "white" households.[12] Professor Stakeman shows that in 1764, the "Black" population was 322 as compared to 23,406 "whites," and by 1820, the number had risen to 929 as compared to 296,406 "whites."[13] Most of these African-Americans lived in the Portland area, so that by the time Russwurm arrived, the region had a little over nine hundred African-Americans, or about .3 percent of the general population. Given their upper class status, Russwurm would probably not have had much contact with these African-Americans, especially since they were spread over ninety-two towns in 1800.[14]

Despite the small numbers, Portland's fifty or more African-Americans were able to form a church, which served as both a place of worship and a social center. Given the extent to which they were distributed throughout the state, it was very difficult for them to form other social institutions. Most (over 50%) lived in towns with less than twenty "Blacks".[15] Professor Stakeman has indicated, however, that despite the small numbers, many of African-American in Maine formed self-supporting communities. Since Maine's laws prohibited interracial marriages, these individuals traveled great distances from community to community seeking companionship and nurturing friendships.

What social status did Africans in Portland have? What were their occupations? For the most part, they were farmers, which was not unlike the majority of working "whites." Professor Stakeman found some evidence of African-Americans working in the manufacturing and maritime sectors as well. In fact, as the maritime trades increased shortly after 1820, other towns, such as Brunswick, Bath, Harpswell, Bristol and Warren attracted as many African-Americans as Portland. In these port towns, African-Americans found work as seamen, fishermen, shipwrights and stewards.

The senior Russwurm was determined to have his young son brought up in the best of the aristocratic traditions of Maine. The manner in which young Russwurm was presented to Maine is recorded in records of the Maine Genealogical Society:

> The elder John Russwurm when he came to Portland brought with him a young mulatto boy 13 years old, who was named John Brown...He was proud of his son. He introduced him into the best society in Portland where he was honored and respected. He attended the best schools and had all the privileges that other boys of the best of families enjoyed.[16]

Hebron Academy

Shortly after his arrival in Maine, the senior Russwurm enrolled the boy in the finest private school in the District of Maine, Hebron Academy, located in the Town of Paris. The dates of his attendance at the all boys school is unclear, but school officials estimate that it must have been between 1813 and 1819. He remained there until 1819, the year that he left for Boston.

After being brought from Quebec to the exclusive school, he suddenly found himself alone in a strange new land, among people he did not know. To make matters even worse, on April 3, 1815, his father died. Whether his father left provision for the continuation of his education is unclear. What is clear, however, is that Susan, his step mother, continued to support the young man in his studies at Hebron Academy. His only link to his father was his half brother, Francis, who was born in 1814, and another brother, Edward.

The father had left his son, however, prepared to meet the rigorous challenges of the Hebron curriculum. In order to gain admission, John needed to meet the following requirements:

1. be 10 years old, at least
2. be able to write

3. be able to read English correctly
4. be of good moral character

he prospective student also had to be examined by the Preceptor, Williams Barrows, Jr., in the presence of the Standing Committee. The President of the school, during Russwurm's tenure, was Samuel Parris, who held this position from 1807-1827.

The school consisted of a Trustee House, the Academy and the Chapel. The students stayed in the town, or in a boarding place, which was one mile south of the school, or at the house of Deacon William Barrows. His favorite saying was "I fear God and know no other fear." Unfortunately, his barn, which was used for student residences, burned down on December 14, 1814. The school was quite prone to fires, because another fire at the school destroyed many records including those pertaining to Russwurm's enrollment. The Academy was an unattractive one-story building, needing painting, with a huge chimney. The room was divided by large folding doors, and had a stage and row of chairs for the students.

Hebron Academy was one of only a few select private schools east of Exeter Academy. The charter for the new school was granted by Governor Caleb Strong on February 10, 1804.[17] The original incorporators were Reverend James Hooper (Pastor of the Baptist Church at Paris); Ezekiel Whitman (Attorney at New Gloucester-later Chief Justice of the Supreme Court of Maine), Dr. Cyrus Hamlin, Samuel Parris (father of Governor Albion K. Parris) and John Greenwood (magistrate).[18] Most of these incorporators subsequently became trustees. As is clear from the background of the incorporators, the school would reflect religious and social values of the upper-classes in the community.

Russwurm was one of approximately a little over forty students at Hebron. At this early point in his stay at the school, he was exposed to Bowdoin College through his second Preceptor, John Eveleth, who served in that role between 1814-1816.[19] Eveleth was a graduate of the college and therefore encouraged his brightest students to seek admission. Bowdoin was one of the few prominent New England colleges that would accept Africans. Harvard College, though much older than Bowdoin, did not accept its first Black student until 1848, and then only after sustained student protests.[20]

Once admitted, young Russwurm had to master Greek and Latin as well as read the following books in the morning and evening before prayer: the Holy Bible, the Beauties of the Bible, Columbia Orator, Webster's 3rd Part, Welch's Arithmetric, Morse's Geography, Murray's or Alexander's English Grammar.

Soon after John's father died in 1815, Susan Russwurm married William Hawes, but she remained committed to providing support for young Russwurm. She made it clear to him that he would remain an integral part of their family. Despite the death of his father, John was able to complete his studies at Hebron before moving on to Boston, where he would make his first encounter with a large and thriving African community.

Russwurm in Boston

When Russwurm arrived in Boston in the year 1819, he discovered a vibrant and free African community that was attempting to survive economically as well as struggle to end slavery in the South. Simply because Russwurm did not have to confront the evil of slavery in Boston when he arrived, did not mean that it had never existed in this city. The earliest estimate is that slavery began in Boston between 1624 and 1630.[21] By 1696 New England colonies had become more heavily involved in the slave trade as a result of England's revocation of the monopoly given to the Royal African Company. The Assiento of 1713 enabled Britain to gain even more control over the slave trade by cutting Spain off from its Spanish slave markets. Soon Boston became the major slave port in the United States with many prominent Bostonians engaged in the trade. Among the leading families involved in the trade were those of James Bowdoin, Andrew Fanueil and John Hancock.[22] By the American Revolution, 5,249 Africans lived in Massachusetts, making up 1.8 percent of the general population.[23] In 1790, the year of the federal census, the number had increased to 5,369, or 1.4 percent of the general population.[24] The majority of these individuals resided in Boston. A year after Russwurm arrived in Boston the total population of Boston was 43,298, of which 1,690 or 3.9 percent were Africans.[25]

The community that Russwurm became apart of was extremely self-directed and determined. The people had taken deliberate steps to secure a meaningful presence in the city. In 1796 they founded the African Society as a vehicle to promote self-improvement. It gave assistance to those members of the community who had need of charitable assistance as well as helped individuals obtain employment.[26] In order to address the religious needs of the community, they founded the African Baptist Church on August 8, 1805 and the Bethel Methodist Church in 1818.[27] The first pastor of this first church was Thomas Paul. Approximately, two thousand Africans lived in the city by 1825.[28]

Even though Russwurm had left behind friends and a step family, he still followed political developments in Maine closely. Moreover, his step-family in Portland were the only family that he had in America. Even though he was forging new bonds in Boston, he believed that it was important to stay in touch with them. For example, on July 19, 1819, he corresponded with his family concerning the controversial issue of Maine statehood. The District of Maine had existed as a political appendage of Massachusetts from its creation and a great many people wanted the District to separate from Massachusetts. Though recognizing the importance of autonomy, Russwurm believed that the District could no longer sustain itself economically.[29]

Upon his arrival in Boston at the age of twenty, Russwurm was one of the best educated persons in the city, regardless of ethnicity. His training in education made him an excellent leader in the African community's efforts to establish educational institutions for the free Africans. He became an immediate asset to the community. He served as Principal of the Primus Hall School, which was located in the basement of the African Meeting House, a facility that had been erected by Africans as a meeting house and later served as the first African Baptist church.

Prior to the arrival of Russwurm, free Africans in Boston had established schools for the education of their people. In 1798, they established a school in the home of Primus Hall for the education of their children and hired the teacher, Elisha Sylvester. By 1808 the school was relocated to the basement of the African Meeting House and in the same year its members hired Prince Saunders, the second teacher.[30] The school was supported by both public funds and contributions from the African community. Given the cordial relations between some African-Americans and European-Americans in the city, Prince Saunders was able to convince a wealthy Bostonian, Abiel Smith, to donate securities in his estate to the Boston School Committee to benefit African school children.[31] For the five years that Russwurm was in Boston many educational developments occurred. In 1822 the West End Primary School opened in the African Meeting House.[32] Russwurm as well as other prominent African Bostonians, taught in these schools people such as Thomas A. Paul of Dartmouth's class of 1841 and son of Rev. Thomas A. Paul.[33] In the first thirty years of the nineteenth century African men and women of extraordinary abilities converged to create a unique educational experience for themselves and their children. Even before Massachusetts enacted the first state school law in the country, Africans had asked the Commonwealth for separate African schools.[34]

The city could boast of other enterprising Africans during the nineteenth and the latter part of eighteenth centuries. For example, Prince Hall, a wealthy free African, and the father of, Primus Hall, established the first African masonic lodge in America. The African Masonic Lodge, recognized by the Grand Lodge of England in 1787, aided many African Bostonians, who needed shelter, fire wood or other necessities. Prince Hall, a Methodist minister had served in the colonial army during the American Revolution and in 1755 sought membership in the St. Andrew Masonic Lodge of Boston. After he was denied membership, he launched the African Masonic Lodge. Boston's African Lodge 459 inspired other Africans in New England to form lodges. For example, in 1799 a lodge was formed in Providence, Rhode Island.[35]

The spirit of Prince Hall symbolized the overall tenor of Boston's African community. Even before he received a response from England concerning his new African Lodge, he organized his group and continued to agitate for full inclusion into Boston society. On November 26, 1787, he wrote James Bowdoin, Governor of Massachusetts and offered to organize 700 African men to fight against a horde of rebellious farmers in the western section of the state, which would later be called Shay's Rebellion. In the letter to Governor Bowdoin, Hall stressed several key points that clearly reflected his views on government and the role of African citizens. First of all, his fraternal order required its members to be "...peaceful subjects to the civil powers..." Secondly, it prohibited them from engaging in any "...plot or conspiracies against the state where we dwell;..."[36]

This was not the first petition of Hall, however. In January, 1777 he and seven other Africans in Boston petitioned for the freedom of all slaves in the Commonwealth. In 1787 Prince Hall and 73 African

Masons petitioned the General Court to be returned to Africa. Even though slavery had been outlawed in the Commonwealth for seven years, they still felt that life in the Commonwealth was extremely oppressive and that life in Africa would be more suitable. He wrote:

> "...This leads us humbly to propose the following plan to the consideration of this honourable Court...They who are disposed to go and settle there shall form themselves into a civil society, united by a political constitution, in which they shall agree...and...write...into a religious society, or christian (sic) church; and have one or more blacks ordained as their pastors or Bishops; And being thus formed, shall remove to Africa and settle on said lands...we are poor and utterly unable to prosecute this scheme or to return to Africa without assistance. Money is wanted to enable those who shall be appointed, to go to Africa, and procure lands to be settled upon; and to obtain passage for us and our families."[37]

The Boston that Russwurm encountered, therefore, was one where the African community had engaged in all forms of African expression, including both accommodation and repatriation. One of the most significant influences upon Russwurm was the teachings of Rev. Thomas Paul. While in Boston, Russwurm eagerly joined in the struggle to educate the African children of his community. Yet, he still struggled with the question of what a talented young man should do with his future. Even though his work in Boston was stimulating and fulfilling, could he spend the rest of his life in a precarious existence, avoiding the ever present slave catchers who sought to snatch Africans from the streets and send them south. Russwurm's involvement with the Primus Hall School put him in the middle of the debates over colonization, especially over emigration to Haiti. The free African community in Boston had a favorable view of Haiti. In 1823, Rev. Paul traveled there and met with President Boyer. During this meeting they discussed the importance of Africans in America emigrating to Haiti. When Rev. Paul returned to the United States, his letter to the Columbian Centinel, in which he encouraged emigration, was published on July 1, 1824. His article read in part:

> ...I am fully persuaded that it is the best and most suitable place of residence which Providence has hitherto offered to

> emancipated people of color, for the enjoyment of liberty and equality with their attendant blessings...[38]

By 1826, when he graduated from Bowdoin College, he too had placed Haiti at the center of his political perspective. As a commencement speaker, Russwurm spoke of liberty in Haiti and made plans to eventually emigrate to the island.

His most important acquaintance, however, was David Walker, a militant leader who published a pamphlet urging Africans to take up arms against slavery. Although Walker came to Boston in 1825, a year after Russwurm had gone to Bowdoin College, it appears that the two made contact with each other, and stayed in touch even after Russwurm graduated from college and moved to New York City. Walker was born a free man in Wilmington, North Carolina on September 28, 1785. Before moving to Boston he traveled throughout the South, where he witnessed the horrors of slavery, which upset him so much that he resolved to leave the South before he was killed as a martyr:

"If I remain in this bloody land, I will not live long. As true as God reigns, I will be avenged for the sorrow which my people have suffered. This is not the place for me-no, no, I must leave this part of the country. It will be a great trial for me to live on the same soil where so many men are in slavery; certainly I cannot remain where I must hear their chains continually, and where I must encounter the insults of their hypocritical enslavers. Go, I must."[39]

His mother was a free woman, his father a slave, who died before David was born. In Boston he learned to read and write and ran a new and used clothing store on Brattle Street in the heart of Boston's African community, which was located on Belknap (Joy) Street on Beacon Hill. In 1828, he married a woman by the name of Elisa and had one child, Edward Garrison Walker. David Walker was a tall (6 feet) man who became active in African politics. He became a member of the Massachusetts General Colored Association and worked closely with leaders, such as John T. Hilton, Grand Master of the Masonic lodge in providing shelter to runaways and the poor.

By 1827, after Russwurm had gone to New York, Walker agreed to become a general agent for the newspaper, *Freedom's Journal*. Walker and Reverend Paul worked diligently among the African community to foster support for the paper. In 1828, Walker organized support for George Horton, a North Carolina African who was attempting to obtain his freedom from slavery in North Carolina, but was caught.

In that same year, Walker disagreed with Russwurm over how the paper should be run. His anger reflected the larger disappointment that was felt among Boston's African community. The major concern was over the paper's liberal attitude toward colonization. This conflict ultimately led to the break up of the partnership between Russwurm and Cornish. After Samuel Cornish left the paper as co-editor, Russwurm increasingly became sympathetic toward colonization. Despite this mounting criticism in Boston, Walker continued to support Russwurm and the paper, even until its last publication in March 28, 1829.

Walker, nevertheless, maintained a militant posture in his outrage over slavery and the condition of free Africans in America, who were uniformly denied an opportunity to compete for good paying jobs. Most, Walker wrote, were relegated to low paying occupations such as bootblacks, barbers and cleaners. Africans were not hired as carpenters and mechanics, for example, because these jobs were reserved for the "white" working class.[40] In addition, Walker wrote and argued that Africans were discriminated against in the provision of public schooling as well, that in segregated public schools Africans were not taught grammar. He also lambasted segregation and discrimination in the "white" churches of the city. For example, an African man purchased a pew in the Park Street Church, but once the church leadership found that he was African, they had him removed by force.[41] Walker, therefore wrote and published his Walker's Appeal so that these indignities in the North and slavery in the South could be better known throughout the United States. The pamphlet caused considerable alarm in the South. The southern slave holders were incensed that someone, and an African at that, would launch such an assault upon their way of life. The Governor of Georgia tried to suppress the further release of the book by writing Harrison Grey Otis, Mayor of Boston. The Mayor refused to intervene informing the Governor that he would not attempt to censor the lawful publication of Walker's thoughts.[42] A group of Georgia planters then pledged to kill Walker, placed a bounty of $1,000.00 upon his head and $10,000.00 if captured alive. This type of retaliation caused both Walker, his friends and family concern over his life. Many urged him to run to Canada for safety. He resolutely pledged to stand his ground:

> I will stand my ground. Somebody must die in this cause. I may be doomed to the stake and the fire, or to the scaffold tree, but it is not in me to falter if I can promote the work of emancipation.[43]

On August 6, 1830, Walker was found dead in Boston of mysterious causes; some say he was poisoned. Most believe that he was murdered by individuals who wanted to silence his militant teachings. At the time of his death he was 34 years old.

Outside of Philadelphia there existed no more developed and militant African community than Boston. And Russwurm was fortunate to be apart of its leadership. It was in Boston that he first attached himself to a striving community that was dedicated to the social uplift of not only the free African community, but to those held in slavery as well. This community had established itself as innovative and persistent in its efforts to liberate African people from slavery, racial oppression and economic exploitation. They were pioneers long before European-American abolitionists, such as William Lloyd Garrison, Wendell Phillips, Harriet Beecher Stowe captured national attention. As early as the eighteenth century Abijah Prince, a free African, left Massachusetts to become one of the founders of Sunderland, Vermont.[44] Another prominent member of this community was Lucy Terry Prince, a poet who tried to get her son admitted to Williams College and argued her case, involving a land dispute, before the United States Supreme Court. Then there was Lemuel Haynes, pastor of congregations in Vermont and New York; Paul Cuffe, famous shipbuilder in New Bedford; Frederick Douglass, abolitionist and Lewis Temple, inventor of harpoon toggle in New Bedford; and Phillis Wheatley, poet in Boston.[45] It is noteworthy that Rev. Lemuel Haynes became the first African-American to receive an Honorary Degree in the United States (Middlebury, 1804) and may have been the first to turn down admission to a college (Dartmouth in 1779).[46]

Russwurm at Bowdoin College

When Russwurm began classes, at age 25, in Brunswick, Maine on September 20, 1824, he re-emerged himself into upper class New

England culture. This re-entry into New England culture was significant in two regards. First, he became the first African student to matriculate at Bowdoin College and one of the first three to enroll at an American college. Higher education in this early century was, for the most part, closed to Africans. Before 1840 less than fifteen Africans had been admitted to American colleges and universities.[47]

Russwurm, though not the first African graduate of an American college, was undoubtedly the most influential. He was preceded by Alexander Lucius Twilight of Middlebury's class of 1823 and Ernest Jones of Amherst's class of 1826. Russwurm graduated fourteen days after Jones.

The first college graduate was a native Vermonter, born in Corinth, and the first African member of a state legislature. He built a huge granite school house in Brownington, Vermont, with his own funds, and was a prominent educator in his community for twenty-five years.[48]

Unlike Boston, where he was a part of a sizeable African community, at Bowdoin, Russwurm was the sole African student, and one of approximately 200 Africans in the Brunswick-Portland area. The only other African person on the campus was Phebe Ann Jacobs, a servant to President William Allen. She came to Brunswick from Dartmouth University with William Allen and his wife Marie Malleville Allen in 1820. Phebe was believed to have had religious powers and was buried in Brunswick in 1828.[49]

At the college, Russwurm would meet several men who would have profound influences on his life. Most of these men were from old New England families who had been "bred" for schools like Bowdoin because the competition for admission to the college was stiff. A student had to produce certificates of good moral character and demonstrate by an entrance examination competency in geography and arithmetic. In addition, a prospective student had to translate passages from Cicero's *Select Oratory*, Virgil's *Bucolics, Georgic*,and *Aeneid,*[50] readings that would be accessible to only well to do families.

Once admitted, students had to follow a rigid schedule of academic work and received severe punishment if they deviated from any of the rules. The faculty, known then as the Executive Government adopted rules of conduct that were strictly enforced. A sampling of the rules for which violations resulted in severe penalties was:

1. Negligence in Study
2. Negligence in Declamation
3. Absence from Private Declamation
4. Ignorance of Euclid
5. Whispering at Prayers
6. Reading in Public Worship
7. Wrong Position at Prayers
8. Leaning Head on Seat in Front at Prayers
9. Causing Drum to be Beaten in College Yard
10. Playing Cards for Money
11. Eating or Drinking at Woodworth's Tavern
12. Smoking a Segar on the Street
13. Making Bon Fire in Yard
14. Walking Unnecessarily far on the Sabbath [51]

When students abridged these rules and regulations, they were assessed fines for each offense. For example, the fine for tardiness at prayers was .03 cents, absence from prayers .06 cents and absence from public worship on the Lord's day .20 cents. The school was administered under the tight leadership of President McKeen and the Executive Government, consisting of Parker Cleveland, William Smyth, Thomas Upham, Samuel Phillips Newman and Alpheus Spring Packard.

The college day for students was replete with prayers and study. As soon as it was daylight, students had to be out of bed and at prayers in the chapel, which was unheated. They, then had to spend an hour in recitation before breakfast. After breakfast there was three more hours of study before noon, three hours of study in the afternoon, prayers, then the evening meal.[52]

Bowdoin was a young college when Russwurm entered. It had been incorporated in 1794 by the General Court of Massachusetts. Tuition at the college was $8.00 per term, or $24.00 per year and room an additional $3.74 per term and board $1.75 per week.[53] John, however, did not reside on campus, but rather in Brunswick, in the home of a carpenter. There is little evidence that he lived off campus because of ethnic prejudice, since the college had a policy that required students to live on campus unless all dormitory rooms were occupied.[54] It may have been that Russwurm preferred to live off campus given that he was one of the oldest students on a campus of 136 men where it was not unusual for students to be as young as thirteen or fourteen. For example, in the class of 1825, of the nineteen students, one half were under sixteen.[55]

Despite living off campus, Russwurm was active in campus activities and had quite a few college friends. He, like many students, met many of them for snacks at Ward's Tavern, located on the edge of the college. To the shock of this small community, in September, 1820, the owner of Ward's committed suicide and the tavern, which was also an inn, came under the control of his daughter. She was described by students as about thirty years of age, good looking and friendly. It was a place where students could get supper on credit from time to time.[56] John interacted with these students off campus, without any overt encounters with prejudice.

Life on the Bowdoin campus however was not totally free of ethnic insensitivity, however. Periodically, students would start bonfires on campus, and it was not unusual for them to blacken their faces with cork.[57] As the only African student on campus, this practice undoubtedly caused John embarrassment.

Even though Russwurm was aware of the fires and the blackening up, he also had genuine relationships with fellow students. Fellow schoolmate Nathaniel Hawthorne, who befriended John, writes that Russwurm lived outside the limits of Brunswick. He was described as "dignified, easy in his manners, and too sensitive because of his color to return visits."[58] Hawthorne and friends, however, would periodically slip out of their rooms and away from studies to visit Russwurm. They found him and his life quite different from anything they had encountered in their upper class backgrounds.[59] Hawthorne's observations revealed that Russwurm did in fact have some difficulty adjusting to the all "white" Brunswick environment after his five years in Boston's African community. In Boston he had lived among a community that was both poor and victimized by racism, yet in Brunswick, he was cast in the midst of upper class students.

Hawthorne and his other classmates, Franklin Pierce and Alfred Mason, all came from well to do New England backgrounds. Hawthorne's father was a sea captain, but his college expenses were paid by his uncle, Robert Manning. In order to prepare Nathaniel for entrance to Bowdoin, he was tutored by Benjamin Lynde Oliver.[60] When he entered the college, Nathaniel was fifteen and lived in Maine Hall where he shared a room with Alfred Mason. Mason had many ties with Bowdoin. His brother, George had recently graduated, his cousin, William Appleton was a student, and his uncle, Jesse Appleton had served as President. His cousin, Jane Appleton later married Franklin Pierce,[61] a Bowdoin graduate who later became President of the United States.

Despite the class differences, Russwurm's new friends welcomed him into campus organizations and activities. Soon after arriving at the college, he was invited by Hawthorne to join the prestigious student organization, the Athenaeans. He wrote back to them: "Gentleman of the Athenaean Society, with alacrity, I accept your kind invitation."[62] From his activities with this literary society, he became close friends with Hawthorne and Horatio Bridge. Another student, whom Russwurm knew at the college, was Calvin Ellis Stowe, who had graduated from the college as valedictorian in 1824 and served as the first Librarian of the college. Stowe and Russwurm were both in their early twenties. In 1836 Calvin married Harriet E., who later wrote *Uncle Tom's Cabin.* This book, which had a profound impact on raising the nation's consciousness about slavery, was written in Brunswick.

Another student, who remained a life long friend, and perhaps had the greatest impact upon Russwurm's career was James Hall. Hall was a member of the class of 1824, who maintained close contact with Russwurm throughout his life.

William Pitt Fessenden was another Bowdoin graduate who maintained close ties with John after he left Bowdoin. Fessenden was born on October 16, 1806 and entered the college at the age of twelve. After graduating, he entered the practice of law in 1827.[63] Fessenden, however, did not graduate with his class because he was caught drinking at Wardsworth Tavern in his senior year,[64] a place of debauchery that was strictly forbidden by college rules.

After practicing law in the Portland area, Fessenden became involved in politics. He was especially moved by the anti-slavery movement, and early in his career raised his voice against the evil institution. In February, 1854, he was elected to the United States Senate and served for a period of six years. He was elected despite the divisive controversy in the state, but due to his political acumen he was able to garner the votes of the Whigs and the anti-slavery Democrats. In the Senate he took a clear position against slavery and delivered a speech in opposition to the Kansas-Nebraska Act which placed him squarely in the congressional anti-slavery camp.

The Kansas-Nebraska Act, like the Fugitive Slave Act, was a Congressional enactment that significantly curtailed African freedom. The debate was over whether the people of Nebraska and Kansas or Congress would decide whether the two new states would be slave or free. There was a lot of pressure to leave this decision to the two states, thus effectively repealing the Missouri Compromise of 1820 that kept slavery out of territories north of latitude 36 30'. Despite the efforts of Bowdoin alumni, such as Fessenden, the Kansas-Nebraska Act passed on May 26, 1854. Despite this defeat, from June, 1864 to March, 1865, he served as Secretary of Treasury under Abraham Lincoln and was supportive of the administration's anti-slavery posture.[65]

His opposition to slavery was absolute. In 1850, before Russwurm had finished his term as Governor of Maryland in Africa and before Fessenden went to the Senate, the two men met. Russwurm had come to the United States to get medical attention for his longstanding rheumatism ailment. At a meeting in Maine, Fessenden tried to persuade him to remain in the United States for medical treatment and to take his rightful place in the anti-slavery campaign.[66] Russwurm refused the invitation, returned to Africa and died roughly a year later in June, 1851. The fact that Russwurm could not be convinced to give up his tenure in Africa is a testimony to the resolve he held toward African nationalism. Even though his close friends in the United States sought his assistance in their fight against slavery, he would not abandon Africa and his dream of self governance.

Although it is clear that Russwurm had a warm and supportive relationship with some fellow students, significant influences upon the development of his political views came from two professors, William Smyth and Thomas Upham. Both men opposed slavery, but took different approaches in seeking its end. Smyth was a staunch abolitionist who disdained any compromise with slavery, while Upham supported colonization as the most important means to overcome the racial problem in America.

Smyth was a Professor of Mathematics who was actively involved in anti-slavery activities in Brunswick, Maine. He shared one half of a building on campus with Professor Alpheus Spring Packard. His side of the house was reputedly used as a stop off point for the Underground Railroad, where he concealed escaping slaves on their trek from the South to Canada.[67]

It is interesting to note that in January, 1970, Bowdoin College named this building that had been occupied by Smyth as the Afro-American Center and on January 27, 1979 rededicated the house as the John Brown Russwurm Afro-American Center. The rededication symbolized the important legacy of the college and its early faculty in fighting slavery. Michael Henderson, Chairman of the Afro-American Society spoke at the dedication: "It is no longer simply an Afro-American Center...It is an historical and cultural part of the college. The dedication formalizes the recognition of the rich history of this house."

Roger Howell, who was President of the college in 1970, spoke at the re-dedication and re-visited the reasons why the Afro-American Center was established in 1970. He recalled the eloquence with which Virgil Logan, an African-American student, pled the cause before the Board of Trustees. President Howell then spoke of Russwurm:

> John Brown Russwurm was a man of courage and fortitude; he spoke to the issues that touched him and through him all of mankind in a language that was forceful, direct and never wavering. Were he alive today, I am sure he would speak with vigor to the sorts of issues I have attempted to raise. [68]

President Howell did, in fact, connect in eloquent terms the college's fundamental commitment to equality, that was manifest as early as the nineteenth century. Russwurm and Smyth symbolized this institutional commitment. The two men were undoubtedly attracted to each other if not because of their similar political beliefs, then certainly because of their similar ages. Smyth was born in 1797 and graduated from Bowdoin in 1822, four years before Russwurm. In 1825, he was appointed Adjunct Professor of Math and in 1828 Professor of Math and Natural Philosophy.

There was another professor, whose views caught the attention of Russwurm. Thomas Upham, who had been often referred to as "sensitive and saintly," was the same age as Russwurm, having been born in 1799. In 1824 he was elected Professor of Mental and Moral Philosophy and served in that role until 1867. He was the son of a Congressman and in 1825 married Phebe Lord, who was from a wealthy York County family. She was an early advocate for women's rights and abolitionism and spoke often around Brunswick on these subjects.[69] As a result of his wife's wealth, Upham was able to travel extensively around the world, which contributed to the development of his liberal world views. To Upham the people of the world shared a common heritage:

> I thought I was an American, but I have found out the world is my country. I am one of those who are willing to testify that man in his central nature is the same everywhere. In his joys, his griefs, his hopes, his affections, he is one.[70]

In 1855, he published his views on the world's peoples in his Letters: Aesthetic, Social and Moral, Written from Europe, Egypt and Palestine.

This notion of the universality of the human race was significant for the nineteenth century. Throughout the United States numerous prominent individuals believed the opposite: that there was a fundamental difference between Africans and Europeans and that Europeans were superior to Black African people. In fact, many justified slavery by the theory and belief that Europeans were ordained by God to bring civilization to a heathen African people, who had otherwise been cursed by God. Upham, on the other hand, recognized the contradictions between alleged Christian principles and slavery and warned that Africans had the capacity to understand this hypocrisy. Despite these views, he could not envision the two groups coexisting in America, but rather that Africans should be returned to their homelands, from which they had been taken. Slavery, for him, was an abomination and the most human solution to it was the resettlement of the Africans. Through colonization, Africa would be redeemed by the efforts of free and educated returning "colored man." Two years before he died, Upham wrote in 1870 the following:

> But I did not, and could not, at any period of my life, disconnect the interests of Africa from the interests of the negro race in this country. [71]

For him, nationalism should be an essential component of the solution to the "colored" problem in America. He firmly believed that Africans were equal to Europeans and expressed this sentiment in a poem, written in 1850. The poem was called:

> Yanko, The Noble Negro Judge not of virtue by a name, nor think to read it on the skin; Honor in black and white's the same, the stamp of glory is within. Whate'er his color, man is man, A negro's heart like any other; And Heaven, in its capacious plan, Bids us treat him as a brother.[72]

Within a short century he envisioned African republics flourishing under a single flag of the "United States of Africa."

Africa, he envisioned, would achieve this unity of purpose through peaceful means, as he was an early pacifist and his *Manual of Peace* was one of the earliest treatises against war. He believed that war had to end because it had devastating effects upon people, both on and off the battle field.[73] He knew that the slavery conflict would lead to war, and colonization was a means of avoiding bloodshed. War, he wrote, was contrary to the gospel and inconsistent with civilization, humanity and religion.[74] For Upham, armies should be disbanded and cannons melted into church bells.

Although John Russwurm, by senior year, was not firm in what he would do upon graduation, his political philosophy had firmly taken shape. He had already concluded that he would not remain in the United States, but would wait for an invitation from the Haitian Government, and settle in Haiti. If an invitation was not forthcoming, he would study medicine in Boston. In preparation for this potential medical career, he attended lectures in anatomy and chemistry.[75] The fact that Russwurm chose Haiti indicated an attraction to revolutionary nationalism. The people of Haiti provided to the young thinker an example of how a protracted revolutionary struggle against tremendous military forces, such as the French, could ultimately lead to freedom. The revolt of more than a half million Africans began in August, 1791 in Saint Dominque and ended with the establishment of the Republic of Haiti in January 1, 1804.

Russwurm may have been unsure of precisely where he would live and work upon graduation, but his views on nationalism were firm. His commencement speech, given on September 12, 1826 applauded the goals of revolutionary struggle. Excerpts of the speech were printed in several national newspapers, including the "Eastern Argus" and the "Boston Courier." The title of his speech was The Condition and Prospects of Hayti:

> The changes which take place in the affairs of this world show the instability of sublunary things. Empires rise, and fall, flourish, and decay. Knowledge follows revolutions and travels over the globe. Man alone, remains the same being, whether placed under the torrid suns of Africa, or in the more congenial temperate zone. A principle of liberty is implanted in his breast, and all efforts to stifle it are as fruitless as would be the attempt to extinguish the fires of Etna.
>
> It is in the irresistible course of events that all men, who have been deprived of their liberty, shall recover this precious portion of their indefeasible inheritance. It is in vain to stem the current; degraded man will rise in his native majesty, and claim his rights. They may be withheld from him now, but the day will arrive, when they must be surrendered.
>
> Among the many interesting events of the present day, and illustrative of this, the Revolution in Hayti holds a conspicuous place. The former political condition of Hayti we all doubtless know. After years of sanguinary struggle for freedom and a political existence, the Haytiens on the auspicious day of January first 1804 declared themselves a free and independent nation. Nothing can ever induce them to recede from this declaration. They know too well by their past misfortunes; by their wounds which are yet bleeding, that security can be expected only from within themselves. Rather would they devote themselves to death than return to their former condition. Can we conceive of anything which can cheer the desponding spirit, can reanimate and stimulate it to put every thing to the hazard? Liberty can do this. Such were its effects upon the Haytiens-men who in slavery showed neither spirit nor genius: but when Liberty, when once Freedom struck their astonished ears, they became new creatures; stepped forth as men, and showed to the world, that though Slavery may benumb, it cannot entirely destroy our faculties. Such were Touissant L'Overture (sic), Desalines (sic) and Christophe.

The Haytiens have adopted the republican form of government: and so firmly is it established, that in no country are the rights and privileges of citizens and foreigners more respected, and crimes less frequent. They are a brave and generous people. If cruelties were inflicted during the Revolutionary War, it was owing to the policy pursued by the French commanders, which compelled them to use retaliatory measures.

For who shall expostulate with men who have been hunted with bloodhounds-who have been threatened with an Auto-da-fe-whose relations and friends have been hung on gibbets before their eyes-have been sunk by hundreds in the sea-and tell them they ought to exercise kindness towards such mortal enemies?

Remind me not of moral duties, of meekness and generosity. Show me the man who has exercised them under these trials, and you point to the one who is more than human. It is an undisputed fact, that more than sixteen hundred Haytiens perished in the modes above specified. The cruelties inflicted by the French on the children of Hayti have exceded the crimes of Cortez and Pizarro.

Thirty-two years of their independence so gloriously achieved have effected wonders. No longer are they the same people. They had faculties, yet were these faculties oppressed under the load of servitude and ignorance. With a countenance erect and fixed upon Heaven, they can now contemplate the works of Divine munificence. Restored to the dignity of man to society, they have acquired a new existence- their powers have been developed: a career of glory and happines unfolds itself before them.

The Haytien Government has risen in the neighborhood of European settlements. Do the public proceedings and details of its Government bespeak any inferiority? Their state papers are distinguished from those of many European Courts, only by their superior energy and non-exalted sentiments; and while the manners and politics of Boyer emulate those of his Republican neighbours: the court of Christophe had almost as much foppery; almost as many lords and ladies of the bed- chamber;and almost as great a proportion

> of stars, and ribbons, and gilded chariots, as those of his brother potentates in any part of the world.
>
> Placed by Divine Providence amid circumstances more favourable, than were their ancestors, the Haytiens can more easily than they, make rapid strides in the career of civilization-they can demonstrate that although the God of nature may have given them a darker complexion, still are men alike sensible to all the miseries of slavery, and to all the blessings of freedom.
>
> May we not indulge in the pleasing hope, that the Independence of Hayti has laid the foundation of an Empire that will take a rank with the nations of the earth-that a country, the local situation of which is favourable to trade and commercial enterprise- possessing a free and well regulated government, which encourages the useful and liberal arts: a country containing an enterprising and growing population, which is determined to live free, or die gloriously: will advance rapidly in all the arts of civilization.
>
> We look forward with peculiar satisfaction to the period when like Tyre of old, her vessels shall extend the fame of her riches and glory, to the remotest borders of the globe;-to the time when Hayti treading in the footsteps of her sister republics, shall, like them, exhibit a picture of rapid and unprecedented advance in population, wealth and intelligence."

This pro-nationalism speech was the first of its kind to be given by an African person in the nineteenth century. More importantly, it demonstrated the depth of Russwurm's understanding of the nature of struggle and the importance of African national independence. It was a declaration that African freedom could only be sustained when it was rooted in separation, national pride and development.

Even though he was ultimately invited to emigrate to Haiti, Russwurm chose America by moving to New York City, where he and Samuel Cornish began work on a new African-American newspaper.

Russwurm in New York City

The opportunity to chart new ethnic progress by establishing an African newspaper, temporarily distracted Russwurm from his nationalist leanings. Therefore, it was with some misgivings that John joined

"RIGHTEOUSNESS EXALTETH A NATION."

CORNISH & RUSSWURM, Editors & Proprietors

NEW-YORK, FRIDAY. MARCH 30, 1827

[VOL. I. No. 3.

MEMOIRS OF CAPT. PAUL CUFFEE.

PEOPLE OF COLOUR.

JOHN B. RUSSWURM

Founder of the Negro Press

An exact reproduction of the original paper by permission of the New York Historical Society, Copyrighted 1891 by Willey & Co., Springfield, Mass.

The first page of ***Freedom's Journal***

Reverend Samuel Cornish to start the newspaper on March 16, 1827. The paper's motto "Righteousness Exalted a Nation," both represented Reverend Cornish's religious zeal and Russwurm's comitment to nationalism. It boldly stated "We wish to plead our own cause."Africans, through their free brothers and sisters declared to the world that their cause would be exalted through the print media, just as earlier American patriots had proclaimed their right to freedom through pamphlets. The cost of a yearly subscription was set at $3.00, one half payable in advance, in an effort to make it affordable to its impoverished readership. The paper had several agents, including Reuben Ruby, Portland, Maine; John Rhymond, Salem, Massachusetts and David Walker, Boston.

Russwurm felt very prepared for this new venture since he had devoted himself to rigorous study and had substantial experience in community development in Boston. However, with pleasure he looked at the new opportunity to serve his people and advance the cause of African liberation. The paper would play a critical role in advancing the interests of Africans in America. Russwurm and Cornish were in agreement that the paper would urge the abolition of slavery and agitate for the right to vote. They realized that free status in the North was incomplete without the franchise.

They agreed that new paper would involve itself solely with the issues facing Africans in America. The fact that its initial offices were located in the middle of the Black community, at 5 Varrick Street, symbolized this commitment. The Five Points section of New York City was considered by whites to be dangerous and overcrowded because it was the first stop many free Africans made when they arrived in New York. Outside of Baltimore, Maryland, more free Africans lived in New York City than in any other city. A total of 500,000 free Africans existed in the United States at the time, as compared to two million who were enslaved primarily in the South.

The paper recognized the needs of this community both enslaved and free, to advance politically and economically. A particular focus of the early issues was on the youth of the community. Education was seen as a key to advancement of the race. In order to facilitate the development of a literate population, the paper called for the institution of free public libraries and the creation of additional African Free Schools. In addition to its support of education, the paper took a firm position against lynching throughout the country. It reported all lynchings and called for the prosecution of those involved in the activities.[76]

Another important public service was the publication of information about the infamous "Blackbirders." These individuals were white bounty hunters who patrolled the northern states in search of fugitives and free Africans who did not have in their possession manumission papers.

Even though Russwurm had agreed with Cornish to concern themselves with issues facing Africans in America, he could not ignore the centrality of Africa in the public discourse. Africa was at the top of the public agenda and *Freedom's Journal* could not avoid the raging debate over colonization. While many free Africans wanted Russwurm to stay clear of the issue, he believed that a responsible paper had to print articles of different points of view. Furthermore, Russwurm brought to New York City his own individual commitment to Africa. America was not his home. He ultimately hoped to settle in Haiti, but saw the paper as an important contribution to the struggle for abolition in the United States.

In the first six months of the paper, Russwurm avoided the controversial issue of colonization. Prominent free Africans, such as Bishop Richard Allen of the African Methodist Episcopal Church and James Forten of Philadelphia had hoped that Reverend Cornish, co-editor of the paper, would keep Russwurm's views on colonization under control. Many had hoped that the Reverend's strong opposition to colonization would insure that the paper did not become another vehicle for the American Colonization Society. Even though Russwurm did not explicitly endorse colonization in the first half of the year, he openly supported the efforts of the first and most prominent supporter of repatriation, Paul Cuffe. To highlight his support of Cuffe, Russwurm published on the first page of the paper, the Memoirs of Captain Paul Cuffe. He also ran leading articles on the "Haytien Revolution." In order for the African public to understand foreign affairs, the paper had a weekly foreign news column and a magazine format. In addition to domestic and foreign news stories, it contained information on new marriages, poetry, advertisements for cheap clothing stores and for B.F. Hughe's School for Colored Children of Both Sexes, which was located under St. Philips Church.[77]

The free African population in New York City welcomed these types of articles. Within a year after Russwurm's arrival, free Africans had already begun to meet and organize themselves in anticipation of the abolition of slavery in New York State. On March 27, 1827, they met in Albany, New York at the African Meeting House to plan activities for July 4, 1827, the date that the law abolishing slavery would go into effect. The page helped them disseminate information on their meeting and the progress made in the freedom efforts.

Within a few months after its founding, the paper moved to larger office space at 152 Church Street, which signaled to both the European and African communities that the paper would continue to grow. Russwurm was determined to show to the world the cruelties of slavery and racial discrimination. He was particularly aware of the difficulties faced by free Africans in the North. For many, freedom meant uncertainty as they faced segregation in housing and menial or no employment. For those who resorted to criminal activity, in an effort to survive, they were dealt with severely by the legal system as the paper explained in the case of William Henison in Warren County, North Carolina. Mr. Henison, a free Black, was convicted in Superior Court of forcibly breaking into a house and stealing a few inexpensive articles. He was convicted and sentenced to death by Judge Ruffian.[78]

After six months of cooperation, Rev. Cornish dissolved his partnership with Russwurm because of the paper's increasing endorsements of colonization. In fact, in the issue announcing the dissolution, Russwurm explicitly stated the paper's new policy of freely discussing colonization. On February 14, 1829, Russwurm allowed several pro-colonization articles to appear in the paper, including an excerpt from the Lancaster Gazette which read in part:

> Every acre was honorably and regularly bought of the rightful owners and the whole is guarantied to the colonists as neutral ground by all the respectable naval powers of Europe. The soil is highly productive, and agriculture is highly rewarded. The inhabitants are comfortably housed, fed and clothed. Many families, in addition to the necessaries, and what are called the comforts of life, enjoy some of the luxuries...They realize the right of suffrages...The seeds of commerce have germinated and become visible in Liberia.[79]

Russwurm was convinced, by this date that Africans, even if free, would not be considered the equals of European. He firmly believed that Europeans would not stop viewing Africans as an "odium of inferior and degraded caste."[80] Russwurm's epiphany was a culmination of extensive research and contemplation over colonization and the Society. He wrote:

> ...We have carefully examined the different plans now in operation for our benefit, and none, we believe, can reach half so efficiently the masses as the plan of colonization on the west coast of Africa...The evidence has now so nearly reached the point of moral certainty that the coast of western Africa will, at a date not far remote, be covered with a dense

> and enterprising population, composed partly of immigrants from the United States and partly of native Africans."[81]

What is clear from this speech is that Russwurm was more concerned with the welfare of the African masses, than with himself and any personal gains he may achieve through repatriation. Although his decision may have been ridiculed by many African leaders, who earnestly felt that the locus of their struggle for liberation had to be waged in the United States, Russwurm was convinced to a "moral certainty" that repatriation represented the most pragmatic alternative for African people. Furthermore, Russwurm reasoned that the legal concepts of master and servant would not be compromised by repatriation.[82] This notion formed the basis of a widespread philosophical argument throughout the country. The various state courts had clearly established rules with respect to the rights of masters over their servants and the Society was one of the major organizations that recognized this legal principle. By Russwurm acknowledging this concern, he gained greater credibility not only among those who favored colonization, but also among southern plantation owners. Colonization was not viewed by many southerners as a threat to their plantation system. It is most likely that this fact most irritated militant African leaders who saw slavery as the sole and most important object of their activities.

These favorable depictions of Liberia outraged some free Africans. Many saw the paper as going too far in the direction of the American Colonization Society, which they did not trust. Criticism against Russwurm was both direct and harsh. Many felt betrayed by the most educated African of the period. Finally, amidst mounting public outrage, on March 28, 1829, he resigned from his position as publisher of the paper, and returned to Bowdoin College, where he pursued a Master's Degree. It was ironic that he retreated to Maine, rather than Boston his other home, at a time of such personal turmoil.

As news of his resignation and endorsement of colonization spread throughout the African community of New York City, the chant of "traitor" could be heard in the Five Corners. One group hung an effigy of him in the central square and pelted it with rocks and mud, before setting it on fire. A sign around the neck of the effigy contained Russwurm's name.[83]

Russwurm's conversion to repatriation was not frivolous, as the mob insisted, rather it was based upon close personal considerations. He weighed all of his options, including that of remaining in the United States. More than any other African of the period, Russwurm had more intimate contact with Europeans. Despite this contact, he concluded that African people's future rested with Africa. He did not believe that whites would ever treat Africans equally. He wrote: "We consider it a mere waste of words... to talk of ever enjoying citizenship in this country."[84]

Furthermore, Russwurm did not believe that freedom could come to Africans in America without a violent confrontation. He was particularly concerned about his good friend and associate, David Walker, who had recently called for slaves to take up arms. Russwurm believed that if free Africans engaged in violent revolts and assaults against the plantation owners, these actions would only worsen the condition of slaves in the South. The plantation owners would retaliate against the slaves for the actions of the abolitionists.[85]

Even more importantly, Russwurm had developed an Afrocentric perspective that gave intellectual underpinnings to his decision to go to Africa. During the nineteenth century, more than any other, Europeans attempted to debase African people, thereby making them believe that they were inferior and had made no contributions to world civilization. Russwurm rejected these notions and the view that Europeans were superior to Africans. In an article, "The Mutability of Human Affairs," written by Russwurm in 1827 and published in Freedom's Journal, he discussed the longevity of African history and the role of Egypt and Ethiopia in bringing culture to the world. He boldly challenged the mounting European views that ancient Egyptians were not "Black," but "white" or Caucasian. Russwurm wrote:

> ...Mankind generally allows that all nations are indebted to the Egyptians for the introduction of the arts and sciences; but they are not willing to acknowledge that the Egyptians bore any resemblance to the present race of Africans. Though Herodotus 'father of history' expressly declared that the Egyptians had black skins and frizzled hair.[86]

Consequently, when Russwurm repatriated to Africa, he did not do so as an individual who considered himself inferior, but rather as a man who recognized the centrality of Africa to human development.

Despite the criticism that was widespread, Russwurm abandoned New York City for Brunswick, Maine and ultimately for Liberia. Free Africans in New York City, however, disputed the laudatory claims of the American Colonization Society and Russwurm. They argued that Liberian authorities denied trading privileges to returning Africans and denied them a voice in government.[87] Other rumors flourished that free Africans were, in fact, sold back into slavery. The American Colonization Society tried to combat many of these rumors, but met with little success. For Russwurm, however, "full citizenship in the United States was impossible..."[88] The only viable choice that he saw was Africa. After returning to Maine, he did not know what he would do, but an offer from the American Colonization Society made his decision easier. The society offered him a position in Liberia as Superintendent of Schools,[89] which he accepted.

The word spread quickly throughout the African community that Russwurm had joined with the hated colonization society. In September, 1830, a convention of free Africans convened in Philadelphia that was organized by James Forten, Hezekiah Grice, Reverend Peter Wiliams and Reverend Samuel Cornish launched a new organization. The "American Society of Free Persons of Colour, for Improving Their Condition in the United States; for Purchasing Lands; and for the Establishing of a Settlement in Upper Canada would offer Africans an alternative to Liberia."[90] It was ironic that these men could envision Africans emigrating to Canada, rather than to Africa. Yet they saw in their efforts, as opposed to the other, Africans playing a pivotal role in the resettlement efforts.

These Africans found quick support among prominent white abolitionists. In William Lloyd Garrison's *Liberator*, a successor to *Freedom's Journal*, Russwurm was vilified and free Africans urged to continue their fight for liberation in the United States. In 1831, Garrison re-established the New England Anti-Slavery Society and its members denounced colonization as another form of slavery. *The Liberator* published the following letter on April 16, 1831 in criticism of Russwurm and colonization:

> Sir – Notwithstanding the many preposterous arguments of colonizationists, and their wild and incoherent freaks, in support of their imaginary scheme of civilizing Africa, by

> draining the people of color from their original and only home; notwithstanding the many hyperbolical accounts, which they so assiduously and conscientiously circulate about that pestiferous clime;- I never felt so indignant at any of their manoeures (for every step they take to facilitate their plans, tends but to expose their inconsistency) as at a piece of composition which appeared in the twelfth number of the 'Liberia Herald,' written by its editor John B. Russworm (sic). This John B. Russworm (sic) is known, I presume, to every one of us; his ingratitude is but too deeply stamped on the minds of many, who have been requited in a manner, which neither time nor space will ever obliterate. After he subverted the pledge he made to his brethren, he left, to our satisfaction, his country-suffused with shame-and branded with the stigma of disgrace-to dwell in that land for which the tempter MONEY caused him to avow his preferment. He has resided there more than a year, publishing doubtless to the satisfaction of his supporters, their many glorious schemes, and eulogizing to the very skies the prosperity of his goodly LIBERIA. Not contented with lauding the retreat in which and about which he may flame with impunity, he has the audacity to reprove those with whom he played the traitor. Out of much he said, let this suffice as an example: 'Before God, we know of no other home for the man of color, of republican principles, than Africa. Has he no ambition? Is he dead to everything noble? Is he contented with his condition? Let him remain in America.' To this we reply, that before God, we know of no surer burial place than Africa, for men of any color; that we will never envy John B. Russworm his ambition; and that we will pray God, that his notions of nobleness may never enter our hearts, and that we will not be contented with our condition, but will make it better in this our native home. R. Philadelphia, April 8th, 1831.

Russwurm in Monrovia

Russwurm's repatriation to Africa represented a significant milestone in African history. His decision meant that one of the most educated of all free Africans in the nineteenth century made a calculated decision to forgo the promises of American society, and seek his future in Africa. Although he had initially turned down an invitation from the A.C.S. to work in Monrovia in 1827, by 1829, he was ready to make his exodus. Many factors contributed to this readiness. First, he found that it was extremely difficult to make *Freedom's Journal* profitable. While free Africans openly supported the paper, many, as a result of precarious financial conditions, were unable to provide the type of continuing financial support that was necessary to insure its survival. Secondly, he did not believe that the future for Africans in the United States could be reconciled with that of "Whites." In Africa, he believed Africans would have an opportunity to be free and independent, and those Americans involved with the colonization efforts would be allies in his nationalist efforts. Thirdly, and most important, he was offered the position of Superintendent of Monrovia's schools and asked to run the colony's newspaper, *The Liberia Herald,* which had not been in operation for some time.[91] Russwurm was, therefore, confronted with an opportunity to make a significant contribution to African development and to be a leader in such efforts. Never before had an African person assumed such responsible roles in Liberian government since the American flag was first raised on April 22, 1822.

In September, 1829, he set sail for Liberia. He was excited by the possibilities of self-governance in Africa. The problems would be immense, but, quite different from those in the United States. The major difference and one that satisfied Russwurm tremendously, was the absence of slavery. Rather, the tasks that confronted the government involved reconciliation and trade with the indigenous people and general issues of nation-building. He would have a direct role in resolving complex public policy issues relating to education, public administration and communication. Russwurm for the first time would be in the forefront of an effort to bring about a positive national outcome.

On November 15, 1829, he arrived in Monrovia, determined to stay. He did not go to Africa as a missionary, but rather as a repatriating African. His decision to forsake America was clear and final. There would be no looking back. As he arrived in Monrovia, at the age of thirty, he envisioned a new world in which to work and build a future. Unlike other repatriates, he would be a leader in the colony and would interface with and influence people at all levels of the social system.

His first challenge would be to provide leadership to the common schools of Monrovia. He would not have to develop a system of education because the colony had already established one that was separate from several missionary schools in the area. To his surprise, upon arrival, he found the schools under the leadership of George McGill, another African who had brought his family to Liberia at an earlier time. McGill would later become vice agent of the colony, and remain an influence upon Russwurm throughout his stay. For Russwurm, McGill was a symbol of what an African person could achieve in Africa if he possessed the skills and determination.

Contrary to what was believed among Africans in the United States, repatriates could chart a future for themselves. Each repatriate was given a parcel of land to develop for their families. The size of the land depended upon the size of the family and marital status. The A.C.S. ran classes on how to cultivate the soil and to use local fertilizers. The success or failure of the settlers depended upon the extent to which they mastered the techniques for farming and continued to work hard. Although the settlers lived under a government that was primarily controlled by white men, they nevertheless, had immediate control over their own land. Social advancement, therefore, was commensurate with the skills and drive of the settler.

Russwurm quickly received greater responsibility in the colony. In 1830 he was appointed Colonial Secretary and served in that capacity for four years. He was responsible for all the records of the colony, including legal documents and official correspondence.[92] Despite this advancement, he encountered racism in the colonial administration. While both Russwurm and McGill could advance to responsible positions, there was a limit to how far Africans could go. The A.C.S. remained primarily an American organization, controlled by American men in Washington, D.C. The Colonial Agent in Monrovia remained American, and this fact, caused Russwurm considerable discomfort. Even though Russwurm possessed more and better education than most of the men who had responsibility over him, there was very little that he could do to change the situation.

Despite these problems, Russwurm remained optimistic. This optimism, no doubt, stemmed from the very pragmatic approach that he took toward Liberia. It was not the best of worlds, but at least it was better than America. He even wrote his half-brother Francis and inquired whether he wanted to settle in Africa. But the one event that most cemented him to the continent was his marriage in 1833 to Sarah McGill, daughter of George McGill. A year later, the couple had their first child, whom they named George Stockbridge Russwurm. John had a lot to be grateful for. He had successfully made the transition to Africa, married, and published the colony's only newspaper, *Liberia Herald* for four years.

While he may have achieved personal satisfaction, many of the other settlers did not share in his joy. In 1834, disagreements between the Colonial Agent, Robert Pinney and many of the settlers, particularly Hiliary Teague and Jacob Prout, reached a crescendo. Under the leadership of the two men, settlers seized the courthouse, disrupting the trial of a fellow settler. The settlers voiced several complaints relating to the fairness of the judicial process, and demanded that Robert Penney resign.[93] Pinney refused to resign and the demonstration quickly subsided.

Soon, the frustration of the settlers resurfaced with Russwurm at the center of a developing controversy. Shortly after the courthouse incident, Robert Pinney attempted to clamp down on the leaders of the social unrest. He immediately issued a proclamation that the leaders were engaged in an illegal rebellion and ordered Russwurm to print his statement in the *Liberia Herald.* John Russwurm found himself in a delicate dilemma. If he printed the statement, he would be perceived as a puppet for a government that many settlers felt was insensitive and racist. If he refused, he could risk the charge of insubordination. Furthermore, Russwurm believed that he, alone, should exercise control over the paper and its contents. If he gave into Pinney he would forever lose his autonomy.

After much deliberation, he printed Pinney's statement. The uproar was immediate and threatening, as a group of settlers stormed into the office of the paper and confronted John Russwurm. The settlers talked of burning the press and accused Russwurm of cooperating with a government that was not representative. They wanted more of a voice in how policies were decided and control over their own lives. Russwurm acknowledged their dissatisfaction with the government, but argued that destruction of the press was not the appropriate way to resolve the conflict. The men listened to his plea and left the press room without destroying the equipment.

The controversy did not, however, end for John Russwurm. He did not like the compromising position that the A.C.S. had placed him. The men, who led the revolts, were honorable men and merely wanted full independence. They wanted to control their own lives, rather than be controlled by American whites who did not fully understand them. Russwurm thought hard and long about his predicament in. In protest over how he had been manipulated by Pinney, in 1835, Russwurm resigned as editor of the paper. He felt that his integrity had been compromised and that he was powerless to change the perception that many settlers had of the administration. He had made a courageous decision in siding with administration, but his decision had forever destroyed his relationship with the settlers of the colony.

Being alienated from his fellow settlers, he began to feel homesick, not for America but for Maine and his friends and relatives. In a letter to his half brother Francis, he wrote on March 31, 1834: "Mr. C. Stockbridge...the most regular correspondent and the one who seemed to take the deepest interest in my welfare; in this distant land." Even at this late point in his life, Russwurm questioned whether his white friends in Maine failed to write because of his color. He continued to write:

> Mrs. A. Blanchards...I also answered directly and I know not again why you all seem to forget poor me here. I will not be foolish enough to impute it to the darkness of my complexion, because color is nothing in Africa: what is then the reason for so long a silence?[94]

Not only did Russwurm have to ponder the reasons why his relatives and friends did not write, but he also had to experience, on a daily basis, evidence of the African slave trade. He explained to his cousin Francis that the Liberia coast "...is completely overun with vessels of all nations..." engaged in the slave trade. A year later his frustration intensified as his health began to deteriorate due to rheumatism, which he initially contracted in 1833. These difficult times in Liberia dampened significantly his enthusiasm about Africa in general. On September 27, 1835, he wrote again to Francis Edward:

> ...I suppose I shall live and die in Africa, but I hope not in Liberia, for more fanaticism, bigotry and ignorance I

> never saw amongst men not excepting the last agents of the A.C.S.[95]

In this letter he was clearly upset over the leadership of the colony, and with his inability to exert meaningful change. Even though he had the skills to make greater contributions to development of the country, he was denied an opportunity, primarily because of his color. Despite these problems, John appeared to be satisfied as a business man. He urged Francis to write his partner, Mr. Dailey, who had business at Miss Rogers and Co. on Exchange Street, New York City.

He also found joy in being a parent, despite his dismay at the lack of letters from his relatives. He wrote:

> Our George Stockbridge Russwurm is now over 13 months old and is as fine a child as you would see in any part of your happy land. I have not the time to write more but beg you to remember me to every member of the family individually, beginning with Mr. and Mrs. Hawes and ending with Mrs. R. Stockbridge and family. I live in Africa but my friends in America can never be forgotten.[96] His agony over whether his people had forgotten him continued:...Why so much silence on the part of my family. I suppose they have cast me off because I am in Africa. I hope not however...[97]

Fortunately, a Bowdoin alumnus rescued him from his intolerable anguish. A year before the confrontation over the press, Russwurm had welcomed to Monrovia Dr. James Hall. Hall had been dispatched by the new Maryland in Africa movement to explore the west coast of Africa for possible settlement of Africans from Maryland. The movement to establish the Maryland colony was a direct result of revolts in the southern part of the United States. Maryland was the first American state to adopt colonization as an official policy. This decision was motivated by concern over the recent uprisings in Virginia, most notably the Nat Turner revolt. Colonization would free the state of free Africans, and therefore control the agitation for the abolition of slavery. Hall had been given the authority to found a new colony, and Russwurm was glad to know that a personal friend of such high character would be nearby.

Russwurm in Cape Palmas

Hall soon asked Russwurm to become apart of the new Maryland colony. It was in the new Maryland colony that Russwurm was able to expand his administrative and leadership skills. Many of the founders of Maryland in Africa believed in the gradual abolition of slavery, and the Maryland government adopted such position as its official policy. In 1832, the state appropriated $200,000.00 for the establishment of a colony on the west coast of Africa. Fortunate for John, the first expedition into the region was led by Dr. James Hall, his Bowdoin school mate. Hall traveled to Africa with twenty-five emissaries and acquired 800 square miles of land, approximately 270 miles south of Monrovia. In 1836, when he returned to Baltimore, he recommended that Russwurm be appointed Governor of the colony. Hall had absolute confidence in both his integrity and ability to lead the colonial government.

Even though Russwurm had encountered many difficulties for several years in Africa, he had not abandoned any of his commitment to repatriation. On the contrary, he saw repatriation as a more pragmatic approach to the racial problem in America. In 1836 he urged the United States Government to expend its surplus of $16,000,000.00 for the expansion of repatriation efforts.[98] He argued that repatriation was of equal importance as the Louisiana Purchase and would benefit both free and slave populations. More importantly, he saw benefit both to Africa and the United States.[99] This symbiotic aspect of his philosophy should have been more palatable to both Africans and Europeans. Russwurm was looking at the racial problem from an international perspective, while most others could not get beyond the national obsession with slavery. Russwurm envisioned an Africa that went beyond Liberia, while most free Africans in the United States could not see beyond their immediate restrictive environments. Such near sightedness was ironic given, that slavery was nothing more than the kidnapping of African nationals for profit by European nationals, in a diabolical international conspiracy to exploit African labor.

Russwurm, moreover, was clear that Africa had to be the ultimate destiny of Africans in America. While some may have opted for Canada, he was convinced that such notions were short-sighted:

> Our brethren of color are beginning to view it in a more favorable light. And though a few of them misled them-

> selves, have endeavored to mislead the more ignorant to Canada, have they succeeded? Do not the resolutions of Upper Canada speak volumes? Are they not viewed as intruders?[100]

He rejected Canada as a national base for Africans in America. Africa for him was the place where prerogatives of national government could be exercised. He marveled at the successful experiment in nation-building that was unfolding in Liberia:

> You here behold colored men exercising all the duties of offices of which you scarcely believe...Many fulfill the important duties with much dignity. We have here a republic in miniature...Before God, we know of no other home for the man of color, of republican principles, than Africa. Has he an ambition? Is he dead to everything noble? Is he contented with his condition?[101]

He saw Africa as the next situs for European national development. For him, neither Europe nor Asia represented a viable choice for national development for Europeans. Even the West Indies had proven unfruitful for these European explorers.[102] But Africa, however, provided them free labor, abundant land and rich natural resources. Africa could, he believed, also provide Africans in America a national alternative to American racism and economic exploitation.

The transition to Maryland in Africa was exactly what Russwurm had wanted. He too, had tired of the A.C.S.'s refusal to extend leadership roles to African settlers. He knew that he was better qualified than many of the European-Americans in Monrovia. He, therefore, accepted Hall's offer and gladly moved his wife and two sons to Cape Palmas. When he took up residence at the Governor's mansion, he made history. Never before had an African person, returning from the west, assumed such a position of responsibility.

He immediately established a government that was both fair and demanding. One of the first laws passed by his Governing Council was an ordinance that specified that no settler could receive aid from the Society Store unless he had cultivated at least "one acre of land in potatoes, cassada, plantains, cotton or rice." There would be no free rides and everyone would have to learn principles of scientific farming. In addition, children had to attend school and adults were encouraged to learn to read and write. Literacy, he believed, was necessary in order for citizens to know their rights that had been written in a constitution and bill of rights.

As Governor, Russwurm continued to conduct his affairs in a deliberate and responsible manner. In periodic letters to J.H.B. Latrobe, President of Maryland State Colonization Society, he outlined the steps that he was taking to both preserve peace and order as well as extend the boundaries of the colony. In March, 1846, he indicated to Mr. Latrobe that he had been in contact with the Kings of the Tabou, Bassa, Half Bereby, and Grand Bereby concerning the possible annexation of additional land.[103] The annexation of this land would have two important results. They would help cement the security of the colony by expanding citizenship to other African people. Annexation would carry with it immediate citizenship in Maryland in Africa. Secondly, it would mean that trade could expand into new territories. The positive results would be, therefore, both political and economic. These negotiations were successful, in part, due to the help that Russwurm was able to obtain from King Freeman, King of the Kru People in the Monrovia area, who had become a personal friend of Sarah Russwurm, his wife.

The annexations did not, however, occur without additional problems for the Russwurm administration. Annexation meant that his administration had to become more intimately involved in the internal affairs of various ethnic groups. For example, it had to police new territories and settle disputes that had heretofore been the sole province of the various kings. Ultimately, many of these disputes were resolved by Russwurm when he threatened to cut off trade if the hostilities did not stop. If trade sanctions were not imposed, then fines were levied upon individuals responsible for the offending conduct.

On the positive side, the administration established two free schools in Cape Palmas, and the missionaries established others. Russwurm believed that free schools modeled upon New England schools would lead to better citizenship. Furthermore, he believed that Maryland should provide to the colony a printing press. He wanted the laws and ordinances to be printed and distributed to all colonists.

By 1848, after twelve years as Governor, Russwurm's health began to decline even further. The pace he had set for himself was exhausting and unrelenting. On May 4, 1848, he wrote his good friend Dr. James

Hall to inform him that he had returned from his nine week trip to the United States and the Caribbean islands. The voyage had taken him to St. Thomas and a number of other islands, and he had returned feeling much better, but still feeble.[104]

Despite the restful trip, events on the west coast of Africa continued to be challenging. The King of Appolonia killed the Governor and other officials of the French settlement on the Assinee River. As a result, the English, French and Dutch engaged in war against the king. As many as ten warships docked off the coast of Appolonia.

The King was subsequently driven from the beach to the interior where he was captured and transported to New South Wales. Since he had control over the gold trade with the Europeans, he lost this advantageous role. Appolonia was taken over by the British, which quickly resulted in the arrival of British settlers, who set up factories and took over the King's trade in gold and ivory.

Russwurm was unable to control this expansion of European colonialism. He wrote James Hall on January 18, 1849 to express his frustration:

> Alas! That even in the 19th century, the greatest foe to human happiness is man- What has so depopulated the country around Monrovia, in some parts of which the heart is pained to see a fine Champaign region for miles without an inhabitant! And yet in your free country there are men who solemnly declare that Liberty cannot exist without slavery being tied to its car! Oh Liberty! Thou art, indeed a by-word for oppression in the mouths of such hypocrites!

It seemed that Africans were being resettled in West Africa from many areas of America and Europe. Hundreds of recaptured slaves from Brazil were settled in Accra and possessed great reputations as traders. The Dutch opened a gold mine thirty miles into the interior of Elmina, and brought several families from the Dutch island of St. Thomas to work the mines at a fee of $1,000.00 per family.

By November 22, 1848, peace still had not been restored to the region. Russwurm, had been assured, however, by his friend, King Freeman that he would help restore harmony between the Appolonia group and the European powers. The fighting had curtailed the importation of rice from the interior, which forced the colonists to rely heavily upon their cultivation of potatoes. These misgivings, notwithstanding, Russwurm continued to exercise his duties faithfully. In November, 1850, he successfully purchased the entire Garroway Country. Although several ethnic groups in the interior were at war, he received assurances that the conflicts could be resolved. The colony would receive from the acquisition, favorable navigation routes into the interior, rice, palm oil and camwood.

In the same year, President Roberts from Monrovia visited Russwurm, and discussed the possibility of Maryland being annexed to Monrovia. Russwurm informed Roberts that Maryland did not desire to unite with Monrovia, and that they could discuss the matter further in several years. Although the Monrovia papers stated that a great majority of the Maryland people wanted this annexation, Russwurm discounted such news. The major difference of opinion surrounded the nature of the unification. Would Cape Palmas be a county or an independent state?

For Russwurm there was no need to unite with Monrovia. Maryland was doing fine on its own. In January, 1850, the colony had peace at last and a bountiful harvest. New colonists arrived from Maryland to find plenty of the following agricultural products: rice, palm oil, potatoes, plantains, cassadas, cabbages, beets, radishes, turnips, lettuce, mustard, cape coast onions, egg-plants, ochras, squashes, cantelopes, watermelons, sappadella, bread-fruit, jack-do, rose apple, patanga, shaddock, avocado-pear, grapes, oranges, lemons, sour and sweet sops.[105]

Although the colony was prosperous, Russwurm's health continued to deteriorate. In early 1850, he had to temporarily relinquish his authority to Dr. McGill as a result of a severe bout with rheumatic fever. In June, 1851, he died and was buried in Cape Palmas, West Africa. No other nationalist of the nineteenth century could boast of such a successful return to the continent.

Notes

1. Mary Sagarin, *The Story of Freedom's Journal, Freedom's Journey* (New York: Lothrop, Lee and Shepard, 1970), p. 14.
2. Beryl M. Brown, *A Short History of Portland* (Kingston: Minister of Education Publications Branch, 1976, P.O. Box 498), page 17.
3. Ibid., page 18.

4. Ibid., page 18.
5. This information was obtained from the National Archives of Jamaica, in the "Register of Baptisms, Parish of Portland," pages one through thirty-five, by Amy Merrill, co-author of *Freedom's Journeyman*, a play about the life of John Brown Russwurm that premiered at Bowdoin College.
6. Sagarin, page 15.
7. Janice Borzendowski, *John Brown: Publisher* New York: Chelsea House Publishers, 1989), p. 21.
8. Roger Magnuson, *A Brief History of Quebec Education* (Montreal, Harvest House, 1980), p. 13.
9. J. Donald Wilson, Robert M. Stamp, Louis-Philippe Audet, *Canadian Education: A History* (Scarborough: Prentice-Hall, 1970), page 157.
10. Wilson, et al, page 160.
11. D.S. Penton, *Non Nobis Solum*, "The History of Lower Canada College and its Predecessor St. Johns School" (Montreal: Corporation of Lower Canada College), page 3.
12. Randolph Stakeman, "The Black Population of Maine, 1764-1900," *New England Journal of Black Studies*, November 8, 1989, page 17.
13. Stakeman, page 18.
14. Stakeman, page 25.
15. Stakeman, page 25.
16. Borzendowski, page 22.
17. *The Hebron Semester*, Vol. XIII-No.1, November 1, 1891. The seeking of a charter was a usual procedure in the early development of towns. The first institution established by New England towns was a church, and then a charter for a school was sought.
18. Ibid., page 9.
19. *The Hebron Semester,* Vol. Vno.2, Spring Term, 1885.
20. *The Hebron Semester*, Fall, 1974, page 10.
21. Lorenzo Johnson Greene, *The Negro in Colonial New England* (New York: Atheneum, 1974), page 16.
22. Ibid., page 353-354.
23. Ibid., page 74.
24. Ibid., page 76.
25. Richard A. Ballou, *Even in Freedom's Birthplace: The Development of Boston's Black Ghetto*, Volume I-II, University Microfilms, International Dissertation Information Services, 1987, page 285, Table 6-1.

26. George A. Levesque, *Black Boston: African American Life and Culture in Urban America 1751-1860*, Library of Congress Cataloging-in-Publication Data, 1994, page 323.
27. Ibid., page 289.
28. Donald M. Jacobs, "David Walker" Boston Race Leader, 1825-1830," *Essex Institute Historical Collection*, page 94.
29. Manuscript Section, Tennessee State Library and Archives, Russwurm, John Sumner, 1739-1860, Papers, 1786-1914. Letters from John Brown Russwurm, July 19, 1819.
30. Henry L. Allen, Sam Barnes, James W. Fraser, *From Common School to Magnet School* "Selected Essays in the History of Boston's Schools" (Boston: Trustees of the Public Library in the City of Boston, 1942), page 20.
31. Robert C. Hayden, *African-Americans in Boston: More Than 350 Years* (Boston: Trustees of the Boston Public Library, 1991), page 46.
32. Even after Russwurm left Boston in 1824, the educational vitality of the Black community continued to spread. In 1838, the Adelphic Union Library Association was formed to promote intellectual debates. Several years later in the 1840's the Histrionic Club was formed for the same purpose.
33. Adelaide M. Cromwell, *The Other Brahmins* "Boston's Black Upper-Class, 1750-1950" (Fayetteville: The University of Arkansas Press, 1994), page 35.
34. George A. Levesque, *Black Boston* "African American Life and Culture in Urban America, 1750-1860" (New York: Garland Publishing, 1994), page 166. The petition for separate schools was made in 1787 and denied by state officials.
35. William D. Piersen, *Black Yankees* "The Development of an Afro-American Subculture in Eighteenth-Century New England" (Amherst: The University of Massachusetts Press, 1988), page 59.
36. Allan D. Austin, Editor, *Sidney Kaplan, American Studies in Black and White, Selected Essays* (Amherst: The University of Massachusetts Press, 1991), page 35.
37. Ibid., page 37.
38. Fritz Daguillard, *A Jewel in the Crown*, "Charles Sumner and the Struggle for Haiti's Recognition" (Washington, D.C.: Haitian Embassy).
39. Frederick Douglass, *Rochester North Star*, July 14, 1848, page 4, column 2.
40. Jacobs, page 103.

41. Jacobs, page 104.
42. Douglass, *Sketch of the Life and Character of David Walker.*
43. Ibid.
44. Lorenzo Johnson Greene, page 83.
45. Lorenzo Johnson Greene, page 314.
46. Andrew Wentink, Directory Special Collection at Middlebury College provided this information, which is contained in *General Catalog of Middlebury College, Bicentennial Edition*, compiled by Travis Beal Jacobs, Proctor Professor of History, Middlebury College Press, Middlebury, Vermont, 2000, page 977.
47. Ibid.
48. *Middlebury*, Spring, 1974, "The Iron-Willed Black Schoolmaster and his Granite Academy."
49. Calhoun, Charles C. *A Small College in Maine* "Two Hundred Years of Bowdoin" (Brunswick, 1993), page 60.
50. William Brookings Mitchell, " A Remarkable Bowdoin Decade, 1820-1830," (Brunswick: Bowdoin College, 1852), page 17.
51. Mitchell, page 25.
52. Borzendowski, page 36.
53. Cantwell, page 95.
54. Sagarin, page 34.
55. Sagarin, page 29.
56. Cantwell, page 68.
57. Cantwell, page 74.
58. Cantwell, page 79.
59. Cantwell, page 80.
60. Cantwell, page 54.
61. Cantwell, page 69. Another useful record of the Bowdoin years is Horatio Bridge's *Personal Recollections of Nathaniel Hawthorne* (New York: Harper + Brothers, 1893).
62. Sagarin, page 41.
63. Nehemiah Cleaveland, Alpheus Spring Packard, *History of Bowdoin College* (Boston: James Ripley Osgood + Co., 1882), page 263.
64. Michael D'Antonio, "Fessenden: Fierce Foe of Slavery" *Portland Press Herald*, May 29, 1982.
65. George Henry Preble, *William Pitt Fessenden: A Memoir* (Boston: David Clapp + Son, 1871), page 13. Another useful article on Fessenden can be found in *Maine Historical Society*, Vol. II, No. 2, Fall, 1971.

66. Sagarin, page 136.
67. American Association of University Women, Bath-Brunswick Branch, page 6. Further evidence of Professor Smyth's house being used on the Underground Railroad can be found in Louis c. Hatch, *The History of Bowdoin College* (Portland: Loring, Short + Harmon, 1927) page 57. In fact, Bowdoin was one of the few New England colleges that had an unofficial role in the railroad. Undoubtedly, college officials and the Brunswick community had some inclination of what Professor Smyth was involved in. See John Clair Minot, Donald Francis Snow, *Tales of Bowdoin* (Augusta: Press of Kennebec Journal, 1901), page 275.
68. *Dedication of Afro-American Center*, January 27, 1979, Remarks by Professor Roger Howell, page 6.
69. John Calhoun, page 61.
70. *Lewiston Journal*, February 27, 1915.
71. Letter from Professor Thomas C. Upham, April 20, 1870. This letter can be found in the rare manuscript section of Hawthorne-Long fellow Library at Bowdoin College.
72. Thomas C. Upham, *American Cottage, 2nd Edition*, "A Series of Poems," (Brunswick: Joseph Griffin, 1850), page 64.
73. Thomas C. Upham, *The Manual of Peace*, "The Evils and Remedies of War" (Boston: American Peace Society, 1842), page 36.
74. Thomas C. Upham, *Letters: Aesthetic, Social and Moral*(Brunswick: The Free Press of J. Griffin, 1855), page 110.
75. Borzendowski, page 36.
76. Borzendowski, page 47.
77. *Freedom's Journal*, Friday, April 6, 1827.
78. *Freedom's Journal*, Vol. 1, No.10.
79. *Freedom's Journal*, Vol. No. 98, February 14, 1829.
80. William M. Brewer, "John B. Russwurm," *Journal of Negro History* , Vol. XIII, No. 4, October, 1928, page 416 (*African Repository*, Vol. XII, page 86).
81. Ibid., page 417 (Woodson, C. G., *Mind of the Negro as Reflected in Letters Written During the Crisis*, 1800-1860, page 163).
82. Ibid., page 418 (*African Repository*, Vol. XII, page 86).
83. Borzendowski, page 11.
84. Borzendowski, page 13.
85. Borzendowski, page 63.

86. Mia Bay, *The White Image in the Black Mind* "African-American Ideas About White People, 1830-1925" (New York: Oxford University Press, 2000).
87. P.J. Staudenraus, *The African Colonization Movement, 1816-1865* (New York: Columbia University Press, 1961), page 188.
88. Staudenraus, page 191.
89. Borzendowski, page 65.
90. Staudenraus, page 193.
91. Sagarin, page 72.
92. Sagarin, page 93.
93. Borzendowski, page 77.
94. Manuscript Section, Tennessee State Library and Archives, Russwurm, John Sumner, 1739-1860. Papers, 1786-1914. Letter to Francis, March 31, 1834.
95. Ibid, Letter to Francis Edwards, September 27, 1835.
96. Ibid, Letter to Francis Edward, September 27, 1825.
97. Ibid. Other letters are available in this collection that reflect on his melancholy state: Letter from Susan Hawes, 1826, page 8; Letter from James Hall to A. Cleveland, page 8.
98. William M. Brewer, "John B. Russwurm," *Journal of Negro History*, Vol. XIII, No. 4, October, 1928, page 419 (*African Repository*, Vol. XII, page 86).
99. Ibid., page 419 (*African Repository*, page 86).
100. Ibid., page 420 (Woodson, *Mind of the Negro...*, page 162).
101. Ibid., page 421 (Woodson, *Mind of the Negro...*, page 161.
102. Ibid., page 421 (*African Repository*, Vol. XXVII, page 357). Additional information on Russwurm can be found in *African Repository* Vol. XV, page 324; Vol. XXVII, page 356; Vol. XII, page 272 and Vol. XXVII, page 358.
103. *Maryland Colonization Journal*, August, 1846.
104. *Maryland Colonization Journal*, July, 1848.
105. *Maryland Colonization Society*, January, 1850.

Chapter Nine

THE AFRICAN NATIONALIST IDEOLOGY OF EDWARD WILMOT BLYDEN

The work to be done beyond the seas is not to be a reproduction of what we see in this country. It requires, therefore, distinct race perception, and entire race devotion.[1]

While John Russwurm achieved unprecedented political power in Cape Palmas, he failed to articulate a clear philosophical rationale for the political development of the colony and the region. He was, in short, a pragmatist who, though highly educated, did not struggle with broad concepts such as African nationalism and Pan-Africanism. However, from 1847 to the end of the century, a clear Pan-African ideology did emerge from the continent. Its architect was Edward Wilmot Blyden. No one in the nineteenth century articulated a more profound philosophical rationale for repatriation than did Blyden. He and, to a lesser extent, Alexander Crummell struggled with a theoretical paradigm that made Africa the center of the African person's worldview. It was Blyden, however, who created a rationale that grew out of the rich legacy of African communalism and spirituality. Blyden, born in St. Thomas, West Indies, in 1832, and brought to the United States by the American Colonization Society, was convinced that national consciousness could be planted and nurtured in Liberia.[2]

Blyden arrived late on the Liberian scene. By the time of his departure for the new African nation, John Brown Russwurm had died and Lott Cary had already returned to the United States. As soon as Blyden arrived in the United States, the Colonization Society placed him in contact with the American Missionary Association, an American Christian organization that supported African-American relief programs. Within a short time Blyden convinced the association to send him to Liberia as a missionary, arguing that he would be more effective in converting the Africans than would American missionaries.[3] While on the surface it would appear that missionary activity was his motivating reason for going to Africa, it was merely a means to a clear end: return to Africa.

From the beginning of his stay in the United States, Blyden had to contend with racism. He had hoped to enroll in college on arrival, but none would accept him. Liberia, therefore, seemed to be a welcome alternative to blatant American racism that prevented him from realizing his full human potential. Even though he had to compromise his values by attaching himself to the missionaries, this was more satisfying than constantly being subjected to the indignities in the United States.

In Liberia he would find an African political independence that was not perfect, but still a significant improvement from America, where Africans had virtually no political power. Even though Liberia was under the nominal control of African politicians, it was still a neo-colony of the United States, given that the republic remained dependent upon the colonization society for settlers and finance.

After Haiti, Liberia represented the most significant experiment with nationalism in the nineteenth century. Nationalism in Haiti and Liberia were fundamentally different, however. Unlike Haiti, independence in Liberia did not result from armed struggle or protracted political negotiations or a militant social movement that could form the basis of African nationalism. The leadership of the Liberian colony did not agitate for political independence, instead they negotiated for a gradual shift in the power relationships that would result in a greater sharing with the American administration.[4] This leadership failed to articulate an overall nationalist purpose that would galvanize the people toward a common goal. For example, Joseph Jenkins Roberts, an African-American agent for the former American administrators of the colony, founded the first political party of the republic and kept himself and his followers in office from 1847 to 1869 without an election. This new African political elite in Liberia deliberately sought to fulfill selfish and narrow political objectives, rather than pursue a strategy of empowerment for the repatriates. Even though this leadership had experienced racial oppression and economic exploitation in the United States, many of them felt superior and more sophisticated than the indigenous people because they spoke the English language and worshiped the Christian God.[5]

Ironically, this same African leadership had no control over who came to the new republic. The American Civil War resulted in a significant decrease in the number of Africans going to the republic, as the efforts of the American Colonization Society were curtailed due to the bloody conflict between the states. After the Emancipation Proclamation in 1863, the Thirteenth Amendment in 1865 and the Fourteenth Amendment in 1868, the flow of settlers to Liberia decreased even further. The only significant resettlement consisted of 346 Barbadians in 1864.

The reasons for this downturn in repatriation were complex. First, since over 60 percent of the settlers had been emancipated specifically for colonization, southerners felt that it was in their best interest to hold on to their property and not put them under the control of the enemy, that is, the leadership of the American Colonization Society. Furthermore, freedom for the slaves in 1865 sparked a belief that a better life could be obtained in America.

Particularly during the period 1867 to 1877, known as "Reconstruction," Africans found that they could for the first time obtain access to political privilege in the South. Consequently, many looked away from Africa and saw America as the land of opportunity at last and envisioned the day when they could gain total access to the benefits of American society. Furthermore, agencies such as the Freedmen's Bureau promised them good jobs, adequate health care and an education throughout the South. The federal government, for the most part, delivered on its promise. African-American colleges such as Morehouse, Fisk and Howard received substantial aid.

This philanthropy caused African-Americans to feel that the American government was at last on their side and would help them gain their rightful place in America. Consequently, the Freedmen's Bureau succeeded in diverting the allegiance of millions of newly freed slaves from Africa, thereby depriving Liberia of the most committed and talented leaders. On the other hand, the payoff was considerable. African-Americans gained political leverage by accepting this governmental assistance that helped them to utilize the political process in the southern states. The federal government needed the allegiance of African-Americans who comprised the majority of the southern population, and therefore stood in an excellent position to determine the political direction of the region. Through sheer numbers, African-Americans were able to amass enough political leverage to gain election to influential positions of leadership throughout the South. For example, in South Carolina (1860), out of a population of 703,000, 412,000 were African-American. As a result, in the first South Carolina legislature a decade later, eighty-four African-Americans were elected to the legislature as opposed to seventy-three European-Americans. This trend continued throughout the South. In Mississippi between 1870 and 1881 two African-American men, Hiram Revels and Blanche Kelso Bruce, were elected to the U.S. Senate. In Louisiana, Lieutenant Governor P.B.S. Pinchback became governor after the impeachment of the elected European-American governor. An African-American became secretary of state in Florida, another was appointed to the Supreme Court in South Carolina and a third became mayor of Natchez, Mississippi.[6]

To most African-Americans it seemed as though America was finally living up to its national creed and becoming concerned about the plight of African people. In reality, this change across the southern landscape resulted from African-Americans registering to vote, and exercising that vote in a fashion to benefit themselves. Progress did not result from benevolence. Many European-Americans were still unsure as to whether African-Americans should even remain in America. Even Abraham Lincoln, the author of the Emancipation Proclamation, asked Ben Butler, a Massachusetts politician, to develop a plan for deporting freed slaves. Many African-Americans, unaware of Lincoln's true feelings about their destiny, hailed him as their liberator. The murder of Lincoln on the heels of emancipation served to reinforce even further the myth that Lincoln fought the Civil War to free them. This inaccurate belief that the president of the United States had placed his life in jeopardy in order to ensure freedom for African people endeared many to America. As a result, interest in Liberia was displaced by devotion to Lincoln and the Republican Party.

It was in the context of an economically powerless republic that Blyden had to plant the seeds of African nationalism. Blyden, considered the father of West African nationalism, developed a philosophical rationale for repatriation that projected Africa as the center of the African person's universe.

Blyden, though fully aware of the motives of the Colonization Society, felt that the organization was the most effective vehicle to achieve his goal of African repatriation to Liberia. He believed that every race of people commanded respect from others by being part of a strong nation, and that in order for Africans to gain respect, whether in America or the West Indies, they had to develop and support the continent of Africa. Blyden went further to say that nationalities were as natural as creation, and that Africans were divinely predestined to repatriate to Africa and build a strong nation.

Central to Blyden's concept of a strong nation was the necessity for fervent race pride. In order for Africa to regenerate itself, Blyden believed, Africans had to develop positive attitudes toward themselves. Blyden's teachings were badly needed as many leaders of the Liberian government believed that because of their lighter complexion they were socially superior to the mass of the people. Blyden, on the other hand, taught that the darkest of the race constituted the purest and that the more mixed the race became, the more degenerate African people became. Consequently, he envisioned a Liberia consisting of pure black people. To that end, he urged the American Colonization Society to send only pure blacks to the republic.[7]

Blyden realized that Africans had to resurrect their self-image; particularly after the pervasive attempts by missionaries during the nineteenth century to portray Africans as heathens and savages. Many missionaries taught the Africans that if they wanted to be saved by God, they had to abandon their inferior traditional customs.

Blyden started to develop his theories of racial purity at an early age in the West Indies. The society he saw there approximated that of Liberia to the extent that many of the people who were afforded social status by the colonialists had light skins. Blyden held disdain for the light-skinned West Indians and unsparingly lashed out at those in Liberia. He taught that the greatest attribute of African people was to be pure black, of unmixed African parents, and to have a love for Africa. He thought that as long as African people remained in close contact with European culture, they would lose their sense of self-worth:

> From the lessons he every day receives, the Negro unconsciously imbibes the conviction that to be a great man he must be like the white man. He is not bought up...to be the champion, the equal, the comrade of the white man, but his imitator, his ape....To be himself is to be nothing.... Every intelligent Negro, in the lands of his exile, must feel that he walks upon the face of God's earth a physical and moral incongruity. [8]

However, Blyden did not believe that African people would always be ignorant of themselves, but that the inevitable redemption of Africa would lead to the rise of African people throughout the world. He saw the interest in Africa and repatriation as a manifestation of God's will to create a strong Africa. Therefore, he urged Africans to partake of the glorious moment of African development: "We need some African power, some great center of the race where our physical, pecuniary and intellectual strength may be collected."[9] In order for "African Power" to become a reality, he envisioned a fundamental change in the minds of African people in America and Africa. In order for Africans, who had been in America, to establish their correct relation with Africa and its people, they must purge themselves of poisonous Western values and settle in Africa. Despite the problems involved in massive repatriation, Blyden believed it was feasible; and in 1891 he addressed a group of Yoruba people to explain the positive effects the repatriation of 100,000 African-Americans would have on their country.

Blyden believed that religion had an important role to play in the development of African nationalism in Liberia and Africa. According to him, African traditional cultures were models of righteous societies. For instance, in African traditional society, because of its communalistic nature, no one was oppressed or starved. The individual received his first training in the family, which prepared him to work within the confines of the village. The family would, in turn, insure that the individual had security. If one member of the family acquired a great deal of wealth, it was incumbent upon him to help the less fortunate members. Unlike capitalist societies, African society compelled the individual to work within the framework of the group for the benefit of the group. When the family unit encountered severe handicaps, it could then turn to the village or community for aid, since the land, water and all community wealth belonged to the entire village. The members of the family could call upon the village because they had helped in communal projects like defense and land clearance.[10]

Blyden saw African society as the one example to the world of how people should live together. African society was not based upon the exploitation of man by man, but upon cooperation. Blyden believed that the African traditions closely paralleled the teachings of Jesus. In Western societies he saw a contradiction between the principles of socialism that Jesus professed and materialistic individualism. He even asserted that religion originated in Africa, and that Africa would have a critical role to play in teaching the world righteousness:

> Africa may yet prove to be the spiritual conservatory of the world.... when the civilized nations in consequence of their wonderful material development, shall had their spiritual perceptions darkened and their spiritual susceptibilities blunted through the agency of a captivating and absorbing materialism, it may be that they may have to resort to Africa to recover some of the simple elements of faith.... Perhaps there is no people in whom the religious instinct is deeper and more universal than among Africans. And, in view of the materializing tendencies of the age, it may yet come to pass that when, in Europe, God has gone out of date ... or when that time arrives in the development of the great Aryan race ... when the belief in God will be as the tales with which old women frighten children, when the world will be a machine, the ether a gas, and God will be a farce; then earnest inquirers after truth leaving the seats of science and the "highest civilization" will take themselves to Africa to learn lessons of faith and piety; for "Ethiopia shall stretch forth her hands unto God."[11]

However, Blyden did not believe that Africans alone possessed divine favor, but that all mankind had the potential to be good. Although Edward Blyden received training in the Christian tradition, he respected Mohammed just as much as Jesus. After his voyage to Egypt and the Middle East in 1866, he developed a good knowledge of the Arab language and the Muslim religion.

Nevertheless, he saw Christianity playing a significant role in the development of nationalism in Africa. However, it was to be different from that brought to Africa by the missionaries or taught on the plantations by the slaveowners. It was to inspire the African with a feeling of preeminence in God's plan for the rejuvenation of mankind. No doubt Blyden saw himself as an African Moses compelling his people to leave their oppressors and build for themselves in their own land. If they stayed in America, they would eventually lose their African virtues and adopt the ways of their oppressors. Repatriation was, therefore, the only answer to both spiritual and physical degradation of black people in America:

> We have been dragged into the depths of degradation. We have been taught a cringing servility. We have been drilled into contentment with the most undignified circumstances. Our finer sensibilities have been blunted. There has been an almost utter extinction of all that delicacy of feeling and sentiments which adorns character. The temperament of our souls has become harder and coarser, so that we can walk forth here, in this land of indignities, in ease and in complacency while our complexion furnishes ground for every species of social insult which an intolerant prejudice may choose to inflict.[12]

Edward Blyden undoubtedly qualified as one of the most original African thinkers of the nineteenth century. As with most repatriates of the period he was sponsored by the American Colonization Society, but he did not allow those who controlled his finances to influence his philosophy. In a period when many of the African leaders had not come to any firm conclusions about African people's destiny, Blyden offered a clear and convincing philosophical basis for repatriation. He recognized that Africans in Africa had a role to play in the larger world that could never be realized when a portion of its people were scattered around the world. In that sense, he was one of the earliest repatriates who had a Pan-African perspective. He envisioned the day when Africa would be strong, respected and loved by all African people. Before he died in 1912 he had already left African people of the world a rich legacy and a clear challenge. For him African consciousness constituted a richness and uniqueness that would add new dimensions to world culture.

The nationalist philosophy of Edward Blyden had little chance of success in Liberia. Essentially two forces prevented the young republic from adopting an ideology that would give it a philosophical basis for its existence. The first was caste discrimination demonstrated by the elite class toward the indigenous Africans. These settlers even engaged in the military conquest of the interior of Africa in complicity with the beliefs held by nineteenth-century European explorers that African land could be claimed by discovery. The pursuit of territorial gains invariably led to wars between Africans in the interior and the settlers. Unfortunately the Africans were easily defeated by the guns of the settlers. Some ethnic groups, such as the Gola, Grebo and Kru, however, resisted the settlers for a while as a result of their guerrilla warfare tactics, but were soon overcome. These conquests led to the deepening of suspicion and hatred between the groups.

Even in the twentieth century, hostility between the two groups remain considerable. The following letter from an African in Kpelle University, Liberia epitomized the division that continued to prevail in Liberia:

> We students had to elect a class president. Some of the Americo-Liberians got together and said they didn't want anyone from the tribes. So we interior students got together, and we agreed to elect a Gio boy. We felt we had a majority. These people are too hard in their hearts, they cannot change ... there will be a civil war. They think so much of themselves and who are they. You know, they think they are better than us, but they are all sons of slaves - they were slaves here in Africa before they went to America, that is how they were sent.[13]

The second factor that prevented Liberia from adopting the nationalist philosophy of Edward Blyden was economic. After the Civil War and the Emancipation Proclamation, interest in emigration among Europeans and Africans declined. As a result, as interest among whites shifted from Liberia, so did the finances that supported the colony. In addition, the new republic failed to stimulate economic growth. The bulk of the economic aid received by the republic came from Great Britain in the form of long-term loans. Liberia remained dependent upon Britain until 1908, when it sought economic aid from the U.S. government.[14]

During this period the greatest need as seen by the country's leaders was economic aid and expertise. Blyden brought neither when he came to the republic. The sixty-one years of independence stretching from 1847 to 1908 was a time of grave economic uncertainty. Immediately after independence, the nation had to procure loans from European bankers at a high interest rate in order to set up its military. In addition, the political leadership of the republic embezzled large sums of money; President Edward Roye was impeached in 1871 for conspiracy to embezzle.[15] The fledgling republic constantly faced the possibility of bankruptcy and, had it not been for the loans, the country probably would have fallen.[16]

Independence fell upon the shoulders of its leaders before any of them had an opportunity to prepare for it; therefore the results were disastrous. In an atmosphere of economic instability, the nationalist philosophy of Edward Blyden fell upon deaf ears. Furthermore, the adoption of Blyden's philosophy would have meant a radical reapportionment of the meager resources that existed in the republic. The integration of the indigenous Africans within the republic would have required more equitable distribution of the national wealth, which would have affected the social position of the republic's leaders. Social class divisions and privilege constituted another factor that had a bearing on the future of African nationalism in Liberia. Essentially the republic had to choose between economic independence and neocolonialism. The choice was easy for the leadership that was more concerned with maintaining its privileged positions than with charting a separate economic path involving more reliance upon indigenous Africans. As a result of this type of attitude among the political leaders, the move into the neocolonial camp was inevitable:

> Liberia is not an Independent Republic: in fact, it is not an independent nation at all; but a poor miserable mockery - a burlesque of a government - a pitiful dependency on the American Colonizationist, the Colonization Board at Washington City in the District of Columbia, being the Executive and Government, and the principal man, called President in Liberia, being the echo-a mere parrot.[17]

Finally, economic dependency can be directly related to the failure of Liberia's leaders to forgo Western aid and adopt the nationalist concepts of Edward Blyden. As a result of this failure, Liberia never became an economically independent African state that could have been a symbol of African freedom, but instead became a neocolony of American economic interests.

Notes

1. Howard Brotz, *Negro Social and Political Thought 1850 to 1920, Representative Texts* (New York: Basic Books, 1966), page 137.
2. Gearge Padmore, *Pan-Africanism or Communism* (London: Dennis Dobson, 1965), page 32.
3. Padmore, page 32.
4. J. Gus Liebenow, *Liberia: The Evolution of Privilege* (Ithaca, NY: Cornell University Press, 1969), page 61.
5. Liebenow, page 15.
6. Lerone Bennett, *Before the Mayflower* (Chicago: Johnson Publishing Co., 1962), page 186.
7. Robert W. July, *A History of the African People* 2nd ed. (New York: Charles Scribner), page 412.
8. Blyden cited in July, page 223.
9. July, page 225.
10. July, page 219.
11. Blyden cited in John S. Mbiti, *African Religions and Philosophy* (New York: Doubleday, 1970) page 135.
12. Blyden cited in Brotz, page 113.
13. Fraenkel Merran, *Tribe and Class in Monrovia* (London: Oxford University Press, 1965), page 225.
14. Padmore, page 35.
15. Padmore, page 35.
16. Padmore, page 37.
17. Brotz, page 78.

Chapter Ten

VOLUNTARY REPATRIATION AND NATIONALISM

Repatriation in the nineteenth century was a function of who controlled financial resources, and since Africans did not to any large degree, they had nominal control over the process. With the exception of Cuffe, Africans did not have sufficient control over capital that would have allowed them to be self-sufficient in the provision of their food, medicine, transportation and other necessities. Therefore, Africans had little involvement in such critical questions as who went to Africa, where they came from and how they gathered the resources to make the journey. Despite this overwhelming control by outsiders, voluntary repatriates who returned to Africa either, by their own resources or through that of others, developed and maintained a clear perspective on African nationalism.

Voluntary repatriation began with Paul Cuffe in 1815, but this independent nationalist movement quickly became eclipsed by the American Colonization Society and its policy of banishment of unwanted Africans. Repatriation in the nineteenth century, therefore, became synonymous with the activities of the Colonization Society, the one organization in the first half of the nineteenth century that could marshal enough financial resources to transport Africans back to Africa. Although the motives of the Colonization Society were racist and designed to further its economic interests, Africans, who believed that they would be better off in a country of their own, compromised with the Society in order to get transportation to Africa.

Cooperation with the American Colonization Society did not mean that these African-American leaders shared the racist ideals of the white members of the Society, but rather they wished to use the Society as a means of establishing an African state in Africa. As Africans became more involved in colonization efforts, African newspapers such as *Freedom's Journal* and the *North Star* carried editorials and articles on the pros and cons of colonization. Such frequent and in-depth coverage in these papers insured that most free Africans in the nation had access to information on colonization in general and Liberia in particular.

African repatriation during the nineteenth century did not originate from the activities of the Colonization Society, but from Africans who voluntarily left America for Africa or created the means by which other Africans could leave. Although Africans were torn from Africa by the slavers, many never lost their emotional attachment to the land. Some slaves even committed suicide by jumping overboard from the slave ship rather than face an uncertain future. Still others such as Cinque and a host of other Africans seized one slave ship, the *Amistad,* and demanded that they be taken back to Africa.

A great many Africans who were forcefully taken to the American continent maintained their identity with Africa. Many of the organizations founded by Africans had names such as the Free African Society formed in 1787, and the Sons of Africa formed in 1798. Several black churches also bore the African title: The First African Baptist Church (1798) and the Free African Meeting House (1805).[1]

One of the earliest expressions of African nationalism that developed independently of the colonization efforts was that of Robert Alexander Young who published his *Ethiopian Manifesto* in February 1829. Young believed that the descendants of Africa were Africans wherever they happened to be born in the world. In the *Manifesto* he appealed to African people to come together and form a nation. Young's nationalist philosophy foreshadowed many of the Pan-African sentiments that were expressed nearly a century later by Marcus Garvey and others.

Another nationalist thinker of the first half of the nineteenth century was the Reverend Lewis Woodson, who influenced Martin Delany. Although Woodson did not advocate emigration to Africa, he did urge Africans to form independent settlements in the United States.[2]

What was clear to all of these nationalists was that African-American people were in fact an African people and that they needed to unite and secure their destiny. It was never an easy task to reconcile Africa with the abject exploitation on the plantations. How could one advocate for repatriation when the vast majority of one's brothers and sisters were being deprived of the full value of their labor, and denied their rights as human beings? Although this question represented the toughest of decisions in the nineteenth century, many free Africans confronted the dilemma and opted for repatriation.

Henry Highland Garnet (1815 to 1881)

Henry Garnet was one of these leaders who was able to reconcile Africa with the struggle for emancipation in the United States. As a young boy, Garnet's family escaped from slavery in Maryland to freedom in Wilmington, Delaware. With the help of Quaker friends, the family reached New York City in 1825. In New York City he attended school and lived next door to another prominent African nationalist, Alexander Crummell. The two young men attended the New York African Free School with Ira Aldridge, who later became a famous Shakespearean actor and European emigrationist, who lived most of his life in Europe and was buried in Lodz, Poland.

Henry Highland Garnet, though an African nationalist, favored repatriation to a limited degree. He realized that not all of the free Africans could go to Africa because of the large amount of money required: "There are those who, either from good or evil motives, plead for the Utopian plan of the colonization of a whole race to the shores of Africa. We are now colonized. We are planted here, and we cannot as a whole people, be colonized back to our fatherland."[3]

At the famous Albany Convention of 1840 Garnet supported the "antiemigration" resolution that was passed by the free Africans in attendance. At that point in his career he could not give his undivided endorsement to repatriation, but Alexander Crummell could endorse these "emigrationist" efforts.[4] While growing up in New York, Garnet had considerable contact with Africans from the continent and from the West Indies, which influenced his thinking on Africa. In 1843 he wrote an address to Africans held in bondage that was published in 1848. In his text Garnet called upon all Africans in the United States to rise up against oppression and have pride in Africa.[5]

However, it was not until the 1850s that Garnet began openly to advocate repatriation as a solution to oppression in America. By 1858 Garnet had moderated his views on Africa. In that year, he and a number of other prominent Africans founded the African Civilization Society as an alternative to the American Colonization Society. A person of good moral character, who paid $1.00 per year, could become a member. $25.00 could make one a life member. Article II sets forth the purpose of the organization:

> The object of this Society shall be the civilization and christianization of Africa, and of the descendants of African ancestors in any portion of the earth, wherever dispersed. Also, the destruction of the African Slave Trade, by the introduction of lawful commerce and trade into Africa: the promotion of the growth of cotton and other products there, whereby the natives may become industrious producers as well as consumers of articles of commerce: and generally, the elevation of the colored population of our country, and of other lands.[6]

By 1859 Garnet had resolved most doubts in his mind concerning the value of returning to Africa and therefore became a prime advocate of it. On September 19, 1859, Garnet addressed a group of free Africans in Boston and explained to them the object of The African Civilization Society: "to establish a grand center of negro nationality, from which shall flow the streams of commercial, intellectual, and political power which shall make colored people respected everywhere."[7] Repatriation became the topic of so many of Garnet's speeches that many African critics suspected that he worked for the American Colonization Society. Leaders such as Frederick Douglass avidly sought the opportunity to debate with him on the question of "colonization."

In a special meeting of the African Civilization Society, held on November 4, 1861, Martin Delany, another founder, urged the organization to clarify its goals and objectives. A special committee was formed and chaired by Delany. The committee drafted a supplement to the constitution that clarified the purpose of the organization. The key provisions of the supplement were Articles I and II:

> Article I – The Society is not designed to encourage general emigration, but will aid only such persons as may be practically qualified and suited to promote the development of Christianity, morality, education, mechanical arts, agriculture, commerce, and general improvement; who must

> always be carefully selected and well recommended, that the progress of civilization may not be obstructed.
>
> Article II – The basis of the Society, and ulterior objects in encouraging emigration, shall be Self-Reliance and Self-Government, on the principle of an African Nationality, the African race being the ruling element of the nation, controlling and directing their own affairs.[8]

Lott Cary (1780 to 1828)

Although men such as Delany and Lott Cary possessed nationalist sentiments, they shared many of the popular stereotypes about Africa. Lott Cary, like many "whites" in the nineteenth century, viewed Africa as a land of barbarism and degradation. Christianity to Cary was one factor that could save the benighted continent from damnation by bringing civilization to it. In 1817 he was a leading figure in the founding of the African Missionary Society in Richmond, Virginia. Five years later he journeyed to Africa under the auspices of the Baptist Board of Foreign Missions of the United States.[9]

Cary, like Paul Cuffe, saw repatriation as a means of converting the so-called heathens, while maintaining a firm commitment to Africa consciousness. In 1820 he made the following statement that clearly indicated his identification with Africa: "I am an African, and in this country, however meritorious my conduct and respectable my character, I cannot receive the credit due to either. I wish to go to a country where I shall be estimated by my merits, not my complexion, and I feel bound to labor for my suffering race."[10]

However, after a brief analysis of his writings, it is apparent that the missionary motive played a significant role in his nationalist philosophy. In 1825 while in Liberia, he wrote Mr. William Crane of the Richmond Baptist Missionary Society and boasted that he had baptized nine converts.[11] Later that same year, he and other missionaries established a school for native Africans. He envisioned Christian education uplifting the "sons of Ham" to civilization and salvation: "You must know, that it is a source of much consolidation to me, to hear the word of God read by those native sons of Ham, who a few months ago were howling in the devil's bush."[12]

Liberia therefore lured free Africans who saw in Africa not only a place of refuge for African people, but also a field for missionary activities. Although they shared these missionary designs with many whites engaged in colonization, they never failed to realize and appreciate the African heritage which they shared with the African continental population.

Alexander Crummell (1819 to 1898)

Several other prominent African men who had settled in Liberia left out of frustration. As the motives of the Colonization Society became clearer, they broke from the society and returned to the United States. One such man was Alexander Crummell, who strongly criticized what in the long run proved to be one of the colony's major problems: marginalization of the indigenous Africans. Crummell was born in New York in 1819. His mother was a free African and his father a Temne from Sierra Leone who emigrated to the United States. His childhood was spent in New York where he attended the African Free School and the Oneida Institute. At the age of thirty-three he enrolled at Queen College, University of Cambridge in England and received a degree in 1853. Before going to England, he was ordained an Episcopal minister.

Crummell's significance to repatriation stems from his relentless attacks upon the Liberian government for not adopting a benign governmental policy toward the indigenous Africans. The colonial government excluded the indigenous Africans from governmental service. The independence constitution of 1847 made no mention of indigenous Africans participating and having a voice in the republic. Crummell represented the leadership of a movement of educated settlers who lashed out at these discriminatory policies. The major problem stemmed from the fact that the European-American members of the Colonization Society had no intention of treating indigenous Africans any differently from the way they treated Africans in America.

Nevertheless, it was hoped that upon independence in 1847, the leadership of the new republic would change some of the discriminatory practices. This did not happen. However, the native Africans continued to press for change in government policy. One issue revolved around the question of land.[13] The new settlers introduced the concept of private ownership of land, which was contrary to the African concept of communal ownership. In addition, the settlers were reluctant to marry into tribal families and adopted a general stand off policy toward the native Africans. Crummell warned the settlers that their native policy would lead to the future demise of the republic. His advice fell upon deaf ears and it was not until 1904 under the President Arthur Barclay that citizenship was granted to the indigenous Africans.[14]

Finally, unable to compromise his nationalist consciousness with injustice in Liberia, Crummell returned to the United States in 1873 after twenty years in the West African country. Upon his return he committed himself to nationalist efforts. His most important contribution was the founding of the American Negro Academy in 1897, which included African scholars from England, America, Haiti and Africa. Membership in the new organization was limited to forty scholars who researched topics relating to African people all over the world.

James T. Holly (1829 to 1911)

Some Africans rejected Liberia as a place of resettlement. Such was James T. Holly, a clergyman, and one of the first Africans to advocate resettlement to the Republic of Haiti. He believed that the republic, born out of a revolution led by Toussaint L' Ouverture, provided a stark contrast to Liberia. In 1857 he published his booklet: *A Vindication of the Capacity of the Negro Race as Demonstrated by Historical Events of the Haitian Revolution.* Holly's advocacy of emigration to Haiti was more symbolic than anything else, because his efforts did not result in a large resettlement. His importance stemmed from his outright rejection of Liberia as a place where African people could develop a viable nation.

Martin Delany (1812 to 1883)

However, Martin Delany more than any other leader of the nineteenth century exemplified the rejection of Liberia. Delany absolutely refused to compromise his African nationalist thinking with the oppressive policies of Liberia. Delany, who was born a free man in 1812, first investigated South America and other African countries as possible sites for settlement. Although Delany worked with Frederick Douglass on the *North Star* from 1847 to 1849, he did not share Douglass's disdain for repatriation. Three years after leaving the abolitionist paper, Delany published his book: *The Condition, Elevation, Emigration and Destiny of the Colored People of the United States, Politically Considered.* In his book he began to develop a philosophical basis for African separatism and nationalism. He explained that African people in the United States had never been and never would be considered equal citizens. To Delany, the struggle to win equality within America was futile. In 1859 he used for the first time the phrase "Africa for the Africans," which became popular again during the Garvey era in the twentieth century.[15]

Shortly after Delany left Harvard Medical School in 1852, he moved to Canada where he spent considerable time with many of the escaped slaves. This sojourn in Canada helped him realize that Canada could never be the final home for African people. His search for a home outside both America and Canada led him to South America. In South America the soil and climate yielded prolific harvests of food and grain, which provided the necessary ingredients for his people to become a businesspeople. Delany believed that Africans needed to be able to raise enough food and grain for their own consumption and to export any surplus. Furthermore, he believed that the governments of South America had no official policies of discrimination against Africans, which would make it conducive to massive resettlement.[16]

Soon he turned his attention from South America to Africa once he realized that Africa possessed all of the commercial advantages of South America. From the beginning, he rejected Liberia as a place of possible settlement. He was convinced that the colony was never intended to be African owned and operated. He also believed that Liberia was located in an unhealthy area of Africa, the sixth degree north latitude. Whatever area of Africa Delany chose, he was convinced that the number of settlers should be kept at a minimum. He never intended to foster the emancipation of a multitude of unskilled Africans from the United States. He was interested only in bringing to Africa Christian men and women of good character. Those people who possessed skills in agriculture, the mechanical arts and business would be given preference over others.[17] Most important, Delany refused to come under the auspices of the American Colonization Society; to do so would have meant that he was willing to compromise his nationalist philosophy in order to retain "white" financing.

In 1858 he organized a trip to Nigeria that was sponsored by both the National Emigration Society and the African Civilization Society. Although Delany differed with Garnet on obtaining financial support from European-American people, he endorsed the aim of the society as explained in its constitution: to Christianize the African, bring them civilization, destroy the African slave trade and introduce commerce in cotton in order to make Africans producers instead of consumers.[18] The other sponsoring organization grew out of the National Emigration Convention that was held in Cleveland, Ohio, from August 24 to 26, 1854. Four years after the organization was founded a resolution was adopted by its executive committee to send Martin Delany to explore West Africa for possible resettlement sites.

This involvement of Delany represented a new approach to repatriation in the nineteenth century. The project that Delany undertook was intended by the policymakers of the two sponsoring organizations to be a complete break from the American Colonization Society. To demonstrate their lack of affiliation with the Colonization Society, the African Civilization Society chose to send Martin Delany and Robert Campbell to explore in Nigeria instead of Liberia. Moreover, Delany's method of acquiring land differed from that of the Colonization Society. Delany and Campbell acquired rights to land by negotiation rather than by covert force, which characterized the conquests of the Colonization Society. The entire transaction was carried out in an atmosphere of mutual respect and understanding. Campbell and Delany entered into a written treaty with the Egba people of Nigeria, which granted permission for African-Americans to settle in Nigeria (Egbaland). The Oba (king) of Egbaland did not sign the treaty, but seven chiefs who were his emissaries signed. Article I of the treaty read: "That the king and Chiefs on this part agree to grant and assign unto said commissioners, on behalf of the African race in America, the right and privilege of settling in common with the Egba people, on any part of the territory belonging to Abbeokuta not otherwise occupied."[19]

Delany and Campbell were welcomed by the people of Nigeria as returned brothers. Docemo, the king of Lagos, gave Delany a tract of land called Okai Po. The settlers who would occupy the land would differ from the Liberian settlers in that they would have some political sophistication. Moreover, they would be cognizant of the need for hard work and planning under the masterful direction of Delany and other leaders of the African Civilization Society. According to Delany there were three prerequisites for national development: land, people and production. The first two elements Africa possessed in abundance.

The latter would be developed with time. The production of cotton in Africa would allow Africans to sell it at a much lower price than the southern plantation owners. The settlers would teach Africans to grow cotton, then dump the cheap cotton on the world market and cause the collapse of the plantation system and bring about the freedom of the slaves.[20]

In Delany's book, *The Official Report of the Niger Valley Exploring Party,* he emphasized the suitability of the country for conducting commerce. There was a great need for people skilled in the mechanical arts and technical aspects of agriculture, but the unskilled people would have to compete with the indigenous Africans. He believed that cotton production in Nigeria could be expanded as soon as some cotton gins could be imported there. He urged Africans in America to acquire skills in accounting and other practical disciplines that could be used in building a nation. In all of his writing he stressed that all those who were seriously considering repatriation should be prepared for strenuous work.

Finally, and more important, Delany believed that African people would never be free until they lived as a nation. Nation-building would be a gradual process, and no individual would seek to make a quick fortune. Land in Africa would be free, but it could be used by an individual only as long as he worked it. It could never be transferred to another person. In short, Afro-Americans were to go to Africa, not with the false pride of the Liberians, but with deference to the Africans already living there:

> In going, let us have but one object-to become elevated men and women, worthy of freedom-the worthy citizens of an adopted country. What to us will be adopted-to our children will be legitimate. Go not with an anxiety of political aspirations, but go with the fixed intention of cultivating the soil, entering into the mechanical operations, keeping the shops, carrying on merchandise, trading on land and water, improving property.[21]

African-Americans, he believed, were in desperate need of a nation because of the oppressive conditions under which they lived; and these degrading conditions crippled the people, both morally and economically. Delany firmly believed that in order to determine the position of any people in a society, one had only to look at their females: "No people are ever elevated above the condition of their females; hence, the condition of the mother determines the condition of the child. To know the position of a people, it is only necessary to know the condition of their females."[22]

Nationalism was the key to the uplift of African-Americans according to Delany:

> I have determined to leave to my children the inheritance of a country, the possession of territorial domain, the indisputable national education, and the indisputable right of self-government; that they may not succeed to the servility and degradation bequeathed to us by our fathers. If we have not been born to fortunes, we should impart the seeds which shall germinate and give birth to fortunes for them.[23]

It was clear to Delany that African people were a nation and had to begin to see themselves as a separate sovereignty:

Every people should be the originators of their own designs, the projectors of their own schemes, and the creators of the events that lead to their destiny—the consummation of their desires. We have native hearts and virtues, just as other nations, which in their pristine purity are noble, potent and worthy of example. We are a nation within a nation.... But we have been, by our oppressors, despoiled of our purity, and corrupted in our native characteristics... leaving us in character, really a "broken people." Being distinguished by complection, we are still singled out—although having merged in the habits and customs of our oppressors—as a distinct nation of people.[24]

Despite his very firm ideas about African repatriation, Delany succumbed to the ideals of the American dream. After returning from Africa, Delany visited President Abraham Lincoln and asked that he create an all-"colored" army unit to fight in the Civil War. Lincoln was so impressed with the skill of Delany that he made him the first African field officer. Delany therefore continued to fight for better conditions within this country and never continued to pursue repatriation. By accepting the commission of major from President Abraham Lincoln, he substituted his nationalist dreams for an American ideal over which the nation was deeply divided. He nevertheless continued to be lauded by the American power structure. Once the war ended, he was appointed to a judgeship in Charleston, South Carolina, and was nominated for lieutenant governor in 1874, but could not get enough votes on election day.[25]

Those Africans who chose to repatriate had their greatest impact upon colonization after 1851, the year that John Russwurm died, and a year after the Fugitive Slave Act was passed. From that point on, reports of discrimination against the native Africans circulated widely, resulting in a marked change in sentiments toward the colony. The immediate impact was that more free Africans began to reject Liberia as a possible place for repatriation, as it became clear that the Liberian experiment had failed to reunite African people.

In the early years of the founding of the colony, voluntary repatriates had little, if any, control over policies of the American Colonization Society or Liberia. Some of the leaders who became involved at this early point felt that they could use Liberia for their own purposes, but finding that their goals for the colony were incompatible with those of its American supporters, returned to the United States out of frustration where they continued to struggle for the freedom of their people. The majority of the repatriates had to remain in Africa despite any dissatisfaction they may have felt.

Finally, Africans who voluntarily repatriated had very little impact upon resettlement to Liberia in the nineteenth century simply because they were financially incapable of fostering a significant independent repatriation movement, and only marginally participated in the policy efforts of the American Colonization Society. Therefore, the European-American supporters of the Society must bear much of the responsibility for the molding of Liberia into a neocolonial state.

Notes

1. John Henrik Clarke, "The Image of Africa in the Mind of Afro-American: African Identity in the Literature of Struggle," (Phelps-Stokes Seminars in African-American Relations, October 1973), page 15.
2. Sterling Stuckey, *The Ideological Origins of Black Nationalism* (Boston: Beacon Press, 1972), page 15.
3. Garnet cited in Howard Brotz, *Negro Social and Political Thought 1850 to 1920, Representative Texts* (New York: Basic Books, 1966) page 201.
4. Stuckey, page 20.

5. Stuckey, page 18.
6. Stuckey, page 19.
7. Stuckey, page 183.
8. Brotz, page 194.
9. Adelaide Hill and Martin Kilson, *Apropos of Africa: Sentiments of Negro American Leaders on Africa from the 1800's to the 1950's* (New York: Frank Cass, 1969), page 79.
10. Cary cited in Hill and Kilson, page 79.
11. Hill and Kilson, page 81.
12. Cary cited in Hill and Kilson, page 85.
13. J. Gus Liebenow, *Liberia: The Evolution of Privilege* (Ithaca, NY: Cornell University Press, 1969) page 19.
14. Liebenow, page 25.
15. Harold Cruse, *The Crisis of the Negro Intellectual* (New York: William Morrow, 1967), page 5.
16. Brotz, page 82.
17. Martin R. Delany and Robert Campbell, *Search for a Place: Black Separatism and Africa* (Ann Arbor: University of Michigan Press, 1969), page 6.
18. Brotz, page 192.
19. Delany, Martin, R., *Official Report of the Niger Valley Exploring Party*, (New York: Humanity Books, 2004), page 298.
20. John P. Davis, *The American Negro Reference Book* (Englewood Cliffs: Prentice Hall, 1966), page 675.
21. Delany cited in Brotz, page 87.
22. Delany cited in Brotz, page 92.
23. Delany and Campbell, page 104.
24. Delany cited in "Black Nationalism: The Inevitable Response," *The Black World* (Chicago: A Johnson Publication, January 1971), page 10.
25. William Loren Katz, *Eyewitness: The Negro in American History* (New York: Pitman, 1967), page 142.

Chapter Eleven

AFRICAN-AMERICAN WOMEN AND REPATRIATION

In the nineteenth century, many African-American women repatriated to Africa with their families as either daughters or wives. Some of the most notable were Jane Roberts who married the first president of Liberia; and Sarah McGill, who repatriated with her father, George McGill, and later married John Russwurm. Many of these women, particularly Sarah Russwurm, accomplished a great deal in their own right while in Africa. Sarah, for example, mastered the Kru language and performed invaluable diplomatic services between her husband's administration as governor of Cape Palmas Colony and the Kru people.

In addition, not only did African-American women of the nineteenth century have to confront, on a daily basis, the vicissitudes of blatant racism, but also the debilitating effects of sexism. Prior to the Thirteenth Amendment, the African-American woman had to endure, along with her male companion, the stigma of being labeled property, "without any rights that a white man should respect."[1] After the passage of this amendment in 1865, which ended slavery, her struggle expanded to include an end to racism, enfranchisement and women's rights. Therefore, for all of the nineteenth century, the African-American woman shared with her male companion the common struggle to end slavery/racism and promote civil rights; while with her European-American female allies she shared the common struggle to end sexism and secure the right to vote.[2]

Slavery and Subjugation of Women

Therefore, in order to understand the status of African-American women in the nineteenth century and their responses to repatriation overtures, it is critical that one understand the structural norms of American society and their impacts upon the African American woman.

These norms can be classified in the broad categories of enslavement of Africans and subjection of women. These two social forces insured the debasement of African-American women in the social order and consequently led to the creation of the twin ideologies of racism and sexism. The latter ideologies therefore became justification for the maintenance of the social order that was premised upon male supremacy.

Viewing the social order in the above manner, it was clear to the African-American woman that her struggle had to be bifurcated. Furthermore, she had to accept as allies in her struggle men and women of all colors, who appreciated this analysis of the social order and the means to fundamentally alter it. This necessity therefore created a schism in the thinking of African-American women. While some may have appreciated the promising rewards of repatriation to Africa, the vast majority accepted the prevailing abolitionist criticism of slavery, and rejected repatriation or colonization as an option for African-Americans.

Most women, like many African-American men, accepted the negative portrayals of Africa as a place of heathendom and backwardness. Furthermore, the prevailing ideology of the European-American abolitionist movement rejected colonization as an option because they viewed it as a racist scheme, endorsed at the highest levels of the American government. Some individuals, such as Thomas Jefferson, supported colonization.[3] On the other hand, William Lloyd Garrison, the most prominent European-American abolitionist in the United States, opposed colonization because he believed that the movement was premised upon racism, and therefore chastised several national leaders who viewed Africans as "a distinct and inferior caste."[4] Garrison's views were echoed by other prominent abolitionists, such as William Jay, James Birney and James Russell Lowell.[5]

In addition, the leading European-American women abolitionists and suffragists rejected colonization because of its racist underpinnings as well. Some, such as Lydia Maria Child, challenged the validity of prevailing racist notions of African inferiority and postulated that the degraded condition of Africans resulted from slavery, and that racism, in fact, evolved from slavery: "We made slavery, and slavery makes the prejudice."[6] This prejudice or racism then became the justification for keeping Africans enslaved because they were "unfit" for freedom.

The leading African-American abolitionist of the nineteenth century, Frederick Douglass, expounded on this paradoxical form of thinking:

> Ignorance and depravity, and the inability to rise from degradation to civilization and respectability, are the most usual allegations against the oppressed. The evils most fostered by slavery and oppression are precisely those which slaveholders and oppressors would transfer from their system to the inherent character of their victims. Thus the very crimes of slavery become slavery's best defence (sic). By making the enslaved a character fit only for slavery, they excuse themselves for refusing to make the slave a freeman.[7]

The abolitionists therefore united against this pervasive form of racist thinking. To accept colonization would mean giving into notions of African inferiority. The struggle for the abolitionists became not just against slavery, but also against its prodigy, racism, a scientific and institutional obstacle that had to be fought and defeated as did slavery. What Jefferson began in his philosophical writings, scientists elaborated upon in their efforts to prove the inferiority of the African. Consequently, scholars began to postulate that Africans had smaller brain sizes than Europeans, which corresponded to the Africans' perceived diminished intellectual capacity.[8]

Not only did Frederick Douglass oppose this new "science" and colonization, but so did leading European-American woman abolitionists. Most notable were Harriet Beecher Stowe, through her *Uncle Tom's Cabin or, Life Among the Lowly*, published in 1852, and Angelina and Sarah Grimke. The Grimke sisters, who many believed to be part African- American, left their slaveholding families in South Carolina and fled to the North where they could freely engage in antislavery activities. They, of course, came into contact with Lydia Maria Child and her systematic critique of sexism in American society.[9] In her work, Child drew parallels between the treatment of women around the world and slaves in the South.[10]

These women objected to colonization because they questioned the motives of its supporters. Therefore, they urged women in the South to break away from slavery, and women in the North to oppose racism.[11] In order to oppose racism and slavery, women had to examine themselves, pray, speak against and take action against slavery and racism.

Women also had to oppose sexism, particularly in the churches. Angelina eventually broke with her church because of its insistence that she, and other women, maintain subservient positions. However, Angelina summarized in clear terms the necessity for understanding the relationship between racism and sexism and the need for unified action:

> The investigation of the rights of the slave has led me to a better understanding of my own. I have found the Anti-Slavery cause to be the high school of morals in our land, the school in which human rights are more fully investigated, and better understood and taught, than in any other. Here a great fundamental principle is uplifted and illuminated, and from this central light rays innumerable stream all around. Human beings have rights, because they are moral beings; the rights of all men grow out of their moral nature; and as all men have the same moral nature, they have essentially the same rights.[12]

Sarah Grimke's writings more than her sister's challenged the sexist nature of the American social order.[13] For the Grimkes, women had the God-given right to sit in any seat of authority, be it ecclesiastical or secular. By the middle of the nineteenth century, not only had slavery and racism come under attack from progressive European-American women and men, but sexism and the subjugation of women was also being subjected to intense scrutiny. It was within that context that African-American women challenged both sexism and racism and evaluated the developing back to Africa movements.

Maria W. Stewart: Militant Abolitionist

As among men, African-American women opposed colonization for many of the same reasons as European-Americans. This opposition among African-American women, however, was quite different from that of others, including African-American men. The African-American woman had a special role to play in sustaining the African community in America. It was through her strength and determination that the slave community sustained itself.[14] To leave her community would be to abandon those individuals who depended upon her for so much of their sustenance. Unlike the European-American woman, she opposed colonization for nationalist reasons yet never abandoned her love and identification with Africa. In other words, she opposed colonization precisely because, in her view, it was controlled by racist European-Americans to serve their financial and racist interests.

No African-American woman of the nineteenth century more symbolized this opposition to colonization yet love of Africa than Maria Stewart. From the time that she first spoke out against colonization in September 1832 until her death in 1879, she demonstrated a strong identification with Africa and its people in the African diaspora. Not only did she work to free her people in the United States as other women had done, such as Sojourner Truth and Frances Harper, but she also fought tirelessly for women's rights. As such, Stewart's consciousness expanded beyond a narrow definition of African consciousness to include a feminist critique as well.

Her African consciousness, however, was deep rooted and sprang from the nationalist writings of her friend David Walker. Stewart lived in the African community of Boston, where Walker conducted his clothing business and wrote his revolutionary pamphlets. On August 10, 1826, she was married by Reverend Thomas Paul, the pastor of the African Baptist Church, which was located in the African Meeting House. Reverend Paul was a leading supporter of emigration to Haiti and of African independence from slavery.[15] Therefore, it was clear that the identification with Africa among Boston's free persons of color, was a central part of their community.

After the death of Stewart's husband, James, on December 17, 1829, and the death of David Walker a year later, Stewart assumed a more militant stand against slavery, discrimination and women's rights. Largely due to a spiritual conversion that she experienced soon thereafter, she saw the condition of Africans in America not as a mere North American concern, but as a global one for what she called "oppressed Africa."[16] Africans in America were therefore viewed as primarily Africans and continental Africa as the situs of systematic exploitation.

Like David Walker, she believed that God had chosen her to lead the struggle for African liberation. The fact that she was an African-American woman did not limit her perception of her potentialities. If God had ordained her to lead this struggle for freedom, no man could deny her rightful role. Furthermore, she gladly accepted the call, even if it could ultimately lead to her death. She wrote: "I would willingly sacrifice my life for the cause of God and my brethren. All the nations of the earth are crying out for liberty and equality. Away, away with tyranny and oppression! And shall Afric's sons be silent any longer?"[17]

In order to get her word out to the masses, Stewart began to write extensively. She met with the leading European-American abolitionists in Boston, William Lloyd Garrison and Isaac Knapp, and asked them to publish some of her essays in *The Liberator,* which they did in 1831.[18] She continued to use the paper and her own pamphlets to inform free "Blacks" of their important role in the revolutionary struggle to end slavery, subjugation of women, racism and sexism. She wrote:

> Many powerful sons and daughters of Africa will shortly arise, who will put down vice and immorality among us, and declare... that they will have their rights; and if refused, I am afraid that they will spread horror and devastation around. I believe that the oppression of injured Africa has come up before the majesty of Heaven.[19]

African-American women, she believed, would play a key role in this struggle for liberation. She exhorted them, "Ye daughters of Africa, awake! ... Arise! ... distinguish yourselves."[20] Women, for Stewart, were not inferior to men. They could become instruments for God's will. In her writings she pointed to the scriptures as evidence of women's favor in God's plans for human redemption. She wrote: "What if I am a woman; is not the God of ancient times the God of these modern days? Did he not raise up Deborah, to be a mother, and a judge in Israel? Did not Queen Esther save the lives of the Jews? And Mary Magdalene first declare the resurrection of Christ from the dead?"[21] Through these defiant writings, Stewart not only urged women to assume their rightful places, but she also assailed the hypocrisy of the American Christian churches. In this manner, she allied herself with Angelina and Sarah Grimke in their attacks against false Christian dogma.

However, Stewart believed that Africans, through "moral and religious improvements" could change the way nations perceived them. In her essay "Religion and the Pure Principles of Morality, The Sure Foundation on Which We Must Build," she wrote:

> Have mercy on the benighted sons and daughters of Africa. Grant that we may soon become so distinguished for our moral and religious improvements, that the nations of the

> earth may take knowledge of us; and grant that our cries may come up before thy throne like holy incense.
>
> Grant that every daughter of Africa may consecrate her sons to these from birth. And do thou, Lord, bestow upon them wise and understanding hearts. Clothe us with humility of soul, and give us a becoming dignity of manner: may we imitate the character of the meek and lowly Jesus; and do thou grant that Ethiopia may soon stretch forth her hands unto thee.[22]

Many ideas in her essay appear to be at odds with her earlier writings that urged militant resistance. This ambivalence of perspective explains in large part her inability to endorse repatriation movements in the nineteenth century. While she recognized the universal humanity of African people, she failed to understand that repatriation could give Africans precisely what she hoped Christian conversion would bring, that is, political autonomy and control over one's destiny. Unable to envision a utopian community for Africans, Maria Stewart compromised her views on African consciousness by adopting an overly religious solution to a captive people's problems.

In her writings she eloquently described the outrageous degradation of African people, and called for bold and decisive action to ameliorate these problems. She urged African-American women to "Let every female heart become united, and let us raise a fund ourselves; and at the end of one year and a half, we might be able to lay the corner stone for the building of a high school."[23] This type of advocacy was not new to Boston. Africans in Boston had already built a school. John Brown Russwurm had already served as principal at the Primus Hall School before entering Bowdoin College in 1824 to pursue his college degree. Stewart needed to go further in developing a paradigm for African-American people in Boston.

Near the end of her stay in Boston in 1833, Stewart had succumbed completely to an abolitionist, integrationist philosophy. At the heart of this system of thought was the notion that free "blacks" should work to end slavery and to break down discriminatory barriers to advancement in America. It is ironic that she could understand the depths of African oppression in America, yet resign herself to mere integration, rather than separation. Maria Stewart, more than any writer of the nineteenth century, clearly described the crimes of America and the denigration of a people:

> The blood of her murdered ones cries to heaven for vengence against thee. Thou art almost become drunken with the blood of her slain; thou hast enriched thyself through her toils and labors; and now thou refuseth to make even a small return. And thou hast caused the daughters of Africa to commit whoredoms and fornications; but upon thee be their curse.[24]

Instead of urging Africans either to leave and claim their rightful places in Africa or strike out violently against this oppression, she told them to "sheath your swords, and calm your angry passions."[25] She saw Africa as a "strange land"; and a place that under no circumstances would she desire to go to: "They would drive us to a strange land. But before I go, the bayonet shall pierce me through. African rights and liberty is a subject that ought to fire the breast of every free man of color in these United States, and excite in his bosom a lively, deep, decided and heartfelt interest."[26]

Because she could not see beyond these pressing needs in America, she failed to understand and support repatriation to Africa and to fully understand African-American nationalism. Before she died in December 1879, she had never experienced national freedom or independence in the manner that other repatriates had experienced in Liberia, Haiti and Sierra Leone. Instead, the most that she accomplished in her later years was to work as matron of the Freedman's Hospital and Asylum in Washington, D.C. and to seek a service pension through a widow assistance program.[27]

Sojourner Truth and the Women's Movement

As among the men, African-American women who came from free families were more likely to favor repatriation than those born into slavery. It was as if those who obtained their freedom through escape found it more difficult to break from America. If they did not become extremely religious, they indulged themselves in the woman's movement. A case in point was Sojourner Truth who, upon obtaining her freedom from slavery in New York State in 1827, became more involved with the woman's movement than with the antislavery movement. As with many others, religion played a profound role in her ideological development. In 1843 she changed her name from Isabella Van Wagener to Sojourner Truth after undergoing a religious conversion. She continued her work with the women's movement and by 1851 had become a regular speaker at women's rights conventions. In Akron, Ohio, she gave her famous "Ain't I a Woman" speech and forcefully proclaimed to a doubting male audience the centrality of women in both the spiritual and temporal worlds:

> Then that little man in black there, he says women can't have as much rights as men, 'cause Christ wasn't a woman! Where did your Christ come from? Where did your Christ come from? From God and a woman! Man had nothing to do with Him. If the first woman God ever made was strong enough to turn the world upside down all alone, these women together ought to be able to turn it back, and get it right side up again! And now they asking to do it, the men better let them. Obliged to you for hearing me, and now old Sojourner ain't got nothing more to say.[28]

Nancy Prince as Traveler to Europe and Jamaica

Nancy Prince was a person who never gave into Christianity and limited her sights to the abolitionist struggle. Although Nancy never experienced slavery, being born a free person in Newburyport, Massachusetts, she did learn from her grandfather and stepfather about its hardships. Her grandfather, Tobias Wornton, was stolen from Africa and fought in the Revolutionary War at Bunker Hill. Her mother was born in Gloucester, Massachusetts, and her father, Thomas Gardner, was born in Nantucket, Massachusetts. Her mother's mother was Native American and her father was of African descent. Early on, she recognized the hypocrisy in American Christianity and therefore rejected it. She wrote in her diary of her experience working in the home of a Christian family: "I often looked at my employers, and thought to myself, is this your religion? I did not wonder that the girl who had lived there previous to myself, went home to die. They had family prayers, morning and evening. Oh! Yes, they were sanctimonious."[29]

Not only did this Christian falsehood turn her from America, but more important it helped her critically analyze the causes for the systematic debasement of African people, that is economic exploitation on the plantations and economic exclusion in the workplaces of the North. For example, she became outraged that her sister, Silvia, had been drawn into prostitution. In 1816 Nancy was able to rescue Silvia from the clutches of a brothel in Boston. On February 15, 1824, she married and on April 14 abruptly left America for Russia. Mr. Prince was an African-American, born in Marlborough, Massachusetts, who had been taken by Captain Theodore Stanwood to Russia, where he worked for Princess Purtossof.[30] During the stay of the Princes in Russia they received respect as human beings that they could never expect in America. In fact they were received by the Emperor Alexander and Empress Elizabeth as house guests. Nancy was struck by the lack of racism in Russia: "It was customary in those days, when any one married, belonging to the court, to present them with gifts, according to their standard; there was no prejudice against color; there were there all casts, and the people of all nations, each in their place."[31]

After leaving Russia in 1833 because of illness, she resettled in Boston where she attempted to establish an asylum for poor children. Many members of her family had died (mother, sister) including Reverend Thomas Paul. Her husband soon died as well. Eventually the burden of American racism caused her to look beyond America again for a new nation to live in. This time she looked to the Caribbean and the new nation of Jamaica. While there, Nancy freely moved around, spoke to and observed the people. In Kingston, she was very impressed to see a large outdoor market attended by "colored women." Contrary to the stereotypes of the people, she found: "they are not the stupid set of beings they have been called; here surely we see industry; they are enterprising and quick in their perceptions, determined to possess themselves, and to possess property besides, and quite able to take care of themselves."[32]

On December 6, 1840, she arrived at St. Ann's Bay, ostensibly to continue teaching the children who had recently received their independence from the British. In Jamaica she was able to observe the many negative effects of slavery upon African people. It was clear to her that in order to counter these debilitating effects, the Jamaican people needed to have access to an education. She wrote:

> Most of the people of Jamaica are emancipated slaves, many of them are old, worn out and degraded. Those who are able

> to work, have yet many obstacles to contend with, and very little to encourage them; every advantage is taken of their ignorance; the same spirit of cruelty is opposed to them that held them for centuries in bondage; even religious teaching is bartered for the hard earnings, while they are allowed but thirty cents a day, and are told if they will not work that they shall not work at all.[33]

Nancy Prince did not just observe the condition of African people in Jamaica, she also developed a plan that she hoped would change these conditions. On July 20, 1841, she sailed for Philadelphia, where she solicited funds and supplies for the destitute girls she discovered in Jamaica. She continued her solicitation efforts in New York City and Boston. On April 15, 1842, she set sail for Jamaica again with materials for her Free Labor School.[34] However, because of grave public instability, she was unable to carry forward her plan of running a school there, and on August 1, 1842, left the island. In order to continue her educational efforts in the island, she raised funds in the United States for schools. Although she returned to the United States to live, she was an early example of a Pan-African spirit that reached beyond national borders to aid descendants of Africa.

Mary Ann Shadd Cary and Canadian Emigration

Another woman who developed a strong emigrationist fervor was Mary Ann Shadd Cary. She never considered Africa as an appropriate place for Africans to return, but she did recognize the absolute necessity for Africans to leave America for Canada. Her opposition to colonization can be traced to the early influence of her father, Abraham D. Shadd, a successful businessman in Wilmington, Delaware.[35] From her father, Mary developed a strong sense of self and respect for hard work and independence. However, this grounding did not cause her to look to Africa. This failure to appreciate African nationalism was most likely rooted in her paternal upbringing. Mary was born on October 9, 1823, and from that date forward received exposure to the anticolonization views of her father. Abraham became the leading opponent of the American Colonization Society and firmly believed that free "blacks" should use their resources to help their people escape from slavery. "Free blacks" constituted a potential threat to slavery as their population in the South amounted to 10 percent of the general population by 1810.[36] Once they arrived in the North, he believed free persons should help the fugitives achieve a self-supporting existence.

Abraham Shadd was so opposed to the colonization movement that he became the spokesman for African abolitionists in Delaware. In that capacity he and his delegation took a strong position against the American Colonization Society at the National Convention for the Improvement of Free People of Color that was held in Philadelphia in 1830, 1831 and 1832.[37] By 1833, Abraham clearly established his position as a leader of the antislavery efforts by being elected to the board of managers for Garrison's American Anti-Slavery Society.[38] A year earlier when Garrison published his *Thoughts on African Colonization,* he included an essay written by Shadd, who, in turn, became a subscription agent for Garrison's *Liberator.*

While Mary accepted her father's aversion to African colonization, she was able to embrace the concept of African separation. Separation for her, however, did not mean that Africans would have no social contact with European-Americans. Africans, in her view, should leave the United States for Canada, but once there, should not separate themselves from Canadians. Again, this perspective on "race" relations can be traced to her early experiences in the United States. When it was clear to her father that she could not get an education in Wilmington, he moved his family in 1833 to West Chester, Pennsylvania, and enrolled Mary in a school there where she went to school with Quakers and therefore became used to being in contact with European-Americans. Moreover, she developed a strong commitment to academic excellence. Upon completing her education, she returned to West Chester and then to New York City where she attempted to instill these values into her students. She taught the free African children that they should "avoid any appearance of frivolity and should act for themselves without 'waiting for the whites of the country.'"[39]

These strong views on African uplift were expressed in a pamphlet that she published in 1849, *Hints to the Colored People of the North.* She argued that free Africans should reject materialism and use what meager resources they could accumulate to help the antislavery cause. By this time Mary Shadd had established her place as a respectable and forceful abolitionist, but had not given much consideration to repatriation schemes.

However, this steadfast position underwent a fundamental change in 1850. This was the year that U.S. public policy authorized the hunting of so-called fugitives anywhere in the country. The Fugitive Slave Act made free Africans vulnerable to mistaken or intentional kidnapping by federal officials. Individuals who opposed slavery on moral grounds, or any other grounds, could be conscripted by marshals to aid in capturing runaways. The passage of this legislation constituted a critical turning point for Mary Shadd. She saw her hard work being placed in jeopardy by the act and therefore decided that the best response for her was to emigrate to Canada, where she could continue to teach free Africans. In Canada she would find a large community of people that got even larger after the passage of the Act. In 1850 it was reported that 40 came from Boston; 112 from Rochester; 100 from Buffalo and 200 from Pittsburgh.[40]

Africans had been in Canada as early as 1628, and the gradual abolition of slavery began in 1793 as a result of legislative action. Although Canada had abolished slavery on January 1, 1834, as a result of the Imperial Emancipation Act of 1833, the arriving Africans encountered discrimination in all walks of life. They did, however, find other "coloreds" in Canada West, many of whom (1,000 to 2,000) emigrated in 1830 from Cincinnati.[41] Some arrivals, such as Henry Bibb, a runaway from Kentucky, resisted social integration with Canadians, while Mary Shadd favored integration. As soon as she and her brother Isaac arrived in Toronto in 1851, she joined other emigrants to discuss the Fugitive Slave Act and their stay in Canada. Some scholars estimate that 10,000 Africans resided in Canada by 1850, and that the number increased to 40,000 by 1860.[42] Shadd quickly became appalled at the pervasive fear that many of the Africans in Canada expressed toward integration. Many felt that the Canadians would reject and segregate them, just as the Americans had done. They therefore argued that Africans should live and socialize among each other and avoid contact with Canadians.

Again, Mary Shadd turned to the pen to express her opposition to this view. In a letter to Isaac she expressed her feeling of peace and relief on being in Canada: "I have been here more than a week, and like Canada. Do not feel prejudice and ... if you were to come here ... and buy lands as fast as you made any money, you would do well."[43]

In 1852 she published her second pamphlet, *A Plea for Emigration, or Notes of Canada West, in its Moral, Social, and Political Aspect, with Suggestions Respecting Mexico, W. Indies and Vancouver's Island, for the Information of Colored Emigrants.* She maintained her views even though Martin Delany, one of the leading African nationalists of the time, came to Canada to press an African separatist agenda and to give support to its most vocal advocate in Canada, Henry Bibb. The arrival of Delany in Canada to support Bibb would inevitably lead to ideological conflict with Shadd and her views. Coincidentally, in the same year that Shadd published her pamphlet, Delany published his *The Condition, Elevation, Emigration and Destiny of the Colored People of the United States, Politically Considered.* In his book Delany boldly stated that the destiny of Africans in America had to be tied to African repatriation. A year before the Fugitive Slave Act, Bibb published his *Narrative of the Life and Adventures of Henry Bibb, an American Slave.*

Mary Shadd's opposition to African separation, however, appeared to be contradictory in part. On one hand, she supported the separation from the United States to Canada, Mexico, the West Indies and Vancouver Island, yet she rejected the same separation to Africa. Once in Canada she opposed any further separation, but rather argued for efforts to amalgamate the African into Canadian life. These views were widely disseminated through newspapers in America and Canada. Her views therefore were considered and debated among the leading African thinkers of the period.

In Canada, however, her leading nemesis was Henry Bibb, who had developed the strongest following, particularly in Chatham, Ontario where he and his wife Mary resided. Bibb had proven himself to be an industrious and committed leader in the African community. He published the bimonthly *Voice of the Fugitive,* founded a school, built a Methodist church and created societies for temperance, education and abolitionism.[44] He was clearly a man to be reckoned with. Mary was not afraid, however, to challenge his ideas and his position in the small African community. She believed that his views on "black" separatism were wrong. As a direct affront to his views, when she opened up a private school for children in Windsor, Ontario she indicated that it would be open to all students regardless of color.[45] Even though Africans could attend public schools in Canada, many did not desire to attend integrated ones. Consistent with the community's aversion to integration, they turned away from Shadd's private school, thus insuring its closing eight weeks after it opened.

The competing ideals of integration versus separatism continued to clash among Bibb and Shadd. Through his newspaper, Bibb was able to disseminate his ideas much further than Shadd. Realizing that if she desired to get her point of view across on equal terms, she had to have a similar vehicle for dissemination of information, she founded her own newspaper. In 1853, with the assistance of fugitive slave Samuel Ringgold Ward, she published the first issue of *Provincial Freeman.* Ward was a good choice to assist her in the new paper because he was a respected member of the community and later a writer: he published his *Autobiography of a Fugitive Slave* in 1855.

She quickly discovered, however, that due to Bibb and his popularity, it was hard to sustain her publication financially. Consequently, she joined the lecture circuit in the United States where her views were exposed to a broader audience. Bibb continued to attack her ideas and even her person when he called her a "deluded sister."[46] When she returned to Canada full time from her lectures in March 1854, she moved her offices to Toronto. She believed that because of a larger African middle class in Toronto she would be able to get more support for her paper.

However, she soon had to confront trouble. Later in that year Bibb died and her coeditor Ward resigned, leaving her as the sole editor. Blatant sexism now became an obstacle because many men felt that it was out of character for a woman to be an editor of a paper. Unwilling to fight this sexist bias, Shadd asked Rev. William P. Newman to become a nominal editor.[47] It was ironic that she was willing to cave in to the forces of sexism, when she adamantly held her position against separatism.

Perhaps she believed that sexism was too entrenched, but that she could make some progress in her struggle for "racial" equality. Therefore, she boldly continued to speak out against slavery and in 1855 attended the National Negro Convention in Philadelphia as the first African woman to address the group as a corresponding member. After the convention, she returned to Canada and moved her paper back to Chatham. After her speech in Philadelphia, Frederick Douglass stated that Shadd made "one of the most convincing and telling speeches in favor of Canadian emigration I ever heard."[48] And finally in 1856, Martin Delany concluded that "Canada [was) an approved refuge for the black man who desired to flee oppression in the United States."[49]

Even though the newspaper continued to fall upon hard times, she remained active in progressive politics. When John Brown, the fiery revolutionary, came to Chatham on April 29, 1858, to discuss his plans for a new government in the United States, he met at the home of her newspaper, with her husband, Thomas F. Cary, and her brother Isaac. One of her friends, Osborne Perry Anderson became a confidant to Brown and joined him in the courageous raid on Harpers Ferry. Anderson survived the raid and discussed his participation in the revolutionary assault in his book *A Voice from Harper's Ferry,* which was edited by Shadd. After Brown's death, she eulogized him in the New York *Weekly Anglo-African,* and William Wells Brown wrote of her commitment to revolutionary struggle: "Had she been a man, she would probably have been with John Brown at Harper's Ferry."[50]

Furthermore, after the raid on Harpers Ferry, Shadd became more sympathetic to the concept of African repatriation. No doubt she had become increasingly influenced by Martin Delany, whose presence in Canada had influenced John Brown as well as several individuals close to her. Issac Shadd; Amelia Shadd Williamson, her sister, and friend Osborne Perry Anderson became converts to African repatriation. Mary Ann even went so far as to write the American Missionary Association in February 1861, to inquire about a teaching position in Africa.[51] Although she never went to Africa, she did publicize in her paper Delany's ideas and the formation of the American Civilization Society of Canada.

Delany's ideas on repatriation and the support he received from Shadd's close friends and family brought her closer to the heart of African-American thinking on the issue. Delany and Robert Campbell, from Jamaica, did in fact travel to Nigeria and negotiated a "treaty" with the African leaders.[52] Although Delany and Campbell ran into legal difficulties over the interpretation to be given to the "treaty," an understanding was arrived at concerning African American repatriation. In 1861 Robert Campbell wrote to friends in America: "My home shall be Africa, though I be the only person from America; and I am satisfied that any man knowing the circumstances, who is not a fool, and is solicitous for his own welfare, having too a heart to labor for the good of his race, would come to the same conclusion."[53] Campbell sailed with his family for Lagos in February 1862 and never returned to the United States or Jamaica. On January 19, 1884, he died in Lagos after giving great service to the motherland.

Shadd was not as sympathetic to the developing Haitian efforts. Ironically, much of her opposition was to the leadership of the envoy in the Americas, James Redpath, a European-American, who had been hired by the Haitian government to recruit emigrants. She was particularly upset that Redpath bought the *Weekly Anglo-African* on behalf of the Haitian government and renamed it *Pine and Palm.*[54]

The developing events below the Canadian border caused Shadd to focus her attention upon the African struggle for freedom in the United States. After the Civil War broke out, she decided to aid the North in recruiting "colored" soldiers. She therefore served as a recruiting army officer for the states of Michigan and Indiana.[55]

After the war was over, she worked as a teacher in Washington, D.C., and attended Howard Law School as the first African-American woman to be admitted to an American law school. In 1878 she spoke at the National Woman's Suffrage Association convention. She eventually died in 1893.

Amanda Berry Smith as Missionary

Amanda Berry Smith stands out as an African-American woman who had impact upon Liberia in the nineteenth century. Unlike Shadd, she endorsed the concept of repatriation early in her career. She was born in Long Green, Maryland, on January 23, 1837, to slave parents, Samuel and Mariam Berry.[56] Her father bought himself out of slavery and once his mistress died, his wife and children were set free.

This steadfast determination to be free greatly influenced Amanda. She was fortunate to have parents who were not only free, but also literate and Quakers. More important, she came into contact with slaves escaping from the South through the Underground Railroad. Through this contact with runaways and her parents' involvement with helping to marshal these individuals to freedom, Amanda developed deep affection for African people.

In addition, her religious involvement helped her look beyond America for personal enrichment and identity. In 1860 she experienced a religious conversion and by 1879 had been invited by Rev. W.B. Osborne to accompany him to India.[57] The trip to India was a turning point for her. For the first time she met people of a different culture and language and began to see herself within a global context. At various meetings in India she met individuals from China, Japan and South America.[58]

Her consciousness soon turned to Africa. She remembered as a child that her parents spoke of Africa. They taught her that Africa was their home and tried to instill in young Amanda certain memories that they had retained of the continent. She remembered that when she was child, her parents had pictures of Africa *The Brother Jonathan Almanac*, with Africans dressed in colorful clothing and animals of all sizes standing tall in their native habitat.[59]

Later in her life Amanda decided that she had to see Africa for herself. On May 23, 1887, she moved to Old Calabar in West Africa to work as a missionary. She never developed an African repatriation ideology and ultimately opposed the work of the American Colonization Society. Particularly, after the end of slavery, she, like many who had looked upon repatriation as a viable option for Africans, endorsed integration. Africa was quite a shock for her. Even though she had been exposed to memories of the culture through her parents, she was not prepared for the profound differences. First, her religious views prevented her from understanding and accepting African traditional religion. She had no way of preparing herself for such a different encounter with religion. Her views of African culture were so naive that she referred to the traditions of the people as "devil worshipping."[60] As a woman, she was offended by the traditional marriage ceremonies that she observed, whereby young girls were given in marriage to much older men.

Her experiences as a missionary changed her view of Africa forever. Her thoughts on this issue were direct and clear:

> But from the standpoint I look at it, I would move its disbandment forthwith, and let the white people who want the Negro emigrate to Africa so as to make more room for the great flood of foreigners who come to our shores, know that there is a place in the United States for the Negro. They are

> real American citizens, and at home. They have fought and bled and died, like men, to make this country what it is. And if they have got to suffer and die, and be lynched, and tortured, and burned at the stake, I say they are at home.[61]

Conclusions

African-American women in the nineteenth century held similar views toward Africa as their men. They struggled against the odds of both sexism and racism and many overcame these odds to stand up for their beliefs in African separation, whether to Canada or to Africa. Many made the voyage to Africa with their husbands, children, friends and loved ones. As mothers and daughters, they sustained their families and helped them adjust to a different and challenging environment. Through their writings and struggles they changed America by forcing it to reexamine the simultaneous institutional debasement of women and Africans. Like men, they were drawn into the ranks of the Christian believers, but to a person, they challenged the prevailing Christian beliefs as being false and hypocritical.

Notes

1. This pronouncement was made by the U.S. Supreme Court in its decision on African freedom, *Dred Scott v. Sandford,* 60 U.S. (19 How.) 393 (1857).
2. Neither African-American nor European-American women secured the right to vote in the nineteenth century. While the Fifteenth Amendment insured African-American men the right in 1870, the Nineteenth Amendment secured the same rights for women in 1920.
3. Thomas Jefferson, *Notes on the State of Virginia* (New York: Palgrave, 2002), pages 135 to 136.
4. William Lloyd Garrison, *Thoughts on African Colonization* (New York: Arno Press and The New York Times, 1968) (originally published, 1832), page 21.
5. See William Jay, *Inquiry into the Character and Tendency of the American Colonization, and American Antislavery Societies* (originally published, 1835), reprinted in William Jay, *Miscellaneous Writings on Slavery* (New York: Negro Universities Press, 1968), at pages 7-206; James G. Birney, *Letter on Colonization Addressed to the Rev. Thornton J. Mills, Corresponding Secretary of the Kentucky Colonization Society* (New York, 1834); James

Russell Lowell, "The Prejudice of Color," in *The Anti-Slavery Papers of James Russell Lowell* (Boston: Houghton Mifflin, 1902), Vol. I, page 19.

6. L. Maria Child, *An Appeal in Favor of Americans Called Africans* (New York: Arno Press and the New York Times, 1968) (originally published, 1833), page 134.
7. "The Claims of the Negro Ethnologically Considered," in Philip S. Foner, ed., *The Life and Writings of Frederick Douglass,* Vol. 2 (New York: International Publishers, 1975), page 295.
8. Child, page 238.
9. L. Maria Child, *The History of the Condition of Women, in Various Ages and Nations* (Boston: Otis, Broaders and Co., 1838).
10. William Stanton, *The Leopard's Spots: Scientific Attitudes Toward Race in America 1815 to 1859* (Chicago: University of Chicago Press, 1960).
11. Angelina Grimke, *Appeal to the Women of the Nominally Free States* (New York: William S. Dorr, 1837), page 43; Angelina Grimke, *Appeal to the Christian Women of the South,* reprinted in Larry Ceplair, *The Public Years of Sarah and Angelina Grimke: Selected Writings 1835 to 1839* (New York: Columbia University Press, 1989), pages 36-79.
12. Angelina E. Grimke, *Letters to Catherine E. Beecher* in Ceplair, page 194.
13. Sarah M. Grimke, *Letters on the Equality of the Sexes and the Condition of Women,* reprinted in Ceplair, pages 204-272.
14. Angela Davis, "Reflections on the Black Woman's Role in the Community of Slaves," in Floyd W. Hayes, III, ed., *A Turbulent Voyage, 2nd ed.* (San Diego: Collegiate Press, 1997), page 109.
15. Reverend Paul's church was one of the first African-American churches in the United States and still stands in the Beacon Hill section of Boston on Joy Street. These black Baptists organized their church in 1809. See Ruth Bogin and Bert James Loewenburg, eds., *Black Women in Nineteenth Century American Life: Their Words, Their Thoughts, Their Feelings* (University Park: The Pennsylvania State University Press, 1976), page 206.
16. Marilyn Richardson, ed., *Maria W. Stewart: America's First Black Woman Political Writer* (Bloomington: Indiana University Press, 1987), page 8.
17. Richardson, page 9.
18. Richardson, page 12.
19. Richardson, page 18.
20. Richardson, page 20.
21. Richardson, page 22.

22. Richardson, page 34.
23. Richardson, page 34.
24. Richardson, page 39.
25. Richardson, page 40.
26. Richardson, page 64.
27. Richardson, page 116.
28. Amy Anderson, *Fifty Black Women Who Changed America* (Secaucus, NJ: Carol Publishing Group, 1999), page 16._
29. Bogin and Loewenburg, page 202; Kathryn M. Silva, "Black Women and Repatriation, Their Thoughts, Ideas, and Actions in the Nineteenth Century" (Unpublished, Boston, 1999), page 5.
30. Bogin and Loewenburg, page 207. Nancy's husband is referred to only as "Mr. Prince."
31. Bogin and Loewenburg, page 209.
32. Bogin and Loewenburg, page 213.
33. Bogin and Loewenburg, page 214.
34. Bogin and Loewenburg, page 216.
35. Hallie Q. Brown, ed., *Homespun Heroines and Other Woman of Distinction* (Freeport, ME: Books for Libraries Press, 1970), page 92.
36. Jane Rhodes, *Mary Ann Shadd Cary: The Black Press and Protest in the Nineteenth Century* (Bloomington: Indiana University Press, 1998), page 5. The only photograph of Shadd can be found at the National Archives of Canada, C29977.
37. Jason H. Silverman, "Mary Ann Shadd and the Search for Equality," in Leon Litwack and August Meier, eds., *Black Leaders of the Nineteenth Century* (Urbana: University of Illinois Press, 1988), page 87.
38. Rhodes, page 14.
39. Floyd J. Miller, *The Search for a Black Nationality: Black Emigration and Colonization, 1787to 1863* (Urbana: University of Illinois Press, 1975), page 105.
40. Rhodes, pages 28 to 29.

41 Rhodes, page 30.

42. Rhodes, page 31.
43. Rhodes, page 34.
44. Silverman, page 90.
45. Silverman, page 90.
46. Silverman, page 92.
47. Silverman, page 94.

48. Silverman, page 94.
49. Miller, page 158.
50. Rhodes, page 131.
51. Rhodes, page 138.
52. Robert Campbell, *A Pilgrimage to My Homeland: An Account of a Journey Among the Egbas and Yorubas of Central Africa in 1859-60* (New York: T. Hamilton, 1861), page 10.
53. R.J.M. Blackett, *Beating Against the Barriers: Biographical Essays in Nineteenth-Century Afro-American History* (Baton Rouge: Louiisiana State University Press, 1986), page 170.
54. Rhodes, page 139.
55. Brown, page 95; Silverman, page 97.
56. Bogin and Loewenburg, page 143.
57. Brown, page 129.
58. Silva, page 12.
59. Bogin and Loewenburg, pages 159 to 160.
60. Bogin and Loewenburg, page 166.
61. Smith cited in Bogin and Loewenburg, page 173.

Chapter Twelve

BISHOP HENRY MCNEAL TURNER AND AFRICAN-AMERICAN INSTITUTIONAL SUPPORT FOR REPATRIATION

> *The Negro race has as much chance in the U.S. ... of being a man ... as a frog has in a snake den ... Emigrate and gradually return to the land of our ancestors ... The Negro was brought here in the providence of God to learn obedience, to work, to sing, to pray, to preach, acquire education, deal with mathematical abstractions and imbibe the principles of civilization as a whole, and then to return to Africa, the land of his fathers, and bring her his millions.* —Bishop Turner

While the American Colonization Society had almost shut down its operations in most regions of the country by the end of the nineteenth century, African-American repatriation efforts had become institutionalized in "black" America. These efforts that had sprung from individual initiatives in the beginning of the century, had, by the 1880s become an essential part of the collective African-American political consciousness.

The emancipation of Africans from slavery, in the second half of the century, meant that African-Americans could dream of a much broader involvement in America and the world. Slavery meant that Africans were forced to accept a less-than-complete view of the world and to limit participation in it. These limitations were enforced by legal restrictions, such as pass laws, which prohibited the free movement of slaves from plantation to plantation without the express written permission of their owners. The end of slavery meant that Africans could dream of a more complete integration into America.

This new freedom, of course, was not unfettered and without racist opposition. After the Civil War, the onslaught against African progress was pervasive, ranging from the mob violence of the Ku Klux Klan to institutional complicity by the American courts. Even though the postwar amendments to the U.S. Constitution and the Civil Rights Acts were designed to insure equality in citizenship, the courts succumbed to racist popular opinion and therefore failed to protect this fragile citizenship.

The Role of African Churches and Other Black Organizations

Consequently, the African-American church, in particular the African Methodist Episcopal Church (AME), began to play an even larger role in helping Africans to cope with these difficulties. In the beginning of the century, the AME Church, through its founding bishops Richard Allen and Daniel Coker, brought the debate over the nature of African-American citizenship center stage.

Both of the men had an undying love for their people, but they differed sharply on the path that African-Americans should take to achieve freedom. Richard Allen, who was born into slavery in Philadelphia on February 14, 1760, opposed repatriation throughout his life, while Daniel Coker, a free man from Baltimore, endorsed repatriation early and settled in Liberia.

Allen, after purchasing his freedom, began to organize African-Americans for the purpose of establishing a separate place of worship. He had been allowed to preach to the African-American parishioners at St. George's Church, who were segregated from the general congregation. Finding this separation demeaning and contrary to the scriptures, Allen called for a separate church, but only three members of St. George would accept his plea: Doras Giddings, William White and Absalom Jones. In 1787, Jones and Allen organized a religious society the Free African Society.[1] The organization would have both benevolent and religious purposes. Allen could not, however, convince the group to form a separate church and it was not until August 12, 1794, that the African Church of Philadelphia was formed under the Protestant Episcopal Church of America.[2] Absalom Jones, despite his friendship with Allen, became pastor of the new Episcopal congregation. Allen continued to work with other Methodists to establish a separate congregation. On April 9, 1799, Allen was ordained as a deacon because African-Americans were not allowed to be pastors by the Methodist General Conference. On May 5, 1794, he and others met to plan their own church and by July 1794, Bethel African Church was dedicated.

Although the Africans had their own church, they could not elect their own pastor because no African-American pastor had been ordained in the Methodist church conference.

These discriminatory policies led to mounting conflicts between African-American parishioners and the Methodist church leadership over who owned church property and who could set church policies. This controversy touched Bethel African Church as well as its parishioners in Baltimore under the leadership of Daniel Coker. As a result of this conflict, in April 1816, African-American delegates met and declared that they should unite under one name: African Methodist Church. At the convention both Allen and Coker were elected bishops, but on April 16, 1816, Allen was elected sole bishop of the new church.

The membership of the AME Church expanded rapidly after its formation. This expansion, under Bishop Allen, included foreign missions but did not include plans to endorse repatriation. By 1818, membership in the church consisted of 6,784 and by 1826 had increased to 7,937.[3] This surge in membership included foreign missions but did not include African missions. By 1827, St. Peter's AME Church had been established in Haiti and missions had been established in Canada as well.

Early Conflict over Repatriation

Bishop Allen's opposition to repatriation was long-standing. After the American Colonization Society was founded in 1817, he published his views on the colonization society in the November 2, 1827, issue of *Freedom's Journal.* For him, American patriotism was crucial because Africans were in fact Americans and should demonstrate total allegiance to America: "This land which we have watered with our tears and our blood, is now our mother country and we are well satisfied to stay where wisdom abounds, and the gospel is free."[4] In 1830, Allen and Hezekiah Grice expressed their opposition to repatriation even further by calling for a national convention to be held at Bethel Church from September 20 to 24. The convention was convened by their new organization, American Society for Free Persons of Color, which promoted emigration to Canada and improvement of conditions in the United States.

While the Negro convention movement, with the encouragement of Bishop Allen and his church, took a posture against repatriation, the other founding bishop, Daniel Coker, had already repatriated and lauded its virtues in his book *Journal of Daniel Coker*. On February 6, 1820, Daniel Coker set sail for Sherbro, West Africa, aboard the ship *Elizabeth*. He left America with about ninety "persons of colour," Rev. Nathaniel Peck, an African-American minister, and Rev. Samuel Bacon, agent for Maryland Auxiliary Colonization Society. On March 9 he anchored at Free Town, Sierra Leone. He felt exuberance at planting his feet upon African soil, and was pained to learn that the slave trade continued. He wrote: "There are several captured slave ships in port, brought in the other day, and the slaves liberated. The sight of them pained my heart, and made me glad."[5]

His initial impression of Africa was positive as he wrote: "Free Town is a place of considerable trade, and is improving. Thank the Lord I have seen Africa."[6] As he walked through the markets he saw African men and women busy at work, buying and selling produce of every kind. In addition, when he visited the seats of government, particularly the courts, he found African men and women engaged in their duties:

> I must say I was pleased when I viewed the court; the grand jury was composed of coloured men. My mind was carried back to America. The reasoning of Mr. Harper, at Baltimore, came to my mind; there is much truth in his argument. Surely, Ethiopia is stretching out her hands unto God.[7]

Although Africans were attempting to build a nation in Africa, he found that the tentacles of slavery and its oppressive methods attempting to subvert this new nationalism. On February 16, Coker wrote of the efforts taken by the British government to stop the illegal slave trade. On that day he personally observed a Spanish schooner with eighty slaves aboard being brought into shore by the British authorities. He was told by two English missionaries that another Spanish ship with 400 slaves aboard had been captured by the British as well, but before the slaves could be released, their food was tainted with poison, killing all but six of the Africans.[8]

In a letter to Jeremiah Watts of Baltimore, dated April 3, 1820, Reverend Coker expressed his conviction that Africa could become a great nation: "I should rejoice to see you in this land; it is a good land; it is a rich land, and I do believe it will be a great nation, and a powerful and worthy nation: but those who break the way will suffer much."[9] To the "industrious...and christian people," he implored them to come to Africa:

> If you ask my opinion as to coming out; I say, let all that can, sell out and come; come, and bring ventures, to trade, &c. and you may do much better than you can possibly do in America, and not work half so hard. I wish that thousands were here, and had goods to trade with. Bring about two hogsheads of good leaf tobacco, cheap calico, and cheap handkerchiefs, pins, knives and forks, pocket knives, &c., with these you may buy land, hire hands, or buy provisions. I say, come—The land is good.[10]

Not only was Rev. Coker satisfied with his decision to repatriate, but so was Rev. Peck, who had come over on the same ship with Rev. Coker. In a letter to his mother, dated March 27, 1820, Rev. Peck wrote:

> I am now treading the soil of my mother country—thanks be to God! and find that it is good-every thing that heart can wish. The natives receive us with joy and gladness. The climate is very mild and good...Land, the king says, we must and shall have-every thing is encouraging-We have no reason to fear, for Africa is our home.[11]

Bishop Henry Turner Endorses Repatriation

This African-American Christian influence in Africa continued until the end of the century. Between the end of the Civil War and World War I, Bishop Henry Turner became the most important advocate for repatriation. In 1878 he worked with Martin Delany to found The Liberian Exodus Company which bought a ship and transported 200 Africans to Liberia.[12] This decision by Delany ran counter to his views on Liberia as a suitable place for repatriation, but Bishop Turner was able to convince him of its feasibility.

After the death of Martin Delany, many short-lived schemes to repatriate developed. These organizations varied in their purposes. Some had hoped to establish viable commercial links between Africa and Europe, while others dreamed of building an African home for the free Africans in America. An example of a company that failed in its goals was the Kansas African Emigration Association, which was founded in 1887. An African doctor from Barbados, J. Albert Thone, attempted to transport Africans back to the Belgian Congo, but failed. In 1915 Alfred C. Sam, a businessmen from the Gold Coast (now Ghana), raised $100,000 in Kansas and Oklahoma for his resettlement scheme and, in January 1915 he transported sixty Africans to the Gold Coast in his ship *The Liberia*.

Bishop Turner, who had such a widespread influence following the Civil War, was born in 1834 of free parents in South Carolina. After running away from the South, he became an evangelist in a Methodist church. As an evangelist he traveled throughout the South, preaching to both races. These years as an evangelist gave him the opportunity to see the terrible conditions under which African people lived. In 1858 he was introduced to the African Methodist Episcopal Church. After receiving short assignments in Baltimore and Washington, D.C., he went back to Georgia where he formed an AME Church, and worked in the Georgia legislature under the auspices of the Republican Executive Committee. Bishop Turner's work was instrumental in helping Georgia to satisfy requirements for readmission to the union under the Congressional Reconstruction Acts of 1867.[13] Four years later he heard Alexander Crummell speak on the merits of repatriation, which had an important effect upon his thinking. Thereafter, he began to integrate repatriation themes into his sermons and often advocated repatriation. In this context, the African church in America played a central role in providing a forum for the free discussion of solutions to the problems faced by African people. The church was the most available place the people could turn to for advice in the face of blatant segregation and economic exploitation through sharecropping and peonage.

The church also became a haven from deadly violence as well. During the 1890s race relations in America reached a critical point for Africans as lynching became prevalent throughout the South. The African church was the only place where Africans could congregate in large numbers, and where an effective response to the racism of the period could be mounted.

Due to his widespread traveling in the South, and his vocal opposition to these acts of terror, Rev. Turner was able to gather enough votes from southern ministers to elect him to the seat of Bishop of the AME

Church. After attaining the highest position in the African church, he did not divorce himself from the grassroots people and their struggles, but continued to speak out against injustices in America.

Legal Setbacks to Civil Rights Efforts in America

Bishop Turner became particularly incensed when the U.S. Supreme Court in 1883 declared the Civil Rights Act of 1875 unconstitutional. The decision by the Court was viewed by many as an important test case on African-American freedom. The case, decided on October 15, 1883, known as the *Civil Rights Cases,* was a consolidation of five cases from the states of Kansas, California, Missouri, New York and Tennessee. Each called into question the appropriate interpretation the U.S. courts should give to the Thirteenth and Fourteenth Amendments to the Constitution and the Civil Rights Act passed on March 1,1875. These postwar amendments, many believed, would not only end slavery, but also create substantive rights of citizenship for African-Americans that would be further enforced by the Civil Rights Act of 1866 (passed on April 9, 1866) and the Civil Rights Act of 1875.

Two of the cases involved African-Americans who were denied accommodations at an inn or hotel. One case involved denial of a seat in the "dress circle" of San Francisco's Maguire Theater. Another involved being denied accommodations at the Grand Opera House in New York City. The fifth case brought by "Robinson and wife" was against the Memphis and Charleston Railroad for refusing to allow Mrs. Robinson, an African-American woman, to take a seat in the "ladies car" because she was accompanied by "a young man whom he [the conductor] supposed to be a white man, and on that account inferred that there was some improper connections between them."[14] The first four appeals were brought by the U.S. government on behalf of the plaintiffs and the fifth case by private counsel.

At the onset, Justice Joseph Bradley stated that the key question was whether the Civil Rights Act of 1875 was constitutional. If not, the plaintiffs could not seek relief for the alleged violations of law. The first two sections of the act were being challenged by the defendants. Section 1 stated:

> That all persons within the jurisdiction of the United States shall be entitled to the full and equal enjoyment of the

> accomodations, advantages, facilities, and privileges of inns, public conveyances on land or water, theaters, and other places of public amusement;...regardless of any previous condition of servitude.

Section 2 set the civil penalty for each violation of Section 1 at $500 and for each criminal violation (misdemeanor) required a fine between $500 and $1,000 (fine) or imprisonment from thirty days to one year.[15]

Justice Bradley, writing for the Court, concluded that the Civil Rights Act of 1875 was unconstitutional, that Congress did not have the authority to make "a code of municipal law for the regulation of private rights." Even though Congress relied upon enforcement language in the postwar amendments, the Court concluded that this reliance was inappropriate. Furthermore, the Court reasoned that these matters were of state concern and the national government should not get involved with substantive legal protections of this nature. With respect to plaintiffs' arguments that the Thirteenth Amendment prohibited slavery as well as the " badges and incidents of slavery," the Court rejected such arguments outright. Justice Bradley wrote that there was no similarity between servitude and denial of accommodations to inns, theaters and public conveyances:

> It would be running the slavery argument into the ground to make it apply to every act of discrimination which a person may see fit to make as to the guests he will entertain, or as to the people he will take into his coach or cab or car, or admit to his concert or theater, or deal with in other matters of intercourse or business.[16]

The Court was not unanimous, however, in this interpretation. Justice John Harlan dissented from the majority opinion and wrote that the Civil Rights Act of 1875 was properly enacted by Congress because it enforced the principles of universal freedom for American citizens created by the Fourteenth Amendment. Furthermore, he wrote that the Thirteenth Amendment also provided a basis for the Act because discrimination constituted a "badge or incident of slavery." For Harlan, the new concept of citizenship that grew out of the Fourteenth Amendment should receive the greatest legal protection from the Courts:

> if the recent amendments are so construed that Congress may not,...provide, by legislation...for the security of rights

> created by the national Constitution;...then, not only the foundations upon which the national supremacy has always securely rested will be materially disturbed, but we shall enter upon an era of constitutional law, when the rights of freedom and American citizenship cannot receive from the nation that efficient protection which heretofore was unhesitatingly accorded to slavery and the rights of the master.[17]

The decision sent a shock wave through the African-American community. The highest court in the land had failed to protect their freedom and indirectly the benefits of American citizenship from the forces of segregation and "white supremacy." The AME Church, through Bishop Turner, took an immediate and forceful stand and issued the following statement: "If the government that freed him cannot protect that freedom, the Black man would no longer enlist in the armies of the government, or swear to defend the United States Constitution. That constitution is a dirty rag, a cheat, a liberal and ought to be spit upon by every Negro in the land."[18]

Bishop Turner's Nationalist Theology

The new Court ruling stripped Africans of legal protections and allowed them to be openly discriminated against by "whites." This betrayal of Africans caused Bishop Turner to advocate even more for repatriation. However, middle-class Africans, who had found a comfortable position in American society, blasted Turner for his back-to-Africa preaching, even in the face of discriminatory public policies. In 1883 the AME's weekly newspaper, *Christian Recorder*, carried an article by Frederick Douglass which reminded Africans that they had been in America for 250 years, and were Americans and not Africans. Despite the constant criticism by integrationist African leaders such as Douglass, Turner continued to attack injustices within the United States.

It was during this period that Turner began to develop a theology that recognized the centrality of the African experience. In his theology he urged his followers to not use songs in their worship services that equated purity with whiteness. As an attempt to combat the "mental slavery" of the people, he taught that "God was a Negro."[19] He rejected the notion that the devil was black and that Africa was the seat of devil worshiping. Furthermore, Bishop Turner made major strides in the fight against sexism in the church by appointing a woman as deacon in 1888.[20] This decision was consistent with his thinking on gender equality established much earlier when he authored a bill in the Georgia legislature to give women the right to vote.

The chance that he had been waiting for came in 1891, when the Council of Bishops authorized him to take an exploratory trip to Africa. His immediate function in Africa was to advise the AME churches that had been recently formed there. This maiden voyage to Africa had a significant impact on his thinking on repatriation. In February 1892 he returned from Africa with renewed determination to take groups of Africans back. In the South his repatriation preaching fell upon eager ears. Lynching had increased throughout the South and many poor Africans were ready to go anywhere. While a student at Fisk University in Nashville, W.E.B Du Bois reacted in disgust to lynching:

> Murder, killing and maiming Negroes, raping Negro women-in the 80s and in the southern South, this was not even news; it got no publicity; it caused no arrests; and punishment for such transgression was so unusual that the fact was telegraphed North. Lynching was a continuing and recurrent horror during my college days: from 1885 through 1894, 1700 Negroes were lynched in America. Each death was a scar upon my soul, and led me on to conceive the plight of other minority groups.[21]

Bishop Turner Seeks Congressional Support for Repatriation

Within a short period after Bishop Turner returned from Africa, some European-Americans, aware of the widespread discontent among southern Africans, joined with Bishop Turner to form organizations that would transport Africans to Africa. One such company was the Congo National Emigration Company, which was chartered in 1886 by three European-American men from Baltimore. The leader of the company was Martin H.K. Paulsen, who recruited an African man to be president. Capitalizing on the back-to-Africa fervor generated by Bishop Turner among the Georgia Africans, Paulsen financed his company by selling stocks to poor Africans. The company, however, could not get congressional approval, so Paulsen abandoned it.

Benjamin Gaston, who took control of the company after Paulsen, was no more successful than Paulsen in making the company viable.

He, like Paulsen, realized the widespread discontent among Africans and saw the company as a means of getting rich by capitalizing on this discontent. Gaston praised Africa as a country of great riches where African people could go and make a lot of money in a short period of time. He claimed that he went to Africa in 1866, stayed twenty years, and came back to the United States a rich man.[22] He did not, however, remain long on the political scene.

The sudden departure of Paulsen raised questions concerning the safety of African-American investments in the company. Gaston reassured all of the people who had spent their last savings for the stock certificates that the money was safe in a bank. Nevertheless, Gaston knew that the capitalization stock would not sustain any serious repatriation scheme. As a result, he ordered his treasurer, William O'Brien, a European-American, to investigate the possibility of obtaining funds from the federal government. O'Brien contacted a friend, Robert S. Tharin, who worked in the Treasury. Tharin asked the Treasury for funds and had a bill, authored by Senator Matthew C. Butler of South Carolina, introduced into Congress that would repatriate every African in the southern states who desired to leave for Africa. The bill never passed, but Gaston raised enough money, through other sources, to sail for Liberia in March 1894 with thirty African people.[23]

The bill, which never became law, nevertheless did allow southern political leaders to express their fears and prejudices toward Africans in the South. Senate Bill 1121 was filed by Senator Butler on December 12, 1889, and debated between January 6, 1890, through January 30, 1890.[24] Senator Butler marshaled voluminous testimony in support of his racist thesis that African-Americans, though U.S. citizens, should not remain in the southern states. Through testimony from several leading senators from the South, he presented arguments that purported to demonstrate the unfitness of Africans to remain in the United States, and of the service that they would render to Africa.

The first senator to speak on behalf of the bill was Senator John Morgan of Alabama. First, he expressed fear that African-Americans would eventually take control of the southern state governments. For him, the end of Reconstruction in 1877 was a welcome end to African-American control of the political apparatus in the South, and that southern leadership should never let such a state of affairs develop again. He stated:

> I have reached the conclusion, after mature reflection, and, I hope, without prejudice or any feeling that relates to the political or sectional strife in which the negro race has been a conspicuous and dangerous element in this country for a century, that there is a natural incongruity, "an irrepressible conflict" between the races that nothing will cure, except their final separation.[25]

Senator Morgan argued that there existed within the United States "race aversion" that resulted in restrictions on the immigration of Chinese-Americans and, likewise, required the deportation of Africans.

In developing his argument, Senator Morgan examined the "Congo Negro" and concluded that he was superior to other coastal Negroes. The senator believed that the American Negro could civilize those coastal Negroes by imposing slave codes in the same manner that southerners had civilized their African slaves.[26] He envisioned 8 million African-Americans emigrating to Africa to bring knowledge and civilization to "uncivilized" people in the Congo Free State.

On January 16, 1890, the debate continued with Senator Butler taking the floor to speak on behalf of his bill. He started off by discussing how the country dealt with the Indian (Native American), who was savage and "only fit to live on reservations to himself, under coercion." Second, Senator Butler presented data to support his thesis that the racial problem existed throughout the United States. For example, he presented the following data with respect to the numbers of Africans in the northern states:

Ohio	79,537
Pennsylvania	85,109
New York	64,175
Illinois	46,123
Indiana	39,359
Massachusetts	17,750
Connecticut	11,648[27]

He then argued that throughout the North one could not find any of these 343,701 people in responsible positions of authority. By introducing these data he also argued that the South was sharing a disproportionate burden of living with the "Negro." His bill would, therefore, allow for the "gradual, orderly, and voluntary movement of the coloured people out of the Southern States."[28] The precedent for such governmental action, he maintained, was congressional action to remove Indians from certain southern states and congressional appropriations to exclude the Chinese from the country.

The Negro, he argued, had a greater claim to this governmental assistance because he was a citizen, as compared to the Native American. Not only would his bill support the removal to Africa but also to northern states. He believed that when Negroes are in the majority "they not only do not advance satisfactorily in the scale of civilization, but actually retrograde."[29] On the other hand, Senator Butler believed that when the Negro is in the company of the "white" majority, they are "better off and the white man is better off."

Despite this belief that the Negro is better off when he is in the minority, Senator Butler concluded that he must be separated:

> It is conceded on all hands that if the negro is to attain the full stature of his manhood, if he is to become an independent, self-reliant, self-respecting man, and to be made fully competent to discharge well the high responsibilities and duties of life, he must finally rely upon himself; he must elevate himself in the moral, social, and industrial scale by his own exertions, by his own self-assertion.[30]

In support of his position, Senator Butler introduced into the record excerpts from *Christianity, Islam and the Negro Race* by Rev. Edward Wilmot Blyden, a prominent African-American supporter of repatriation. In addition, he quoted Rev. Blyden, speaking at a conference of the African Methodist Church, at which Blyden stated that he hoped Congress would appropriate funds that would allow Africans in America to repatriate.

Senator Butler also introduced into the record writings of prominent American patriots, such as Thomas Jefferson, who wrote in *Notes on Virginia*:

> Nothing is more clearly written in the Book of Destiny than the emancipation of the blacks; and it is equally certain that the two races will never live in a state of equal freedom under

> the same government, so insurmountable are the barriers which nature, habit, and opinion have established between them.[31]

Senator Butler's arguments, however, did not go unchallenged. Senator George F. Hoar from Massachusetts questioned the validity of Butler's claims. First, Hoar stated that there was no compelling evidence that supported the notion that Negroes were so inferior that they would be unfit for American citizenship. In fact, Senator Hoar argued that he had served in the House of Representatives with seven to ten "coloured" men "who were better examples of the legislative character for propriety of conduct, for soundness of judgment, and for ability exhibited in debate than the Representatives of that race."[32] In addition, he made reference to a U.S. senator from Mississippi who conducted himself with "dignity...propriety...and intelligence."[33] Furthermore, he pointed out to Senator Butler that by introducing into the record the writings of Rev. Blyden, he had defeated his own argument that Africans were inferior.

Following the speech of Senator Hoar, Senator Henry W. Blair of Massachusetts took the floor to further rebut the statements of Senator Butler. First, he stated that instead of "exporting" 8 million "coloured people," the government should export 10,000 "white people" who constituted the problem in the country. He stated: "I really believe, sir, that the difficulty, the race problem, exists in the excited imaginations and in the ineradicable prejudices of a few whitemen, and that it by no means exists as a real problem between the races themselves."[34]

On January 23, 1890, the opposition to the Butler bill continued. Senator John J. Ingalls of Kansas reminded the Senate that African-Americans were citizens, some of whom had come to this land in 1619, before the Mayflower. Furthermore, he pointed out that the South was intent on eliminating Africans from the political and social systems. To support his argument that Africans were prevented from voting by violence, he read into the record a correspondent's account of a recent election in Mississippi: "It was the most outrageous thing I ever saw. All the toughs, murderers, etc., in the state were here with their Winchester rifles and took possession of the city. The polls were in the possession of an armed mob, who would not allow a negro to come within one hundred yards of the polls."[35] At one point in his speech, applause erupted from the gallery, composed mainly of Africans. Senator Ingalls assailed the testimony of Senator Wade Hampton of South Carolina, who advocated either migration, extermination or amalgamation. He further presented evidence of 155 Negroes being lynched in Mississippi,[36] and ended his speech by an appeal to justice: "Stack your guns, open your ballot-boxes, register your voters, black and white;... The citizenship of the negro must be absolutely recognized. His right to vote must be admitted, and the ballots that he cast must be honestly counted.[37] Upon the completion of his speech, the gallery erupted into applause again as the debate adjourned at 3:55 p.m.

The session resumed on January 30, 1890, with Senator Zebulon Vance of North Carolina occupying the floor for most of the day. He presented arguments for Negro inferiority, but stated that slavery helped improve the African's condition: "He learned nothing for the benefit of his race from his civilized masters in all these ages. He has made more progress in one hundred years as a Southern slave than he made in all the five thousand years intervening from his creation until landing on these shores."[38] Despite this racist rhetoric, Senator Vance concluded that he could not support the bill because it was impractical to remove from the country 8 million people. He stated that he regretted the presence of Africans in the country: "I should be happy to know that there was not one of them in the United States."[39] His solution to the race problem, however, was to distribute the Negro throughout the northern and northwestern states, thus relieving the South of their burden. The following remark from Senator Vance brought laughter from his colleagues: "If the negro is a good thing we are willing to divide him up. [Laughter.] There is plenty of him to go around."[40] Specifically, he advocated that approximately "500,000 blacks" be removed from the states of Louisiana, Mississippi, Alabama, Florida and South Carolina and resettled in northern states. Six states would not require any removal: North Carolina, Virginia, Georgia, Tennessee, Arkansas and Texas. Such a plan, he believed, would prevent "negro supremacy" from developing within the political arena.

The final speaker of the day in support of the bill was Senator Wade Hampton of South Carolina. He began his speech by asking the Senate if they would vote to import 8 million "negroes" into the United States if none were here. Since the answer to the question was in the negative, then he asked why would it not be beneficial to both "races" if the 8 million voluntarily left? Next, he presented evidence that some Africans in Kansas had chartered an organization entitled The South and Central American Immigration League of the United States of America. Some $80,000 of the needed $2million in capital stock had been raised or pledged by colored people in Kansas. Furthermore, he presented articles from northern newspapers in which colored people expressed their desire to leave the South.[41]

More important, Senator Hampton presented testimony on the cost of transporting 4.5 million Africans to Africa at $32 million per year. The total cost, therefore would be $320 million over a ten-year period. He argued that this amount would be far less than the $800 million that had been paid for pensions between 1861 and 1887. The cost of removing all colored people could be funded, he argued, from the tax on whiskey and tobacco for eighteen months.[42] He believed that the sudden removal of African people would not adversely affect the economy because the jobs would be taken up "by immigrants of our own race."

The Butler bill was never voted into law by Congress. On May 9, 1890, Senator Butler introduced into the record a petition from "colored people" in Williamsburgh County, South Carolina, asking for an appropriation to support their repatriation.[43] The bill was immediately attacked by other prominent Africans in the North and South. *The Savannah Tribune* rejected the emigration scheme of Butler because Liberia had received adverse criticism for its discriminatory treatment of Africans.

Bishop Turner Continues Repatriation Initiative despite Setback

Bishop Turner, on the other hand, gave tacit support to the Butler bill, but attacked it for proposing to send massive numbers to Africa. Criticizing that part of the bill, he wrote: "worship white gods...who are fools enough to believe that the Devil is black and therefore all who are black are consanguinely related to him...who pretend to be serving God and have no aim higher than to get to heaven to be white. Such people would be a curse on Africa."[44] Bishop Turner viewed these American men as opportunists. He realized that in order for Africans to be integrated back into Africa, they had to undergo an ideological conversion.

Given the past history of Liberia, Bishop Turner believed that taking a mass number of Africans who did not have a healthy appreciation of Africa would be disastrous. Therefore, a precondition for repatriation would be a change in mental orientation. At the heart of this ideological change, he believed, was the need for a religious conversion.

Religion formed an essential part of his nationalist beliefs. Bishop Turner stressed that God was black and that African people had been made in the image of God. God had allowed Europeans to bring Africans into European society to learn skills and become civilized, then God had planned for these Africans to return to Africa and help develop it. To facilitate this development, Bishop hoped to repatriate 5 to 10 million people a year. Through his magazine the *Voice of Missions* he propagated his message to African people every month. He urged wealthy Africans to go to Liberia and help it develop as well as make a lot of money, but his appeals to the wealthy Africans continued to fall on deaf ears. By the latter part of the nineteenth century everyone knew of the conditions in Liberia, and therefore would not risk investing money there.

Despite the lack of success, Turner continued to develop means to transport some of the lower-class Africans to Africa. In 1894 he organized the African Steamship Company, which would, in conjunction with the Migration Society, ship approximately 5,000 emigrants to Liberia each year. The United States, he believed, should provide financial assistance to all Africans who wanted to leave America. These payments would be part of a plan of reparations. He believed that the U.S. government owed reparations of approximately $40 billion for the free service Africans provided this country as slaves for 200 years.

Bishop Turner's call for reparations represented a major milestone for African political development. It recognized that the United States had been unjustly enriched through centuries of slavery and that the government should be required to make payments to African people. More important, this restitution would be used to aid Bishop Turner in his repatriation efforts. It is significant that by the close of the nineteenth century, the notion of repatriation as reparations had been placed upon the African-American national agenda.

Unfortunately Bishop Turner was unable to generate much support from the African middleclass. As with Marcus Garvey during the 1920s, this group of African people had too much to lose in America by going to Africa. Southern Africans, on the other hand, lived in almost constant fear of the lynch mob. Jim Crow segregation was beginning to be accepted by most European-Americans as a compromise to those who struggled for full American citizenship rights. The view that Africans should be satisfied with "separate but equal" facilities had begun to grip the American psyche.[45] Africans were subject to being shot, burned or spat upon for any reason. Bishop Turner, a long-time resident and activist in the South, recognized the gravity of this racial crisis when he expressed his fear of extermination: "But the Negro cannot remain here in his present condition and be a man ... for at the present rate his extermination is only a question of time."[46] Repatriation to Africa was the sole means of avoiding this predicament.

Turner's lack of success among the African middle class did not discourage him. In 1898 he took a trip to South Africa to meet with the Ethiopian Church that was formed by Africans who rebelled against the American missionaries. This African church had heard of the AME Church and wanted to become a branch. This liaison would further cement the fraternal bond between "black" America and Africa that Bishop Turner believed was so necessary.

In 1915 Bishop Turner died. In his appeal to the working-class poor, Turner's work and beliefs foreshadowed Marcus Garvey. The genius of Bishop Turner stems from his undying love for his people and a firm belief that in order for Africans to be respected, they had to become a nation. Furthermore, Turner utilized the Christian church, with its large African audience, as a place to teach and aid African people in this period of uncertainty.

Notes

1. Albert J. Raboteau, "Richard Allen and the African Church Movement" in Leon Litwack and August Meier, eds., *Black Leaders of the Nineteenth Century* (Urbana: University of Illinois Press, 1988), page 4.
2. Raboteau, page 7.
3. Raboteau, page 11.
4. Raboteau, page 16.

5. Daniel Coker, *Journal of Daniel Coker, A Descendant of Africa, From the Time of Leaving New York, in the Ship Elizabeth, Capt. Sebor, on a Voyage for Sherbro, in Africa* (Baltimore: Published by Edward J. Coale, 1820), Middlebury College Special Collection, E448C68, 1820, page 21.
6. Coker, page 22.
7. Coker, pages 22 to 23.
8. Coker, page 28.
9. Coker, page 44.
10. Coker, page 44.
11. Coker, page 45.
12. Amy Jacques Garvey, *The Philosophy and Opinions of Marcus Garvey,* Vols. I and II (New York: Atheneum Press, 1970).
13. John Dittmer, "The Education of Henry McNeal Turner," in Litwack and Meier, page 258.
14. The *Civil Rights Cases*, 109 U.S. 3, 5 (1883).
15. The *Civil Rights Cases*, 109 U.S. 3, 9 (1883).
16. The *Civil Rights Cases*, 109 U.S. 3, 24 to 25 (1883).
17. The *Civil Rights Cases*, 109 U.S. 3, 57 (1883).
18. Edwin S. Redkey, *Black Exodus: Black Nationalist and Back to Africa Movements: 1890 to 1910* (New Haven, CT: Yale University Press, 1969) page 41.
19. Dittmer, page 260. The concept of "mental slavery" was popularized in the twentieth century by the late Jamaican poet and singer Bob Marley. In his writings, he described the psychological effects of slavery upon the African mind.
20. Dittmer, page 262.
21. W.E.B. Du Bois, *The Autobiography of W.E.B. Du Bois* (New York: International Publishers, 1970) page 122.
22. Redkey, page 154.
23. Redkey, page 167.
24. *Congressional Record: Containing the Proceedings and Debates of the Fifty-First Congress, First Session of the Senate*, Volume XXI (Washington, DC: Government Printing Office, 1889), pages 154 to 155.
25. *Congressional Record*, page 420.
26. *Congressional Record*, page 420.
27. *Congressional Record*, page 623.
28. *Congressional Record*, page 623.
29. *Congressional Record*, page 624.

30. *Congressional Record*, page 624.
31. *Congressional Record*, page 626.
32. *Congressional Record*, page 629.
33. *Congressional Record*, page 629.
34. *Congressional Record*, page 630.
35. *Congressional Record*, page 804.
36. *Congressional Record*, page 805.
37. *Congressional Record*, page 807.
38. *Congressional Record*, page 970.
39. *Congressional Record*, page 970.
40. *Congressional Record*, page 970.
41. *Congressional Record*, page 972.
42. *Congressional Record*, page 973.
43. *Congressional Record*, page 4364.
44. Redkey, page 71.
45. By 1896 this view had become national policy after the U.S. Supreme Court rendered its decision in *Plessy v. Ferguson*, 163 U.S. 537 (1896). This case involved segregation on the trains in Louisiana. Plessy sued alleging that the Louisiana law that required African-Americans to sit in segregated cars was unconstitutional, in violation of the Thirteenth and Fourteenth Amendments to the United States Constitution. The Court rejected these arguments and upheld the Louisiana law. This decision established a national policy of segregation that remained in effect until 1954 when the Court reversed itself in *Brown v. Board of Education*, 347 U.S. 483 (1954).
46. Redkey, page 184.

CONCLUSION

Colonization in the nineteenth century, a product of the American Colonization Society, represented but another form of political and economic imperialism. As with other forms of imperialist expansion-such as that of the British colonists into America and the Europeans into India, Africa and Latin America—the explicit rationale revolved around the so-called inferiority of the colonized, and the implicit obligation of the colonizer to bring them civilization and culture. Although the real intentions of the colonizers are usually of an economic nature, such humanitarian rhetoric serves to divert attention from the real issue of exploitation. Such was the case with the American Colonization Society, which was founded for the specific purpose of removing politically dangerous free Africans and rebellious slaves who represented a political threat to the economic system of the South. In addition, Liberia was believed to possess commercial potential in view of its abundant harvests or basic food grains and fruits.

As a further extension of its hypocritical rhetoric, the Colonization Society expounded the virtues of national independence in Liberia as many free Africans seized the opportunity in anticipation of citizenship in a "Negro state." Though many of these Africans were cognizant of the racial and economic motives of the white colonizers, they earnestly felt that separation from America and the development of an African nation was a feasible solution to problems facing free Africans in America. However imperfect the vision of these men may have been, it is significant that, in view of the blatant racism in the nineteenth century, they dared dream of such as achievement.

Ironically, those Africans who emigrated to Liberia under the aegis of the Colonization Society found themselves manipulated as pawns as the American colonizers proceeded to subjugate African land and population. However, it must be pointed out again that most Africans had no control over the situation in which they found themselves, because many were emancipated specifically for the colony.

As time passed in Liberia those returned Africans who lived in proximity to the American colonizers began to imitate the colonizers, which is characteristic of the colonized throughout the world. This identification on the part of the settlers was facilitated by their prior socialization in American society. The indigenous African, however, because of his inherent lifestyle that was different from that of the American colonizer and the African agent, was completely relegated to an underclass state and therefore viewed as a threat to the fledgling colony. To the indigenous African, the African-American continued to be an enigma. On the one hand, he espoused the virtues of his return to Africa, while on the other, he practiced the white man's religion and engaged in military raids against fellow Africans and their homes. Liberia became for many continental Africans the symbol of African-American exploitation in Africa.

While the standard of living of the indigenous Africans declined in the colony as a result of the demand for compulsory contributions such as hut taxes and labor exploitation in the form of low wages for menial jobs, the standard for the returned slave remained relatively stable. This discrepancy in social status was a direct reflection of the social position the returned Africans occupied in the colony, a social position that was determined by both class and caste. This group of returned Africans occupied the middle ground of the social hierarchy in the colony. Their authority, although greater than that of the indigenous Africans, was, nonetheless, limited as policy continued to be decided by European-American men in Washington, D.C.

Such a state of affairs, created by the American Colonization Society, resulted in the returned Africans developing an unhealthy disdain for the indigenous Africans and continuing many of the exploitative practices initiated by the colonizers. Independence from the American Colonization Society in 1847 should have been a time when the leadership of the new republic could pause and assess the direction the republic was following, but owing to both personal greed on the part of its leaders and economic pressure on the part of developed countries, such an assessment never occurred on a widespread basis.

However, there were some attempts to instill progressive African nationalist ideas into the debate. The African nationalist philosophy of Edward Wilmot Blyden offered an alterative to caste discrimination prevalent throughout the colony. Blyden advocated that the indigenous Africans be accepted as full citizens in the republic and therefore be given all the privileges and immunities of that citizenship. Such an appeal fell upon deaf ears: The new leaders of the republic continued to manifest the caste and class values taught by the white colonizer. Although African nationalism failed to be implemented in Liberia, such failure must be attributed to the colonization society that feared black unity and its potential threat to the "white" supremacist control.

In assessing the impact that African nationalism in the nineteenth century had upon the future of Liberia, it is important to clearly delineate its various forms. African nationalism for most African emigrants during the nineteenth century can be distinguished from repatriation as propagated by Edward Wilmot Blyden. African nationalism was characterized by a form of chauvinism that placed the African in America at the center of its universe. Despite the close identification with Africa as their ancestral home, many African-Americans, including men such as Lott Cary and Paul Cuffe, viewed the continent in a manner that closely resembled that of American whites. Christianity, a vital force throughout the United States during this period, helped to shape this perspective.

To most Europeans during the nineteenth century, Africa was pictured as a place of barbarism that had to be brought into civilization by the light of Christianity. Therefore, the religious practices of Africans were categorically termed heathen. Such a view of Africa became necessary in order to justify the enslavement of the African race; a view that persuaded many Europeans that they were not enslaving human beings, but rather things. The Christian Church played a primary role in the enslavement of the African, by giving credence to the Biblical myth of the curse of Ham, which maintains that because one of Noah's sons viewed his father's nakedness, God cursed the children of Ham to be black and slaves forever.

These racist views spread far and wide during the nineteenth century, infesting the minds of European and Americans with feelings of racial superiority. It was during the eighteenth and nineteenth centuries, according to historians W.E.B. Du Bois and Eric Williams, that Africa was stripped of its great historical achievements, leading to a process of dehumanization that was essential to the rise of white supremacy. The great civilizations such as Ghana, Mali, Songhay, Nubia, Zimbabwe, Mwene Mutapa and ancient Egypt were completely erased from the history of the African in order to convince the world that the people who were being so brutally exploited, had no history. Dr. Du Bois states in his book *World and Africa* that in the nineteenth century the study of Egyptology was born and received its most significant development, as European historians sought to credit the achievements of the black Egyptians to "hamites," "semites," "caucasoids" and other supposed non-African people.

Several African-Americans did not escape influence of this type of racist thinking about Africa. Christianity, to some degree, helped shape their views on Africa. Consequently, their Christian outlook influenced their nationalist perceptions to varying degrees. As a result, the African-American nationalist during the nineteenth century developed a world view of Africa that in some cases assumed the inferiority of continental Africans and the necessity for the settler to bring civilization. Such a perspective inevitably led to the settlers viewing the indigenous Africans as of a different caste. When the settlers arrived on the African mainland, this difference in worldview manifested itself in Western mannerisms that reinforced these caste differences even further. Returned Africans, for the most part, through no fault of their own, worshiped the God of "white people," ate their food, wore their clothing and spoke their language. This identification with white people led many indigenous Africans to feel that their returned brothers and sisters considered themselves superior. Such antagonisms between the two groups led to suspicion and division on every hand, with the majority of the indigenous Africans ostracized from governmental power.

African nationalism of the nineteenth century was clearly insufficient as a tool for uniting African people on the African continent in a nation-state that recognized the equality of all its people. African nationalism on the other hand, as exemplified by Blyden, was far more encompassing and more universal in its application to African people.

Conclusion

Repatriation, referred to here as Blydenism, recognized in Africa a destiny that would add new meaning to world civilization. It viewed the African as important in God's plan to unfold spiritual wisdom to the world. Therefore, repatriation was seen not as a missionary activity, but as an inevitable stage in the development and liberation of African people. Such a worldview did not allow for the caste conflicts that existed under African nationalism. Blyden understood that Liberia could never become a nation encompassing both settlers and indigenous Africans as long as political power rested solely in the hands of the settlers; to this end, he sought the importation of only pure Africans.

Blydenism was noncompromising with racist Western ideologies and philosophies. African nationalism, on the other hand, accepted the racist assumptions of white missionaries and political leaders. Blydenism refused to accept cultural differences between indigenous and returned Africans as the basis for political participation or lack of it in the African nation. Liberia and the experience of the Americo-Liberians exemplify the pitfalls of nationalist ideologies that are centered around the African-American experience with little appreciation of African history and cultural values. Without a philosophical perspective such as Blydenism, resettlement in Africa must inevitably lead to caste antagonisms between the returned and the indigenous African.

Blydenism, though lessening the caste antagonisms between Africans of differing geographical and ethnic backgrounds, lacked a cogent plan of action that would ultimately lead to the economic development of the continent. Blydenism clearly articulated a philosophy that recognized the universality of the cultural and religious aspects of the African existence. However, its weakness was that it did not postulate a politico economic plan of development under which a unified Africa could strive for self-reliance.

BIBLIOGRAPHY

A

African Repository, Vol. XII.

African Repository, Vol. XXVII.

African Repository, Vol. XV.

Alexander, Archibald, *A History of Colonization on the Western Coast of Africa* (New York: William S. Martien, 1846).

Allen, Henry L., Sam Barnes and James W. Fraser, *From Common School to Magnet School: Selected Essays on the History of Boston's Schools* (Boston: Trustees of the Public Library in the City of Boston, 1942).

American Colonization Society, *Address of the Managers of the American Colonization Society to the People in the United States* (Washington, DC: James C. Dunn, 1832).

American Colonization Society, *Condition of the American Colored Population and the Colony at Liberia* (Boston: Pierce and Parker, 1833).

American Colonization Society, *An Address to the American Society for Colonizing the Free People of Colour of the United States* (Washington, DC: Davis and Force, 1818).

Anderson, Amy, *Fifty Black Women Who Changed America* (Secaucus, NJ: Carol Publishing Group, 1999).

Austin, Allen D. and Sidney Kaplan, eds., *American Studies in Black and White, Selected Essays* (Amherst: The University of Massachusetts Press, 1991).

Athearn, Robert G., *In Search of Canaan: Black Migration to Kansas 1879 to 1880* (Lawrence: The Regents Press of Kansas, 1978).

B

Bacon, Leonard, *A Discourse at the Funeral of Jehudi Ashmun* (New Haven, CT: Hezekiah Howe, 1828), Middlebury College Archives.

Ballou, Richard A., "Even in Freedom's Birthplace: The Development of Boston's Black Ghetto," Vols. I to II, University Microfilms, International Dissertation Information Services, 1987.

Bay, Mia, *The White Image in the Black Mind: African-American Ideas about White People, 1830 to 1925* (New York: Oxford University Press, 2000).

Bennett, Lerone, Jr., *Before the Mayflower: A History of the Negro in America, 1619 to 1962* (Chicago: Johnson Publishing Co., 1962).

Birney, James G., *Letter on Colonization Addressed to the Rev. Thornton J. Mills, Corresponding Secretary of the Kentucky Colonization Society* (New York, 1834).

Blackett, R.J.M., *Beating Against the Barriers: Biographical Essays in Nineteenth-Century Afro-American History* (Baton Rouge: Louisiana State University Press, 1986).

Bogin, Ruth and Bert James Loewenburg, eds., Black Women in Nineteenth Century American Life: Their Words, Their Thoughts, Their Feelings (University Park: The Pennsylvania State University Press, 1976).

"Black Nationalism: The Inevitable Response," *Black World* (Chicago: A Johnson Publication, January 1971).

Bordewich, Fergus M., *Killing the White Man's Indian* (New York: Doubleday, 1996).

Borzendowski, Janice, *John Brown: Publisher* (New York: Chelsea House, 1989).

Bowler, Phillip, Sr. "The Twilight Mystery Solved" (unpublished), Starr Library, Middlebury College.

Bracey, John H., Jr., August Meir and Elliott Rudwick, eds., *Black Nationalism in America* (New York: Bobbs-Merrill, 1970).

Breckinridge, Robert J., *An Address Delivered Before the Colonization Society of Kentucky on January 6, 1831* (Frankfort: A.G. Hodges Printer, 1831).

Brewer, William M., "John B. Russwurm," *Journal of Negro History*, Vol. XIII, No. 4, October 1828 (*African Repository*, Vol. XII).

Bristow, Peggy et al., *Essays in African Canadian Women's History* (Toronto: University of Toronto Press, 1994).

Brotz, Howard, *Negro Social and Political Thought 1850 to 1920, Representative Texts* (New York: Basic Books, 1966).

Brown, Beryl, M., *A Short History of Portland* (Kingston, Jamaica: Minister of Education Publications Branch, 1976).

Brown, Hallie Q. ed., *Homespun Heroines and Other Women of Distinction* (Freeport, ME: Books for Libraries Press, 1970) .

C

Calhoun, Charles C., *A Small College in Maine: Two Hundred Years of Bowdoin* (Brunswick: Bowdoin College, 1993).

Campbell, Penelope, "Medical Education for an African Colonist," *Maryland Historical Magazine*, Summer, 1970.

Campbell, Robert, *A Pilgrimage to My Homeland: An Account of a Journey among the Egbas and Yorubas of Central Africa in 1859 to 1860* (New York: T. Hamilton, 1861).

Cantwell, Robert, *Nathaniel Hawthorne, the American Years*: New York: Rinehart, 1948).

Carlisle, Rodney, "Black Nationalism: An Integral Tradition," *Black World* (Chicago: February, 1973).

Carlisle, Rodney, *The Roots of Black Nationalism* (New York: Associated Faculty Press, 1975).

Catalogue of the Corporation, Officers of the Orleans County Grammar School, Brownington, Vermont, November 1845 (Stanstead: L.R. Robinson, 1845).

Catalogue of the Corporation, Officers of the Orleans County Grammar School (St. Johnsbury, VT.: A.G. Chadwick, 1841).

Child, L. Maria, *The History of the Condition of Women in Various Ages and Nations* (Boston: Otis, Broaders and Co., 1838).

The Christian Statesman, Vol. 1 No. 2 for the week ending September 13, 1851.

The *Civil Rights Cases*, 109 U.S. 3 (1883).

Clarke, John Henrik, ed., *Marcus Garvey: And the Vision of Africa* (New York: Vintage Books, 1974).

Clarke, John Henrik, "The Image of Africa in the Mind of Afro-American: African Identity in the Literature of Struggle." (Phelps-Stokes Seminars in African-American Relations, October 1973).

Cleaveland, Nehemiah and Alpheus Spring Packard, *History of Bowdoin College* (Boston: James Ripley Osgood and Co., 1882).

Clericus (George Smith), *Facts Designed to Exhibit the Real Character and Tendency of the American Colonization Society* (Liverpool: Egerton Smith and Co., 1833).

Congressional Record: Containing the Proceedings and Debates of the Fifty-First Congress, First Session of the Senate, Volume XXI (Washington, DC: Government Printing Office, 1889).

Cohen, William, *At Freedom's Edge: Black Mobility and the Southern White Quest for Racial Control 1861 to 1951* (Baton Rouge: Louisiana State University, 1991).

Coker, Daniel, *Journal of Daniel Coker, A Descendant of Africa, From the Time of Leaving New York, in the Ship Elizabeth, Capt. Sebor, on a Voyage for Sherbro, in Africa* (Baltimore: Published by Edward J. Coale, 1820), Middleb*ury* College Special Collections.

Cotter, Edwin, N., "John Brown in the Adirondacks," *Adirondack Life*, Summer 1972.

Crocket, Norman I., *The Black Towns* (Lawrence: The Regents Press of Kansas, 1979).

Cromwell, Adelaide M., *The Other Brahmins: Boston's Black Upper-Class, 1750 to 1950* (Fayetteville: The University of Arkansas Press, 1994).

Cruse, Harold, *Crisis of the Negro Intellectual* (New York: William Morrow, 1967).

Cropper, James, William Lloyd Garrison, Reverend Nathaniel Paul, Daniel O. Connell and George Thompson, *Speeches Delivered at the Anti-Colonization Meeting in Exeter Hall, London* (Boston: Garrison and Knapp, 1833).

D

Daguillard, Fritz, *A Jewel in the Crown: Charles Sumner and the Struggle for Haiti's Recognition* (Washington, DC: Haitian Embassy, 1999).

D'Antonio, Michael, "Fessenden: Fierce Foe of Slavery," *Portland Press Herald*, May 29, 1982.

Dartmouth College Library, Special Collections, Augustus Washington, N1847.

Dartmouth College Library, Special Collections, *The African Repository*, Vol. 34 (American Colonization Society, 1835).

Dartmouth College Library, Special Collections, Edward Garrison Draper, 1855, "Edward Garrison Draper, A Lawyer for Liberia."

Dartmouth College Library, Special Collections, Samuel F. McGill, M1839.

Dartmouth College Library, Special Collections, "Dartmouth Medical School Graduates."

Davis, Angela, "Reflections on the Black Woman's Role in the Community of Slaves," Floyd W. Hayes, III, ed., *A Turbulent Voyage*, 2nd ed. (San Diego: Collegiate Press, 1997).

Davis, David Brion, *The Problem of Slavery in Western Culture* (Ithaca, NY: Cornell University Press, 1966).

Davis, John P., *The American Negro Reference Book* (Englewood Cliffs, NJ: Prentice-Hall, 1966).

Delany, Martin R. and Robert Campbell, *Search for a Place: Black Separatism and Africa* (Ann Arbor: University of Michigan Press, 1969).

Dittmer, John, "The Education of Henry McNeal Turner," in Leon Litwack and August Meier, *Black Leaders of the Nineteenth Century* (Urbana: University of Illinois Press, 1988).

Douglass, Frederick, *Rochester North Star*, July 14, 1848.

Drew, Benjamin, *The Refugee: A North Side View of Slavery* (New York: Addison-Wesley, 1969).

Du Bois, W.E.B., *John Brown* (New York: International Publishers, 1963).

Du Bois, W.E.B., *The World and Africa* (New York: International Publishers, 1972).

Du Bois, W.E.B., *The Autobiography of W.E.B. Du Bois* (New York: International Publishers, 1970).

Du Bois, W.E.B., *The Suppression of the African Slave Trade* (Baton Rouge: Louisiana State University Press, 1969).

Dunn, James C., *Address of the Managers of the American Colonization Society to the People of the United States* (Washington, 1832).

E

Ebony, February 1972, "Black Political Strategies for '72" (Chicago: Johnson Publishing Company).

Elkins, Stanley, *Slavery: A Problem in American Institutional and Intellectual Life,* 2nd ed. (Chicago: University of Chicago Press, 1969).

Epps, Bernard, "Pioneer Teachers in the Townships: Twilights' Academy in Richmond," *The Record*, Friday, September 9, 1988, Starr Library, Middlebury College.

Examination of Mr. Thomas C. Brown, A Free Colored Citizen of South Carolina, As to the Actual State of Things in Liberia (New York: S.W. Benedict and Company Printers, 1834).

F

Foner, Philip S., ed., "The Claims of the Negro Ethnologically Considered" in *The Life and Writings of Frederick Douglass,* Vol. 2 (New York: International Publishers, 1975).

Forbes, Jack D., *Africans and Native Americans: The Language of Race and the Evolution of Red-Black Peoples,* 2nd ed. (Chicago: University of Illinois Press, 1933).

Fraenkel, Merran, *Tribe and Class in Monrovia* (London: Oxford University Press, 1965).

Franklin, John Hope, *From Slavery to Freedom* (New York: Vintage Books, 1967).

Franklin, John Hope and Loren Schweninger, *Runaway Slaves: Rebels on the Plantation* (Oxford: Oxford University Press, 1999).

Frazier, E. Franklin, *The Negro in the United States,* rev. ed. (New York: Macmillan, 1961).

Freedom's Journal, Vol. 1, No. 4, April 6, 1827.

Freedom's Journal, Vol 1, No. 10, May 18, 1827.

Freedom's Journal, Vol. 8, No. 98, February 14, 1829.

Freeman, F., *Yaradee: A Plea for Africa: Familiar Conversations on the Subject of Slavery and Colonization* (Philadelphia: J. Whetham, 1836).

Freeman, M.H., "The Educational Wants of the Free Colored People," Middlebury College Archives.

Free Public Library of New Bedford, *Cuffee Collection,* Reel 1.

Fyfe, Christopher, *A Short History of Sierra Leone* (London: Longmans, Green, 1962).

Fyfe, Christopher, *Sierra Leone Inheritance* (London: Oxford University Press, 1964).

G

Garnet, Henry Highland, *A Brief Sketch of the Life and Character of David Walker* (New York: J.H. Tobitt, 1848).

Garrison, William Lloyd, *Thoughts on African Colonization* (New York: Arno Press and New York Times, 1968).

Garvey, Amy Jacques, *The Philosophy and Opinions of Marcus Garvey,* Vols. I and II (New York: Atheneum, 1970).

Genovese, Eugene D., *The Political Economy of Slavery* (New York: Vintage Books, 1965).

George, James Z., *The Political History of Slavery in the United States* (New York: Mnemosyne Publishing Co. 1915).

Ginsberg, Eli and Alfred S. Eichner, *The Troublesome Presence* (New York: Mentor Books, 1964).

Glaude, Eddie S., Jr., *Exodus: Religion, Race and Nation in Early Nineteenth Century Black America* (Chicago: The University of Chicago Press, 2000).

Greene, Lorenzo Johnson, *The Negro in Colonial New England* (New York: Atheneum, 1974).

Griggs, Earl Leslie and Clifford H. Proctor, eds., *Henry Christophe and Thomas Clarkson: A Correspondence* (New York: Greenwood Press, 1968).

Grimke, Angelina, *Appeal to the Women of the Nominally Free States* (New York: William S. Dorr, 1837).

Gurley, Rev. R.R. and Daniel Goodloe, eds., *The Christian Statesman*, Vol. I. "Dedicated to African Colonization and Civilization, to Literature and General Intelligence," (Washington, DC: August 9, 1851).

H

Hance, Dawn D., ed., *Early Families of Rutland, Vermont* (Rutland: The Rutland Historical Society, 1990).

Harris, Sheldon, H., *Paul Cuffe: Black America and the African Return* (New York: Simon and Schuster, 1972).

Hatch, Louis C., *The History of Bowdoin College* (Portland: Loring, Short and Harmon, 1927).

Hawkins, Hugh, "Edward Jones: First American Negro College Graduate?" *Schools and Society*, November 4, 1961.

Hayden, Robert C., *African-Americans in Boston: More Than 350 Years* (Boston: Trustees of the Boston Public Library, 1991).

The Hebron Semester, Vol. XIII, No. 1, November 1, 1891; *The Hebron Semester*, Vol. V, No. 2, Spring, 1885; *The Hebron Semester*, Vol. X, No. X, Fall 1974.

Higginson, Thomas Wentworth, *Black Rebellion: A Selection From Travellers and Outlaws* (New York: Arno Press and New York Times, 1969).

Hill, Adelaide and Martin Kilson, *Apropos of Africa: Sentiments of Negro American Leaders on Africa from the 1800's to the 1950's* (New York: Frank Cass and Co. Ltd, 1969).

Hinks, Peter P., *To Awaken My Afflicted Brethren: David Walker and the Problem of Antebellum Slave Resistance* (University Park: Pennsylvania State University Press, 1997).

Hinton, Richard J., *John Brown and His Men (*New York: Ayer Co Publishers, 1968).

Historical Society of Ohio, *The Quarterly Publication of the Historical and Philosophical Society of Ohio,* Vols. VII to IX, "A Brief Exposition of the Views of the Society for the Colonization of Free Persons of Color in America" (Columbus, Ohio 1827).

I

"The Iron-Willed Black Schoolmaster and his Granite Academy," *Middlebury*, Spring 1974.

Irvine, Russell W., "Martin H. Freeman of Rutland, America's First Black College Professor and Pioneering Black Social Activist," *Rutland Historical Society Quarterly*, Volume XXVI, No. 3, 1996.

J

Jacobs, Donald M., "David Walker: Boston Race Leader 1825 to 1830," Essex Institute Historical Collection.

James, C.L.R., *The Black Jacobins: Toussaint L'Ouverture and the San Domingo Revolution*, 2nd rev. ed. (New York: Vintage Books, 1989).

Jefferson, Thomas, *Notes on the State of Virginia* (New York: Palgrave, 2002)

Jenkins, Carroll E., "The Purge of 1851," *Newport Express*, May 23, 1939.

Johnson, Robert, Jr., *Race, Law and Public Policy* (Baltimore: Black Classic Press, 1998).

July, Robert W., *A History of the African People,* 2nd. ed. (New York: Charles Scribner's Sons, 1974).

July, Robert W., *The Origins of Modern African Thought* (London: Faber and Faber, 1968).

K

Katz, William Loren, *Eyewitness: The Negro in American History* (New York: Pitman, 1967).

Kolchin, Peter, *American Slavery, 1619 to 1877* (New York: Hill and Wang, 1993).

L

Lake Placid-North Elba Historical Society, "Lake Placid Publication," July 18, 1938.

Levesque, George A., *Black Boston: African-American Life and Culture in Urban America 1751 to 1860* (New York: Garland, 1994).

Lewiston Journal, February 27, 1915.

Liebenow, J. Gus, *Liberia: The Evolution of Privilege* (Ithaca, NY: Cornell University Press, 1969).

Loewenberg, Bert James and Ruth Bogin, eds., *Black Women in Nineteenth-Century American Life: Their Words, Their Thoughts, Their Feelings* (University Park: Pennsylvania State University Press, 1991).

Logan, Rayford W. and Michael R. Winston, eds. *Dictionary of American Negro Biography* (New York: Norton, 1983).

Loke, Margaret, "In a John Brown Portrait, the Essence of a Militant," *New York Times*, July 7, 2000.

Lovejoy, John, M., "The Life of Ichabod Twilight and the Early Life of Alexander Twilight, 1765 to 1821," (unpublished), Starr Library, Middlebury College.

Lovejoy, John, M. "Ichabod Twilight," (unpublished), Starr Library, Middlebury College.

Lowell, James Russell, "The Prejudice of Color," in *The Anti-Slavery Papers of James Russell Lowell* (Boston: Houghton Mifflin, 1902).

M

Magnuson, Roger, *A Brief History of Quebec Education* (Montreal: Harvest House, 1980).

Maine Historical Society, John Brown Russwurm Papers.

Mbiti, John S., *African Religions and Philosophy* (New York: Doubleday, 1970).

McPherson, James and William Loren Katz, *The Anti-Slavery History of John Brown* (New York: Negro Universities Press, 1969).

Meier, August and Elliott M. Rudwick, *From Plantation to Ghetto* (New York: Hill and Wang, 1968).

Mellon, Matthew T., *Early American Views on Negro Slavery* (Boston: Meador Publishing Co., 1934).

Merran, Fraenkel, *Tribe and Class in Monrovia* (London: Oxford University Press, 1965).

Miller, Floyd, J., *The Search for a Black Identity: Black Emigration and Colonization,* 1787 to 1863 (Urbana: University of Illinois Press, 1975).

Minot, John Clair and Donald Francis Snow, *Tales of Bowdoin* (Augusta, ME: Press of Kennebec Journal, 1901).

Mitchell, William Brookings, "A Remarkable Bowdoin Decade, 1820 to 1830" (Brunswick, ME: Bowdoin College, 1852).

Moore, Barrington, Jr., *Social Origins of Dictatorship and Democracy* (Boston: Beacon Press, 1967).

Morsbach, Mabel, *The Negro in American Life* (Cincinnati: Cincinnati Lithographing, 1966).

N

National Archives of Jamaica, "Register of Baptisms, Parish of Portland."

Nesbitt, Leroy, Jr., "The First African-American to Be Awarded an Honorary Degree," *The Journal of Blacks in Higher Education*, Summer 1995, page 48.

Nicolosi, Vincent, "Twilight Mystery," Starr Library, Middlebury College.

O

The Orleans County Historical Society, *A Walking Tour of Brownington Village Historic District,* Orleans, Vermont.

The Orleans County Historical Society, Brownington, Vermont, "Agreement between Twilight and Orleans County Grammar School Board of Trustees," August 2, 1844.

P

Padmore, George, *Pan-Africanism or Communism* (London: Dennis Dobson, 1956).

Pease, William and Jane H. Pease, eds., *The Anti-Slavery Argument* (New York: Bobbs-Merrill, 1965).

Penton, D.S., *Non Nobis Solum: The History of Lower Canada College and its Predecessor St. Johns School* (Montreal: Corporation of Lower Canada College).

Piersen, William D., *Black Yankees: The Development of an Afro-American Subculture in Eighteenth Century New England* (Amherst: The University of Massachusetts Press, 1988).

Preble, George Henry, *William Pitt Fessenden: A Memoir* (Boston: David Clapp and Son, 1871).

R

Raboteau, Albert, J., "Richard Allen and the African Church Movement" in Leon Litwack and August Meier, eds. *Black Leaders of the Nineteenth Century* (Urbana: University of Illinois Press, 1988).

Redkey, Edwin S., *Black Exodus: Black Nationalist and Back to Africa Movements: 1890 to 1910* (New Haven, CT: Yale University Press, 1969).

Richardson, Marilyn, ed., *Maria W. Stewart: America's First Black Woman Political Writer* (Bloomington: Indiana University Press, 1987).

Rhodes, Jane, *Mary Ann Shadd Cary: The Black Press and Protest in the Nineteenth Century* (Bloomington: Indiana University Press, 1998).

Robertson, David, *Denmark Vesey: The Buried Story of America's Largest Slave Rebellion and the Man Who Led It* (New York: Vintage books, 1999).

Rotberg, Robert I., *A Political History of Tropical Africa* (New York: Harcourt, Brace and World, 1965).

Ruchames, Louis, *John Brown: The Making of a Revolutionary* (New York: Grosset and Dunlap, 1959).

S

Saito, Natsu Taylor, "From Slavery and Seminoles to Aids in South Africa: An Essay on Race and Property in International Law," *Villanova University Law Review*, 45 Vill. L. Rev. 1135 (2000).

Sagarin, Mary, *The Story of Freedom's Journey, Freedom's Journey* (New York: Lothrop, Lee and Shepard, 1970).

Seraile, William, "David Walker and Malcolm X: Brothers in Radical Thought," *Black World*, October 1973.

Sherlock, Philip and Hazel Bennett, *The Story of the Jamaican People* (Kingston, Jamaica: Ian Randle, 1998).

Sherwood, Henry Noble, "Movement in Ohio to Deport the Negro" *Quarterly Publication of the Historical and Philosophical Society of Ohio,* 1912 to 1914, Vols. VII-IX, (Cincinnati: Jennings and Graham).

Shumard, Ann M., *A Durable Memento: Portraits by Augustus Washington, African-American Daguerreotypist.* Washington, DC: National Portrait Gallery, Smithsonian Institution, 2000).

Silva, Kathryn M., "Black Women and Repatriation, Their Thoughts, Ideas, and Actions in the Nineteenth Century," (unpublished, Boston, 1999).

Silverman, Jason H., "Mary Ann Shadd and the Search for Equality" in Leon Litwack and August Meier, eds., *Black Leaders of the Nineteenth Century* (Urbana: University of Illinois Press, 1988).

Stakeman, Randolph, "The Black Population of Maine, 1764 to 1900," *New England Journal of Black Studies*, November 8, 1989.

Stamp, Kenneth M., *The Peculiar Institution* (New York: Vintage Books, 1956).

Stanton, William, *The Leopard's Spots: Scientific Attitudes Toward Race in America 1815 to 1859* (Chicago: University of Chicago Press, 1960).

Staudenraus, P.J., *The African Colonization Movement, 1816 to 1865* (New York: Columbia University Press, 1961).

Stewart. E.A., "Early History of Brownington Academy" *Proceedings of the Orleans County Historical Society*, August 30, 1858.

Stratton, David, "Liberia: The Love of Liberty Brought Us Here," Middlebury College Archives.

Stuckey, Sterling, *The Ideological Origins of Black Nationalism* (Boston: Beacon Press, 1972).

T

Tennessee State Library and Archives, Manuscript Section, Russwurm, John Summer, 1739 to 1860; Papers, 1786 to 1914; Letters from John Brown Russwurm, July 19, 1819. (Hereafter cited as Russwurm Papers.).

Thompson, Thomas Josiah, *The Jubileee and Centenary Volume of Fourah Bay College, Freetown, Sierra Leone* (Freetown: The Elsiemay Printing Works, 1930).

Tyson, George, Jr., ed., *Toussaint L'Ouverture* (Englewood Cliffs, NJ: Prentice-Hall, 1973).

U

Upham, Thomas C., *American Cottage*, 2nd ed., "A Series of Poems" (Brunswick, ME: Joseph Griffin, 1850).

Upham, Thomas C., *The Manual of Peace: The Evils and Remedies of War* (Boston: American Peace Society, 1842).

Upham, Thomas C., *Letters: Aesthetic, Social and Moral* (Brunswick, ME: The Free Press of J. Griffin, 1855).

U.S. Government, *Tables Showing the Numbers of Emigrants and Recaptured Africans Sent to the Colony of Liberia by the Government of the United States* (Washington, DC: 1845).

U.S. House of Representatives, *Report of Naval Committee on Establishing a Line of Mail Steamships on the Western Coast of Africa, and Thence via the Mediterranean to London* (Washington, DC: Gideon and Company, 1850).

W

Walker, David, *David Walker's Appeal* (Baltimore: Black Classic Press, 1830).

Weinstein, Allen and Frank Otto Gatell, eds., *American Negro Slavery,* 2nd ed. (New York: Oxford University Press, 1973).

West, Richard, *Back to Africa: A History of Sierra Leone and Liberia* (London: Jonathan Cape, 1970).

Williams, Eric, *Capitalism and Slavery* (New York: Capricorn, 1966).

Wilson, Henry S., *The Origins of West African Nationalism* (New York: Macmillan Press, 1969).

Wilson, J. Donald, Robert M. Stamp and Louis-Philippe Audet, *Canadian Education: A History* (Scarborough, Ont.: Prentice-Hall, 1970).

Winch, Julie, *Philadelphia's Black Elite Activism, Accommodation, and the Struggle for Autonomy, 1787 to 1848* (Philadelphia: Temple University Press, 1988).

Winks, Robin W., *The Blacks in Canada: A History* (New Haven, CT: Yale University Press, 1971).

Woods, Randall Bennett, *A Black Odyssey: John Lewis Waller and the Promise of American Life, 1878 to 1900* (Lawrence: The Regents Press of Kansas, 1981).

Woodson, Carter G. and Charles H. Wesley, *The Story of the Negro Retold* (Washington, DC: The Associated Publishers, 1959).

INDEX